THE MONUMENTS OF CHRISTIAN ROME

THE MONUMENTS
OF CHRISTIAN ROME

FROM CONSTANTINE TO THE RENAISSANCE

BY

ARTHUR L. FROTHINGHAM, Ph.D.

SOMETIME ASSOCIATE DIRECTOR OF THE AMERICAN SCHOOL
AT ROME, AND PROFESSOR OF ARCHAEOLOGY AND
ANCIENT HISTORY AT PRINCETON
UNIVERSITY

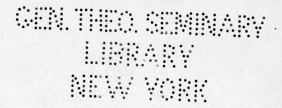
New York
THE MACMILLAN COMPANY
1908

Norwood Press
J. S. Cushing Co. — Berwick & Smith Co.
Norwood, Mass., U.S.A.

TO MY FATHER

CONTENTS

PROLOGUE

I

THE complexity of Rome is at once an allurement and a source of despair. As a growing modern capital it turns its back upon its past, and as a historic museum it bristles with periods and styles so varied they cannot be set forth with the lucidity that makes the art of Athens comparatively easy to grasp.

The present epitome of one group of these phases reflects the artistic life of Rome as a Christian city and the general features of its history and culture from the day when the Emperor Constantine stopped the era of persecution and raised the Christian Labarum as his standard, until that when the mediæval Papacy, after a glorious history, was forced to abdicate its world-power and to leave Rome for Avignon, reducing the city to the lowest ebb of desolation.

When Rome rises again under the Popes of the Renaissance, it will not be by its own efforts or with its peculiar traits unchanged. The new Rome will be a composite picture reflecting the handiwork of Tuscans, of Lombards and of Umbrians: a Rome at war with itself, tearing frantically at its own historic vitals and every day making a mock and travesty of its past. Rome of the Romans is no more.

This old Rome from Constantine to the Renaissance is itself a varied pageant. For nearly two centuries after his death it remained a decapitalized, unambitious Rome, pauperized by imperial bounty, drunk with corruption, hypnotized by vile plays, indifferent to apostles, occupied with a round of baths, games and gossip, clogged with a surfeit of villas, fine raiment and delicate eating, careless of the crumbling away of the ancient world about it under the blows of the barbarians.

In this Rome primitive Christianity was trying to grasp the hearts of the people and the reins of power; reaching out successfully when led by such men as Popes Sylvester, Damasus and Leo the Great. And yet, while fighting indifference and depravity, the Church was itself becoming contaminated with luxury and worldliness. Pagan writers were able to jeer at ecclesiastical dandies and ladies' men; at papal wealth and worldly influence. This was the side of Christian Rome that formed the despair of S. Jerome and sent so many of its saints in flight to the mountains and monasteries of Palestine and the deserts of Egypt, so many of its earnest, ambitious men to Constantinople, so many of its literary lights to Southern Gaul.

But then, before the last echoes of paganism had ceased to reverberate, or asceticism had commenced to supersede the delights of the flesh, the hand of the Lord was stretched out, and there came a blank. For forty days Rome was silent in the wake of the Goths: Senate, Church, corporations, populace, were scattered to all quarters, — Constantinople, Sicily, Gaul, Dalmatia, Egypt, Palestine, — never to be reunited.

When, during the latter half of the sixth century and after the horrors of a great plague had followed the long war, the walls of Rome began once more to shelter a small but motley population, it bore little resemblance in numbers or character to that of the past. There was no aristocracy; there were no organized corporations of the people. The newcomers were mostly of humble birth. They called themselves no longer by the old high-sounding triple Roman names, — no Junius Bassus or Flavius Maximus, — but simple John and Paul. All were poor, but none were pauperized. They worked for their bread instead of receiving it from imperial or papal bounty. They knew of no public baths nor loitering places, no circus nor theatre. They were a Christian people dealing with stern and sad realities, for whom paganism and its delights were as an unreal dream, and the great deserted ghost-like city a weight and a nightmare.

To this people the monks of the East soon came as familiar spirits, and found themselves as much at home on the seven deserted hills as in the deserts of Egypt and Syria. Asceticism was now as much in the eye of the people as self-indulgence had been in that of the Rome of Constantine and Honorius.

This new Byzantine and monastic Rome, some two centuries in the making, was a stern school to retemper the spirit. It bred a people ready to leap forward to the opportunities of the Carlovingian era, a Papacy and a clergy ready to make of Rome once again a city with a mission.

Mission of Rome. — In the days of the Early and Middle Empire from Augustus to the Antonines its mission had been *imperium* with *libertas* and the *pax romana :* the universal pervasion of law and order. To this material and political mission, after a long vacation, the new Rome was about to substitute another *imperium*, equally universal, but less material, an imperium of ideas in which the relation of politics to religion was reversed. For the Roman Empire, the imperial worship that overspread all particular religions had been the necessary handmaid of political unity, as giving the ideal *raison-d'être* of imperialism. With the Roman Church the moves on the political chess-board were subordinated to the supposed exigencies of a religious world-policy which aimed as stringently as the old order had at unity and centralization, at healthy local development under the impulse of the Roman idea. Bishops and abbots took the place of imperial prefects and legates, and under them the local clergy and monks formed the army of occupation. Vaguely groped after as a general system and variously conceived, it was systematized in its religious and moral hegemony during the fifth century by Leo the Great, and afterward by S. Gregory ; it was given a basis of material power through the conception of the political States of the Church under the Carlovingian Popes Hadrian and Leo III ; and it was finally brilliantly perfected in all its aspects in the eleventh century by Gregory VII, the great Hildebrand, at a time when the mediæval mind was both most clearly logical and most deeply religious, at the beginning of the age of scholasticism and the Crusades. Under this Roman banner of reform and Christian democracy, great ideas and impulses swept over Europe, altruism got the better of self-ishness, the great monastic orders redeemed the land and the people, and the arts of civilization took giant strides along national lines during this golden age of the twelfth and thirteenth centuries.

Roman People. — What, then, of the people of Rome and the art of Rome ? What was their part in this long transforma-

Ponte Nomentano, across Anio, near Rome.
Ancient bridge, with mediæval fortifications.

tion ? What was their relation to the Papacy ? That is one fascination of the sphinx-like city. We think of mediæval Rome, if we do not really know it, as identical with the Papacy, as saying its dutiful *amen* to Church policy. How unexpected it is to know the people as they really were, turbulent and hot-headed, the first in Europe to establish a proud and powerful feudal nobility in the Carlovingian era, culminating in their Alberics and their Crescentii; the first to organize a great civilian army of militia in the eighth century, when they were also the first to build a mediæval war fleet and defeat the Saracen invaders.

Riddling their city with towers and fortresses, mostly reared on antique ruins; scattering huge castles over every hilltop and crag in the province; driving out Pope after Pope in jealous defence of their civic rights, and yet so proud of the Papacy as to be unwilling to live without it. Ready to accept imperial aid against the Papacy, and yet rising, regardless of odds and unpreparedness, against any German Emperor who came, with trained armies, to be crowned Roman Emperors of the West, if they happened to offend the fierce and boundless Roman pride. Small wonder that, like any organism without a single aim, this secular Rome never attained to fulness of structure.

This is the heart of Rome: illogical, inconsecutive and passion-tossed, an image of the frowning, rugged, jagged, ruined city, with its harsh contrasts, so different in its lack of unity from the purely mediæval, well-ordered, single-eyed cities of Middle and Northern Italy. The spectre of the ancient world still loomed before the imagination, gigantic and irritating, spurring men on to things they did not themselves understand, as if all afflicted by what alienists call the mania of grandeur, from the days of the political reformer, Alberic, to those of the dreamer, Cola di Rienzo.

Such men as these Romans became incomparable agents when they could subordinate their wills to a system, to an organism like the Papacy. Such a people did not lack imagination. There were always those among them who could turn their peculiar gifts in the direction of art; who could understand how to wield art as an instrument of religion, as one of the greatest means for obtaining the universal dominion in the field of ideas, that always appealed to a Roman; a dominion which Rome alone could gain in those early mediæval days when all Western culture was to be made anew and largely on a Teutonic groundwork.

In fact the Roman clergy and people were in their very race and organization since the Gothic wars, ideally prepared for such a mission, for they were compounded of the antique race, of Byzantine settlers of Greek and Oriental origin, and of northerners of many tribes; yet all, after long seething and attrition, fused into a characteristic and fascinating unit by the two powers of Roman tradition and of the living Papacy. So that it was by no means the Popes alone who were patrons of art in Rome : to the upper clergy and the nobility the majority, in fact, of the monuments was due, and, as we shall see, some of the most flourishing artistic decades were those when the Popes were exiles.

II

Periods. —In a scientific analysis Rome's *epos* from Constantine to Avignon falls naturally into three books. The first tells of the composite pagan-Christian city of the latter days of the Empire, the life in death of ancient culture, the new wine in old bottles full of sediment, with the after-glow of Theodoric the Goth temporarily galvanizing the effete organism until the final fall of the curtain during those famous forty days of the Gothic war when Rome is said to have been completely deserted. There are two centuries and a half in this first book (311–546).

The second book deals with a new Rome hiding within the old, dimly steeped in its memories, but ignorant of the realities of its ancient life and luxuries : an ascetic city weaving fables about a corrupt and decadent society of the past and drawing its real life from Byzantium and its guidance from the Papacy. Its first chapter shows us an almost purely Byzantine Rome ; while in its second chapter the Western elements reassert themselves with the Carlovingian dynasty in the lead and the converted northern nations all bursting into vigorous life. But this life was not fused by a quickening spirit; it went out like the bursting of a rocket, and the second chapter of the epic closes, after a final century of lifelessness, at an even more discouraging and lower level of achievement than the first. It had lasted twice as long, for nearly five centuries (546–c. 1050).

As the second stage had opened with a Gregory the Great, the third and final book of the epic was ushered in by the work of another Pope Gregory, the great Hildebrand, at first the motive power behind several Popes, then himself in the chair. We are now in the creative stage of the Middle Ages, the days of quick living, of self-sacrifice, of idealism, of concentrated purpose. The contest for supremacy between the Imperial and Papal ideas, the movement of the Crusades, the all-pervading work of the monastic orders, the intellectual and moral resurrection of the Church and of society, are among the factors that raise these centuries above the petty policies of the material period that is to follow. Rome was then more than ever a centre of Western life, the main lever and leaven of Europe. What she would have done had not her career been cut short in the midst of strenuous achievement by the flight to Avignon, is one of the unsolved dreams of history !

Art of Christian Rome. — While the supreme rôle of Rome and the Papacy has filled a large place in the scholarly thought that has given us pictures of these ten centuries, almost nothing has been written of her rôle in the sphere of art history. And yet, as the grip of the Papacy upon the Western world grew stronger, Rome was once more called upon to furnish art-types and models, and to give artistic education and direction, exactly as ancient Rome had done for so many of her provinces under the Early Empire.

Why is it that what is so self-evident for the Roman Empire has not been recognized as true for the Middle Ages ? Perhaps because the Christian art of Rome was far from simple, being compounded with Hellenic and Oriental elements, so that its track is not so plain to the eye as that of its less complex pagan predecessor. Perhaps also because its artistic teaching was now so much more in the domain of the spirit than of matter, that its traces are the more subtle and the less demonstrable. But as the fundamental axiom of art criticism for the Christian period is the indissoluble union of art with theology and liturgy, and as it is a truism that all the nations of the North owed their conversion directly or indirectly to Rome, and got from her the form, decoration and furniture, the music and liturgy of their churches and monasteries, and even the relics of their saints; it is the inevitable conclusion that, whatever differences may have arisen through local peculiarities and with certain reservations as to decorative motifs, Rome was the ultimate source of the art of all Europe in the early Middle Ages, even of that of the Frank, the Anglo-Saxon and Germanic nations.

As art had become the "bible of the poor," and its works were dedicated to " the people of God," the Church was now the one common and civilizing centre of the city. And of this art Rome held the double key, that of its technique and that of its ideas. Rome also had in the hollow of her hand, through the organization of the Papacy, the bishops and abbots of all European churches, the men who guided the hands of all the artists of the time.

To know the Christian art of Rome, then, means far more than it seems. It transcends the city and the land; it joins hands with the East and the North throughout the ages of vital Christianity. Yet even now, in this advanced age of art criticism, the knowledge of the history of this Roman art is in a condition that can only be described as infantile.

Problems in Architecture. — Among the causes of this lacuna the first is the unique unity of the Roman style of church architecture and painting during a thousand years of history, a unity which has made critics despair of certainty in dating many of its buildings and their decoration. A second cause is the indiscriminate slaughter and disfigurement of the mediæval records by the prelates and artists of the Renaissance and Barocco periods.

In other countries and other schools there always were, from century to century, such radical changes in style that it would require abnormal critical density to make in most cases an error of over half a century. For example, during this millennium of Roman uniformity France saw a succession of styles, — Merovingian, Carlovingian, Romanesque, Gothic, — not only each instinct with individuality, but each embracing distinct local and chronological variations. Under such conditions, to date a monument approximately without the aid of documents is easy. To give a concrete instance. In almost every province of France during this period we find the successive use of several kinds of covering : wooden roof, tunnel vault, groin vault or dome. And we can control these larger factors by the minor peculiarities of details ; such as the architectural mouldings so rich in the closing centuries of the Middle Ages; such as the capitals where we find a great variety of design, some a more or less imperfect adaptation of the antique orders, some based on geometric forms, some on the imitation of nature — human, animal and vegetable.

Compare this richness with the uniformity of Rome, where no kind of vaulting ever found entrance (except sporadically), but where we are everlastingly confronted by the same wooden roofs; where no system of capitals (except sporadically) ever contested the supremacy of the antique orders; where the classic Roman system of ornament continued in almost unbroken use, hardly interrupted by the Byzantine centuries; where the old thin brick walls, with their plain roundheaded openings for doors and windows, were never replaced by heavy moulded stonework; where no problems in statics troubled the builders' minds and led to new developments.

Such a school requires infinite patience for its decipherment. This patience is severely taxed by the present condition of the churches of Rome. As long as it was Christian Rome that restored its own, there was no incongruity between the new work and the old, but with the Renaissance, and still more with the Barocco period, the Roman Church showed as much destructive ruthlessness for its own past as it did for ancient pagan ruins. What it did not entirely destroy it aimed radically to transform. Not a single church entirely escaped. It was merely a question of scale : from complete destruction, like that of S. Peter, to the less radical transformation of the furniture and decoration, as at S. Maria Maggiore.

We cannot enter any of the Roman churches as we can so many Romanesque and Gothic churches of Northern Europe and have the complete satisfaction of being taken back through the centuries, without a jar or a contradiction. Mutilated as they are, the monuments of classic Rome, in their sombre and ragged nudity, but without discordant additions of other ages, have less to contend with in their appeal to our reconstructive imagination than have the Christian basilicas where Barocco prelates have delighted to hide the lines of classic columns inside hideous plaster piers; to fling riotous and sprawling cupids and allegorical females of colossal size against every apse and chapel; to spread over heavy coffered ceilings the most violent combinations of bright blues, reds and golds; to rip out the wealth of chancel rails, choir screens, pulpits, paschal candelabra, altar canopies that obstructed to their mind the view of the flaunting ceremonial of the age, and yet delighting to fill up the vistas again with portentous altar tabernacles; to cover with whitewash the old mosaics and frescos; to tear down the ancient porticos and plaster against the front one of those meaningless bescrolled and bumptious façades that disfigure most of the streets of Rome. An eminent living prelate and writer has tartly said, "These men make us regret the Vandals."

Yet while allowing the lover of the mediæval Rome that was to voice this lament, it remains true that Rome still contains the most wonderful existing series of Christian works of art in unbroken continuity, and that their history has never been written with any scientific accuracy, though they are most of them familiar inmates of the pages of art histories. Their unity to which I have referred has made it possible to confuse a basilica of the time of a Liberius (352–366) or a Sixtus III (432–440) with one built eight hundred years later by an Innocent II (1130–1143) or a Honorius III (1216–1227). A fresco or mosaic of the tenth or eleventh may reproduce quite faithfully one of the fifth or sixth century.

This confusion is enhanced by misleading documentary evidence. As most of the basilicas were early foundations and were often restored, redecorated and even reconstructed, there are many records of work done which, owing to the vagueness, inaccuracy and exaggeration of mediæval phraseology, leave us in doubt as to the date of the building that now stands before us. The old chronicler's desire to magnify the work done by a contemporary would often lead him to call a mere restoration by the misleading name of reconstruction.

III

Problems in Painting and Sculpture. — All this applies merely to one section of Roman art — to its architecture. If one turns to other branches, one meets with questions just as baffling and problems just as interesting, many of them raised by the recent discoveries which are, every day, emphasizing the importance of the Roman school.

Critics are now asking whether the revival of painting in the thirteenth century did not really take place in Rome. They are asking whether Giotto was not a pupil of Roman artists, especially of Pietro Cavallini, and not at all of Cimabue. The Vasari bubble of the Tuscan origin is being pricked! But who was this mysterious Cavallini? His works are now being identified and discovered, especially in Rome, Naples and Assisi, and he is being hailed as the greatest painter before Giotto and one of the foremost religious painters and decorators of all times, crowning Rome as the source of mediæval and Renaissance painting.

And again, who can say with certainty how much Arnolfo, celebrated as the great Florentine architect and sculptor, who shares with Niccola Pisano the honor of resuscitating sculpture, owed to Rome and her artists as we study his many works in Rome in which he shows himself too completely a leader of the Roman school itself to be classed as an outsider?

I have been convinced for twenty years that in the revival of art in the thirteenth century the Roman school took the foremost part in painting and a prominent share in sculpture. Recent discoveries are leading many foremost critics, such as Zimmerman, Thode, Venturi, Langton Douglas and Strzygowski, to conclusions that involve these results. But we are still struggling for our clews in the obscurity created by the cruel Barocco devastations! The *disjecta membra* of the old basilica now scattered through the Vatican crypt are a symbol of the fate of most of the mediæval sculpture. The absurd copies made before their destruction by unskilled Barocco humanists, such as the series at S. Paolo by Cavallini, and the mutilated fragments that are reappearing from beneath the Barocco whitewash, are a mere apology for the extensive series that rivalled the Assisi frescos in a dozen Roman churches.

If the closing days of the School are full of such puzzles, what is one to say of its earlier work in sculpture and paint-

ing? Only during the past half-dozen years has it been possible to even dream of following the history of fresco-painting
in Rome during the earlier Middle Ages; but now, the discovery of numerous new works of the sixth to the ninth centuries
and the more careful study of others of the tenth, eleventh and
twelfth, have given an embarrassing quantity of material which
no one has yet attempted to classify. How much in all this,
if any, is by Byzantine artists, how much by Italian pupils,
how much is purely Roman in style? The burning Byzantine
question is virulently reopened!

Even the entire system of carved decoration that ruled in
Rome and nearly everywhere in Italy from the seventh to the
eleventh century is cause for bitter controversy, and opposing
critics battle for its Byzantine, its Lombard or its Classic
origin! In this I side emphatically with Byzantium. Everywhere we uncover interesting mare's nests!

For all these reasons this handbook cannot, as such books
usually do, give a summary of recognized facts, but must be
itself often a pioneer and admit a large element of discussion
and hypothesis, and, I may confess, also a modicum of parti-
sanship. To create the right atmosphere I have found a larger
element of history necessary than is at all customary, because
my theory of historic art (*not* of contemporary art) is that it is
as integral a part of civilization as politics, religion, sociology
or literature. As I hope this book may serve in the class-
room, I have also felt it necessary to include a considerable
amount of detailed description of the more important works,
so as to obviate reference to other books for these fundamental
elements. Less serious students may pass this over. I only
regret that I could not make these descriptions more vivid by
a greater number of illustrations: those I have given have
been selected so as to omit no single important type in any of
the arts.

Ever since joining, in 1879, at the age of nineteen, the *Società
dei Cultori di Archeologia Cristiana*, of which De Rossi was
the leading spirit, I have made Christian Rome and its art my
special study. After living in Rome for seventeen years, I
left in 1883, but have returned a number of times, gathering

material and continuing to explore not only the mediæval city but the small towns and monasteries in every part of the Roman province, many of them still gems of sequestered mediæval life. I followed, along the highways throughout this territory, the footprints of Roman art and artists. Before long I expect to publish a history of mediæval art in Rome on a large scale. Of course in this limited space only a part of this work can appear, but even in this handbook I shall include some small part of the material gathered outside of Rome, — I wish it could be more, — because it is a product of the same hands and brains that worked in the metropolis, and many a gap in Rome itself is filled by some work in a country town where Barocco devastation was less active.

PART I

HISTORICAL SKETCH

PART I

HISTORICAL SKETCH

I. THE CITY OF CONSTANTINE AND HONORIUS

BEFORE Constantine's reign (312–337) it had been impossible for Christianity to be adequately represented in works of public art. Whatever metamorphosis it had accomplished in a certain part of the population had been in the domain of the spirit only. Worship had been carried on in various unostentatious ways. At first it had been in the houses of wealthy converts, unchanged in their architecture by this passing use for the new cult. Then, there had commenced, in the third century, with the great increase in the numbers of converts, the custom of building not only special chapels in connection with houses, but even churches of small dimensions. Still, these chapels and churches were either swallowed up in the general splendor or were scattered without the walls at the entrances to the Catacombs, less conspicuous than the thousands of private mausoleums that lined the public highways. The certainty of their destruction or confiscation whenever a persecution was proclaimed helped to determine the modesty of their aspect.

Without the aid of these vanished works above ground the galleries and chambers of the subterranean Catacombs have supplied the only available information for the pre-Constantinian age. It may seem strange that a description of these Christian Catacombs should not form the first chapter of this history. But they really constitute quite "another story," less illustrative of Rome as a city than of the intimate texture of primitive Christian thought and feeling in a form rather desultory than systematic, in an art more private than public, and less an art than a language.

It is only when, after the year of liberation, 312, official Christian art began to succeed official pagan art and to take its place by the side of official civil art, that the new thread in the weave of art history can be started on its way to accomplish its work of reconstruction.

At the same time, while the new art of Constantine bloomed with undoubted and sudden originality in the fields of architecture and mosaic painting, and the pent-up thought of the fathers of the Church found free expression in new artistic ideas for the conversion and edification of the people ; yet there were other branches, such as fresco-painting and carved sarcophagi, which, with an intense conservatism and roots sunk deeply in the two previous centuries, continued in close touch, both of technique and of theme, with what we may call the art of the Catacombs. In fact a considerable part of this subterranean art was actually produced during the course of the fourth century, when the Catacombs were still used for burial as well as for the worship of the relics of the martyrs.

The fourth century in Rome was thus characterized : —

(1) As transitional from private to public Christian art ;

(2) As transitional from pagan to Christian public art ;

(3) As an age of general mutual tolerance, religiously and socially, officially and privately.

In a study of this and the following century it has been the illogical habit of art historians to limit themselves to the ecclesiastical, to the exclusion of civil monuments. But the monumental situation is so completely a reflex of the political and religious duality of the age that the two phases of art, — religious and civil, — with even a sprinkling of the expiring pagan, must be studied separately, for the same school of art produced them all. This will be done after a preliminary study of the exceptional years of Constantine himself.

Constantine's Civil Monuments. — In the early part of Constantine's reign the city was not denuded of imperial engineers and architects, even though some may have been called away to Milan by Maxentius to beautify the new temporary capital.

The most impressive and colossal of existing monuments is the so-called basilica of Constantine; and the Emperor added another to the series of imperial thermæ already erected by Titus and Trajan, Caracalla and Diocletian.

The spectacular triumphal arch on the Via Sacra, the Janus Quadrifrons of the Forum Boarium, the colossal bronze equestrian statue of Constantine in the middle of the Forum and

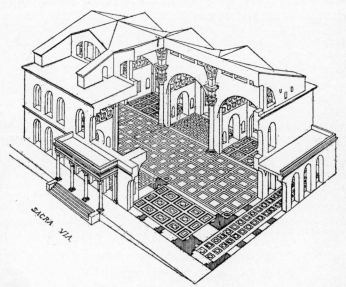

Basilica of Constantine, restored.

his seated statue in the basilica, show that Rome was still the main centre of the imperial school of art, such as it was, even though the city had ceased to have any political importance.

The basilica is, with the Colosseum, the most impressive ruin in or near the Roman Forum. It had been begun by Constantine's rival, Maxentius (306–312), on a plan totally different from all previous public basilicas, which had been long columnar structures with wooden roof. Here, on the contrary, the interior was on an enormous scale covered with a series of

vaults rivalled only by those of the largest imperial thermæ.
The central nave has three high groin vaults supported on piers
faced by enormous shafts, and to these corresponded, on a lower
level, three tunnel vaults at right angles on either side, with
central nave.   The spacious interior was the largest in the history of architecture up to that time, and surpasses even the
largest Gothic cathedrals.   Its architectural details were on so

large a scale that their lack of
finish and their heavy ornamentation were not a glaring detriment.
The curves of the vaults were
covered with heavy coffering and
the pavement with rich marbles.
Owing to its size, it was impracti-
cable for the Popes of the black
century after the Gothic wars to
convert it to any practical use, and
the destruction begun by Honorius
I, who used its bronze tiling for S.
Peter's, was continued and assisted
by earthquakes.   Only the three
lower tunnel vaults, of what we
might term the rear aisle, remain.
Constantine's predecessor, Diocletian, had but a few years before
completed the most colossal of all

Marble Wall-incrustation, Basilica
of Junius Bassus.

imperial baths, one hall of which was converted by Michel-
angelo into the church of S. Maria degli Angeli.   We cannot
say how far Constantine, in his own thermæ, fell short of his
great model, for its ruins, still of considerable extent in the
sixteenth century, afford but a scant basis for reconstruction.
It was, at all events, based on a similar scheme of extensive
vaulted construction.   This entire field of superb structural
architecture I merely allude to, as it passes out of our field and
has no connection with the future of architecture in Christian
Rome.

To the superficial observer the triple triumphal arch of
Constantine, erected to commemorate his victory over Maxen-

tius, in 315, appears to surpass the earlier arch of Septimius Severus. This impression vanishes as we find, on analysis, that it lacks the unity of a single work and age; that it is mainly composed of the spoils of a number of earlier structures; and that it is these borrowed plumes, from the golden age of Trajan and the Antonines, that have given this first impression of artistic value. It wears, metaphorically speaking, bloody garments; for it a great destruction was wrought

Arch of Constantine.

and several memorial arches torn down. The great attic reliefs are from an arch of Marcus Aurelius or Lucius Verus; the medallions from some other early arch; the great battle scenes are from Trajan's Forum. Even the lines of the architectural framework, the main cornice and the columns that support it, are from some destroyed arch of the Antonines. The artists of Constantine contented themselves with the carving of the less prominent features of both figured and decorative ornament, and in both kinds of work they showed themselves below the standard of other Constantinian and even later work in Rome, such as the mausoleum of Constantia

and the church of S. Pudentiana. Another of the imperial
works, the Janus Quadrifrons, shorn of its marble columns, its
niches despoiled of their statuary, stands now in its cold
nudity, incapable of giving us a very definite impression of
its original decorative value. Still, in its massive heaviness, it
is unique as a survivor of what had been a popular and very
early form of city arch, that with four equal sides and double
passageway — a form sometimes placed over the intersection
of two highways. Some fragments of a civil hall or private
basilica, built in 317 by Junius Bassus and preserved when
the hall became a church, show how during these earlier years
of the emperor decorative artists of great value remained. Its
marble incrustations formed a perfect scheme of pictures.

If Constantine was guilty of looting earlier monuments, like
the circus of Nero, to build S. Peter, he also restored some.
It is probably to him that the reconstruction of the temple of
Concord is due. But toward the close of his reign a more
disastrous phase of looting was inaugurated, — worse because
another city than Rome profited by the spoils. After 325 the
Emperor began to transport materials from Rome for the
decoration of the public structures of his new capital, Constantinople, where he was gathering works of art from all parts
of the Empire. He despoiled Hadrian's villa and accepted
columns and marbles from private donors in Rome, so putting
a premium on destruction.

Constantine's Churches. — Turning now to Christian as distinguished from Civil and Pagan monuments, we find the
Emperor assisting the Church in its work of providing buildings for the increasing mass of worshippers and of suitably
commemorating the graves and memories of martyrs and
apostles.

The Roman Church was as yet poor ; it was the Emperor,
not the Pope, who built the first great basilicas. This fact
found its record even in the lives of the Popes. Though com-
piled two centuries later, the life of Constantine's contemporary, Pope Sylvester, shows evidence of being based on
contemporary documents in the Papal archives. In it the only
structure directly attributed to the Pope is a parish church

within the city, — that of Equitius, afterwards called SS. Silvestro e Martino ai Monti. Below the present church, founded above that of Sylvester by Symmachus (498–514), there still exist considerable remains of this primitive church — one of the most historic landmarks of the new free Christianity.[1]

But, aside from this one exception, the monuments of this first generation of Christian art in Rome were due to the personal initiative of Constantine and to the funds of the imperial treasury. The circular letters which the Emperor sent to the

Constantinian Marble Choir Screen at S. Martino ai Monti (Tit. Equitii).

bishops and imperial officials throughout the Empire, the texts of which are given by Constantine's contemporary and biographer Eusebius, show his system of procedure.

Not only the imperial finances and the officials charged with the supervision of monuments, but the state corporations representing every branch of art, were placed at the service of the Church. To a certain extent there must have been limitations, for although in the time of Constantine a considerable proportion of the working classes in Rome were Christians, one may believe that the fact that only Christians could be employed in any works connected with worship would have then shut out many of the most skilled artists and artisans.

In the Emperor's programme he was powerfully seconded by his mother Helena, who appears to have had a more vivid faith than her son. Princely gifts to the Roman Church were two palaces belonging to the imperial family — the Lateran and the Sessorian.

[1] The basilica of Sylvester at the cemetery of Priscilla on the Via Salaria Nova, where the Pope was buried, may also be his work; to judge from the few remaining fragments it may have been of considerable importance.

The Lateran. — The palace of the Laterani had come to Constantine through his wife, Fausta. He gave it to the Roman Church, which gradually established in it its central administration; he built in connection with it, the Cathedral church of Rome and of Christendom, the Lateran basilica, called also the Constantinian basilica, from its founder, and, later, the basilica of the Saviour, and still later of S. John. The large halls of the palace served for meetings of the councils, for the archives and libraries, for bureaus of charity and administration and for Papal residence. However often the Popes might temporarily transfer their residence elsewhere, the tradition that the Lateran was the permanent centre of the Papacy was never shattered until the Renaissance. Part of the ground-plan of the original Roman palace has been recently explored.

The Lateran basilica was the most important church built by Constantine in Rome, but its numerous reconstructions have destroyed all vestiges of its Constantinian features.

The Sessorian. — The Sessorian palace, on the other hand, was not as a whole given to the Church. It was the favorite residence of the Empress Helena, and appears to have remained imperial property as late as the time of Theodoric, when the Council of 501 was held there. The main hall of the palace, however, was converted by Helena into a church, and called " Hierusalem." Here was preserved the principal relic of the True Cross brought from Jerusalem after its discovery ; hence the church received in time the name " Santa Croce in Gerusalemme," and became a sort of appendage to the neighboring Lateran. This basilica still exists, though much mutilated, — the most perfect example of the adaptation of the basilical hall of a private palace to the uses of a church.

But the Emperor's principal group of religious structures was that connected with the tombs of the apostles and martyrs outside the city walls. These are the basilica of S. Peter on the Vatican Hill, that of S. Paul on the Via Ostiensis, that of S. Lawrence on the Via Tiburtina, that of S. Agnes on the Via Nomentana, and that of SS. Marcellinus and Peter on the Via Prænestina. These were all cemeterial basilicas, and were built by the Emperor on a larger scale and with more sumptuous decoration than was the case with most of the cemeterial basilicas erected subsequently by the Popes of this and the following century. Still, they were of very unequal importance. That of S. Peter was by far the largest and most artistic, almost equalling the Lateran basilica. That of S. Paul was comparatively small, and was superseded by another of far greater size and magnificence at the close of the century. The even smaller basilica of S. Lawrence was so changed by Pope Pelagius in the

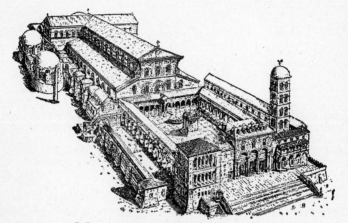

S. Peter and its Annexes in the Middle Ages.
Restoration of Crostarosa.

sixth century that it is difficult to attribute to the edifice of Constantine more than most of the columns of the smaller and lower church. Pope Honorius in the seventh century reconstructed S. Agnes, and of SS. Marcellinus and Peter nothing exists.

The Vatican; S. Peter. — Notwithstanding many restorations, the Vatican basilica remained, therefore, until its destruction in the sixteenth and seventeenth centuries the best example of a Constantinian church, and may well be described here in its general features, following the plan drawn up in 1590 by Alfarano, and the descriptions and sketches by writers and artists of the Middle Ages and the Renaissance. When the

apse was demolished, the proof of its Constantinian age was
found in its stamped bricks, and the mosaic of Constantine presenting the model of the church to Christ, which, as I was able
to prove, existed on the triumphal arch until the end, must
have been original.

The approach to the church was up a flight of thirty-five
steps through a propylæum into a large atrium with over forty
columns enclosing all four sides
of the court.   In the centre was
a large fountain.   The church
was entered by five doors, and
was divided into five aisles supported by eighty-eight columns
and eight pilasters.   The columns, of various marbles, and
of granite, were taken from
antique monuments, the two
nearest the door being of African
marble.   The shafts, bases, and
capitals varied in style, size, and
period so radically that hardly
any two were exactly alike, and
we are reminded of the letter of
Constantine, in which he asked
a bishop to let him know as soon
as the plans for a certain church

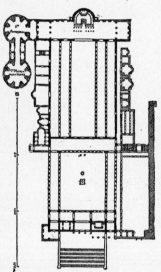

Plan of S. Peter in the Middle Ages.

were completed so that he could
order the columns for it to be
collected from everywhere.   The columns and architraves of
S. Peter's are shown by their marks and inscriptions to have
come from many quarries, and to have belonged to buildings
erected by various Emperors from Titus to Gallienus.

The columns of the main nave supported not arcades but
architraves, and the side-aisles were of diminishing widths.
These architraves were not uniform but varied in mouldings,
ornamentation and proportions.   At the end of the nave the
arch of triumph, decorated with the mosaic already mentioned,
opened into the transept which extended beyond the aisles.

Here stood the confession and altar, above the tomb of S. Peter, and in front of it a double line of twelve superb spiral columns, supporting architraves with sculptures.

In the apse was a mosaic of Christ and the two princes of the apostles Paul and Peter. Constantine's inscription on the arch read, addressing Christ : —

BECAUSE, LED BY THEE, THE WORLD TRIUMPHANT RISES TO THE STARS,

CONSTANTINE, VICTORIOUS, BUILT THIS HALL FOR THEE.

Not long after Constantine, changes and additions took place. A baptistery was added in the right arm of the transept; the

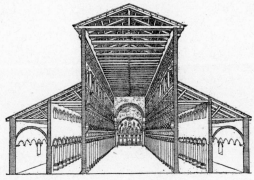

S. Peter (Old Basilica).

atrium was paved, a mosaic was placed on the façade at the expense of the ex-prefect Marinianus (c. 450) ; and two palaces were built to flank the atrium. At this early date the aisles were not, as later, filled with altars and chapels, but the basilica was surrounded by subsidiary buildings, especially by monasteries built by Leo the Great and his successors and by sumptuous circular mausolea, of which two were of especial interest, that of the Anicii Probi, the imperial mausoleum of the dynasty of Theodosius, afterwards called S. Petronilla, and its annex, S. Maria della Febbre. Other buildings were toward the front of the atrium, such as the school for the training

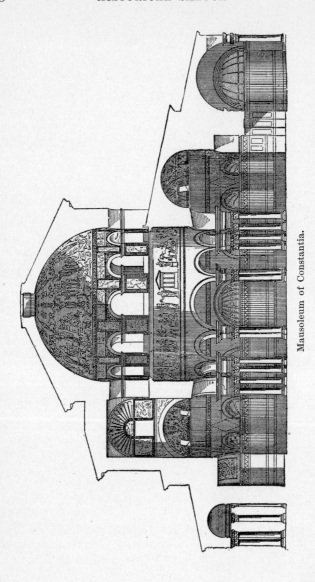

Mausoleum of Constantia.

of singers. Later an entire suburb grew up around the basilica.

When the group was supplemented in the century after Constantine and connected with the mausoleum and bridge of Hadrian by an arcaded boulevard, the general effect must have been imposing, even though the details of the interior may have been defective.

To complete this Constantinian series the imperial mausolea must not be forgotten, connected with these basilicas and their cemeteries, — especially those of the Empress Helena near SS. Marcellinus and Peter, and of Constantia, or, more properly, Constantina, near S. Agnese.

Like all such buildings they were circular in plan. Built with far greater solidity than the basilicas and with vaults instead of wooden roofs, they have suffered less from fire, restoration and time and have remained almost perfect representations of Constantinian structure and decoration, though unequally so, for of the mausoleum of Helena, built on one of the great imperial estates, only the main part of the shell remains, with its dome of terracotta amphorae on a high drum pierced with large openings.

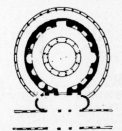

Mausoleum of Constantia.

S. Costanza. — The mausoleum of Constantia was, either originally or shortly after its construction, used as the baptistery of the neighboring basilica of S. Agnese. The closed vestibule has the same oblong form with a hemicycle at each end as the Lateran baptistery, a certain sign of the special liturgical ceremonies connected with baptism. It is also said that traces of the central baptismal font have been found. At the same time the niches in the outer wall were evidently intended for funerary purposes, and the porphyry tomb now near that of Helena in the Vatican was found here and is a proof that the building was actually used as a mausoleum. The apsidal niches are in four groups of three between the doors and the two larger apses. The heavy walls of the dome are too wide to be supported by single shafts, so the twelve arcades rest on twenty-four coupled shafts, whose capitals are surmounted by an architectural member which is equivalent to an interrupted frieze from which the arches spring. The whole arrangement is unique, a summary of Roman achievement up to that time in vaulted and domical construction on a small scale. The

Interior of S. Constantia (S. Costanza).

vertical thrust of the dome is partly received by the vaults and walls of the tunnel-vaulted ambulatory.

We must imagine this mausoleum also as surrounded by a circular colonnade, of which only traces remain, and as fronting on a portico. All around it were minor monuments of the large open-air cemetery attached to S. Agnese — an example of the favorite mode of burial around the suburban basilica, during the fourth and fifth centuries. It was after the Gothic wars that the custom changed and open-air cemeteries became numerous within the walls, such as the one near S. Eusebio.

Endowment.— Constantine was not satisfied with building and decorating many churches. He did two other things: (1) filled their treasuries and sacristies with artistic and precious articles for the religious services; and (2) provided for the adequate maintenance of the building and its personnel by gifts of income-producing real estate. We may conclude that most of the details of this sort given in the Liber Pontificalis — with regard to S. Peter, for instance — were drawn from the church archives and are not imaginary.

This commencement of church endowment was the logical consequence of the religious revolution. At the close of another century the confiscation of the immense properties of the pagan temples, which reverted to the Emperors, was to give an almost inexhaustible source of supply for imperial gifts to the principal churches of Rome.

The City. — By a curious coincidence the only documents that enumerate the monuments of the ancient city, quarter by quarter, belong to the very time of Constantine and his sons. This catalogue which, with the marble plan of Septimius Severus, forms the main basis for its early topography, is drily pathetic, coming just as the curtain is about to be rung down on the imperial city. In the recapitulation which its author makes at the close, he classifies the monuments in categories and enumerates two circuses, two amphitheatres, three theatres, ten public civil basilicas, eleven public imperial baths or thermæ, thirty-six triumphal marble arches, four hundred and twenty-three temples, seventeen hundred and ninety palaces and forty-six thousand, six hundred and two tenements or blocks. Not a single Christian Church is mentioned! The earlier edition of this document, called the *Notitia*, was edited in about 330, on the basis of an earlier document: toward the middle of the century a revision was made called the *Curiosum*.

In population the Rome of Constantine seems, until the latter part of his reign, to have been as large as ever. The area of the Circus Maximus was increased so as to seat nearly three hundred thousand people. The influence of the new faith did not seem to abate one whit the devotion of the people to the circus, the amphitheatre and the theatre. All the

public buildings of these classes were kept in perfect running
order. It was the same with the thermæ and other public
baths, with the basilicas and porticos. There was even one
notable addition to the symmetry and beauty of the city before the close of the century. It was the completion of the
system of porticos by a new and far longer Via Sacra. This
Christian " Sacred Way," destined to supersede the ancient one
through the Forum, radiated in three directions, toward the
suburban basilicas of the princes of the apostles Peter and
Paul and the great martyr, Lawrence. To each of these
centres of worship and pilgrimage there extended several miles
of covered porticos flanking the road and giving shelter from
sun and rain. Focussing toward the centre of the city, these
three lines joined the older imperial porticos and were completed by the *Porticus Maximæ* which bisected the edge of the
Campus Martius and ended at the Tiber in front of the mausoleum of Hadrian. There were even subsidiary porticos leading off to basilicas within the city, like that along the *vicus
patricius* toward S. Maria Maggiore by way of S. Pudentiana.
Triumphal arches were placed here and along the main *Via
Sacra* by Valentinian and Honorius.

The churches built during the fourth century within the
city were not numerous nor conspicuous enough to affect its
aspect; in their exterior effect of plain brickwork they must
have seemed inferior to the average private dwelling. Even
their interiors, rich as they were with color, with hangings
and furniture and sculpture in metal, fell in sumptuousness
below the average of both public and private buildings.

And yet Christianity was affecting art far more than this
would indicate, for this reason, that most of the *new* work was
done for the Church. Imperial legislation before the close of
the century forbids city officials to put up new buildings while
those already existing are in need of repair and unless funds
are on hand sufficient for their completion. The decrease in
the population that set in before the middle of the century
made new work quite superfluous except in the service of the
new religion.

Successors of Constantine; Rome's Doom. — After Constantine's death in 337 there was a lull in building activity. His three sons divided the Empire. Constantius had the East, Constantine and Constans divided Africa and the rest of the West. The hope that Rome would be chosen as the political capital of Constans was deluded. In fact as the fourth century progressed it became evident that as a monumental city Rome was doomed.

The aristocracy of Rome, as represented by the Senate, was not as a majority converted to the new faith. It remained bound to paganism through self-interest if not through conviction. The career of a Roman noble, his *cursus honorum,* so rigidly regulated in its progress through offices of increasing importance, involved more than one charge connected with the pagan religion. Consistent Christians could not rise so easily at first in public office or honors. So it happened that until the fifth century there were many more Christian women than men in the upper ranks. In Rome there was, therefore, great danger that worldly considerations would kill fervor of faith. In fact it was partly in order to be free from these and other trammels of paganism that Constantine founded Constantinople and endowed it with a Senate and with all the privileges which Rome alone had hitherto had as a capital.

The establishment of a Christian state could not be directed from Rome. The Emperors turned their back on her permanently. That her problem was too hard for the intellects of Constantine's successors is shown by the potency of the spell she still exerted on their unwilling spirits ; when there they were once more unconscious pagans, a part of the tremendous past, and were even perhaps galled by an uncomfortable sense of humility as if belonging to a less heroic age. Their *lares* and *penates* were in another atmosphere.

Understanding by the very failure of the persecution of Christianity by the earlier Roman Emperors, how dangerous coercion could become, the Christian Emperors therefore handed over the stronghold of paganism to the Church and the Papacy, so that its moral forces could leaven the lump and mould the masses. Meanwhile conciliation was the watchword of Imperial and Papal policy alike. It was not till 391 that Theo-

D

dosius issued and partially enforced a law forbidding the
celebration of the public rites of pagan worship.

It was only in 416, apparently as a consequence of the last
pagan reaction of 409, that the law formally excluded profess-
ing pagans from public office, both civil and military — a law
which remained largely a dead letter. This date of 416, while
a fatal one for the future of the temples of Rome, was not
immediately so. They always remained public monuments,
in the care of the prefect of the city, still nearly always a
pagan. It was only a few years before that Honorius had
finally confiscated the possessions of the temples.

It will be sufficient to mention a few of the civil buildings

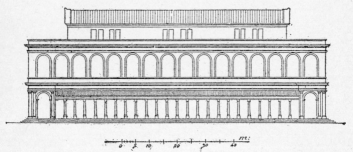

The Basilica Æmilia, in the Fifth Century after Honorius's Restoration.

restored or built at this time. The Grain Exchange (*Statio
Annonæ*) was rebuilt on the old site in the Forum Boarium,
where the church of Santa Maria in Cosmedin now stands,
and in which some of its columns and even the beautiful stucco
decoration in open-work of its arcades were utilized. Not as
a religious structure, but as the public treasure, the temple of
Saturn in the Forum was rebuilt either in the fourth century
or after the fire of Alaric. The present columns are no earlier
and the inscription says: *Senatus Populusque Romanus in-
cendio consumptum restituit.* After this fire, also, the basilica
Emilia was rebuilt and decorated, and apparently also the
basilica Julia. So were the *Curia* and *Secretarium*, where the
Senate met.

The year 367 itself was made memorable by the reconstruction of the *Porticus Deorum Consentium* on the west
edge of the Forum, by the famous pagan prefect Prætextatus.
It was the last building erected in Rome for pagan cult!

Just before this the construction of the great Valentinian
bridge and triumphal arch was commenced, which for years
afforded a subject for correspondence between the Emperors
and the famous Symmachus, who was prefect of the city and
consequently superintendent of buildings, during the latter
stages of their construction. In these letters he airs his
troubles with the architects in charge or appointed to examine into the constructive defects and the cost of the bridge.
We learn something in this way about those court architects
and engineers, — such as Cyriades, — men of senatorial rank
and wealth, who had charge of building and financing such
public structures. The restoration of another bridge, the
Cestian, was being carried on at about the same time.

Finally, under Honorius (395–423), came the restoration
of the walls and gates of Aurelian, planned as a defence
against the invasion of Alaric. Some of the new gates
rise to the dignity of works of art. In the Forum statues
were erected to Stilicho and Honorius to celebrate the
triumph over Rhadagaisus; and others in the Forum of
Trajan.

The last triumphal arches in Rome belong to this time.
That to Gratian, Valentinian and Theodosius (382) framed the
north end of the *Porticus Maximœ*, near Hadrian's bridge, and
was not destroyed until the middle of the fifteenth century.
It was less triumphal than purely a work of civic decoration.
Not so the arch of Arcadius, Honorius and Theodosius that was
built in 405 to celebrate Stilicho's salvation of the Empire
from the mixed hordes of Rhadagaisus. It stood not far from
the other arch and no trace of it remains.

We can judge of the artistic quality of these arches only
from the fragments of a third arch, that of Valentinian and
Valens, built at the entrance to their bridge, a few years
earlier, of which a few fragments were recovered from the
Tiber and are now in the museum of the baths of Diocletian,

including parts of some of the triumphal bronze figures that
crowned it.

Exodus from Rome. — The decreasing population hardly required so many places of amusement; so, while the theatre
of Pompey was diligently restored by Honorius, and the
Colosseum in 442 and 467–472, on the other hand, the prefect,
Symmachus, in the time of Gratian used stones from the
theatre of Marcellus in his reconstruction of one of the
bridges.

Stripped bare of its architects, with its artisan class impoverished and oppressed by imperial officials, Rome was but
poorly equipped either to preserve her old art or to inaugu-
rate a new one. And yet this is what it proceeded to accomplish, with a zeal that was pathetic if we remember its reduced
circumstances, for the Romans remained devoted lovers of
their monuments even until the Gothic wars, as Procopius
then assures us.

The exodus affected art radically because it struck at the
roots of the two classes that had contributed the most to its
development: the aristocracy and the corporations of artisans.
The first blow to the homogeneity of the aristocracy had been
dealt when, in the third century, Rome ceased to be the
political capital of the Empire. Already during the reign of
Diocletian and his colleagues many senatorial magnates had
broken up their great establishments in and about Rome.
But until the foundation of Constantinople the absenteeism of
the aristocracy had been largely temporary. After 325 a new
Roman aristocracy was founded at Constantinople, drawn
largely from that of old Rome. The Senate of the new capital
had the advantage of being at the real centre of the Empire.
The ambitious all left the old stranded ship of State. They
carried away with them from Rome a large retinue of all
classes, and with their departure a large source of Roman
wealth ran dry.

The departure was felt even more disastrously in the country district around Rome than in the city itself. Many large
estates were totally abandoned. There were none wealthy
enough to take up their burden. At the close of this cen-

tury, a document of the year 395 indicates that one of the results had been that five hundred square miles of arable land around Rome had become a morass, and that malaria, the new scourge of the Campagna, had made frightful progress.

Enslavement of the Art Corporations. — The withdrawal of so many of the wealthy affected the prosperity of the artists and artisans of Rome during the fourth century. The Greek artists who had contributed the element of æsthetic beauty in previous centuries had mostly left Rome in the third century, following imperial patronage. The cream of the remaining artists and artisans were called to Constantinople during the decade after 325 to build and decorate the new city. The bulk of those that remained in Rome were the poorer practitioners.

It is a well-known fact that under Diocletian and his successors the imperial authority over the corporations of artisans was absolute, and that only by order of the Emperor could any of them pass from one city to another, so that it was perfectly possible for Constantine to draft as many as he chose of the Roman artisans to form a nucleus for the new corporations in Constantinople. The Theodosian code shows how seriously Constantine and his successors sought to increase the ranks and ameliorate the condition of the artisans and of the better class of artists, — painters and architects, — but it was in the provinces and in Constantinople, not in Rome, that these efforts were put forth.

Their legislation and that of Diocletian show only too clearly how ground down and bound down these men had become. No man could follow an art unless he belonged to his union. Once a member of it, he could not leave it till he died. Nor could he leave the city where he had matriculated. His son was bound to follow the art of his father, who was also his teacher. Each corporation was a distinct wheel in the imperial organism, a State within a State, but subject absolutely to the control of the imperial administration. This went to the extent of forcing each corporation to give to the State as much free labor and free material as was required for the construction, decoration and repair of all public buildings.

No wonder that, enervated by the forced hereditary nature of their occupation, without freedom of choice, without adequate remuneration, they fell more and more into the disastrous habit of scamping the quality and solidity of their work on public buildings. Neither can we blame them if, delivered from the eagle-eyed supervision of the skilled architects and superintendents, long since departed, they plundered the old buildings to build the new and abandoned the old traditions of the masters whose great masses of concrete masonry seemed built for eternity.

Corruption in Rome. — The picture of Roman life drawn by the pagan historian, Ammianus Marcellinus, just after the middle of the fourth century, and during the next half century by men like Salvianus and S. Jerome, show a further cause for artistic decay, for this life was incurably corrupt and devitalized. The Church appeared to make but little impression on its lubricity and self-indulgence. In fact, nearly all the men of culture and refinement, including the aristocracy, were still pagans.

It was to turn this current that we find the leaders of the Church organizing religious instruction by means of art, setting on the walls of the basilicas the landmarks of faith, with a feverish zeal that shows how crucial a moment in the history of Christianity they felt it to be. The origin of monasticism was due to the bitterness of the delusion of the really religious, who saw that, since fashion and authority had stamped Christianity with their approval, the Church as a unit had become infected with most of the soft vices of paganism. But the men with firmest fibre put up a stiff fight, helped by a cohort of the most wonderful women, many of whom were Jerome's friends.

The biography of one of these women, Melania the younger, written by her secretary, has recently been published. She and her husband spent some twenty-seven years in realizing and distributing her immense possessions in the various countries, which are said to have yielded her an income equivalent to $175,000,000 of modern money. She spent the capital in building and endowing churches, monasteries, nunneries and

hospitals and in providing them with sacred and useful vestments, ornaments and utensils, as well as in various forms of
charity. Unless greatly exaggerated, the money thus invested
far surpassed the combined fortunes of the Rockefellers, Car-
negie and the Astors, and the larger part was employed in
the creation of monuments of Christian art in Rome and elsewhere. Others did the same on a smaller scale.

Church Organization. — In selecting sites for such monuments
the Church was prudent. The political shrewdness shown by
the Emperors was emulated by the Popes. As late as the fifth
century the Church hesitated to wound pagan susceptibilities
by planting the standard of the faith in the inner stronghold
of the historic past, in the precincts of the Forums and the
Palatine Hill bristling with the temples of the gods. The
churches were set in inconspicuous and distant quarters, without the walls, on the outskirts, across the Tiber.

The establishment of Christian festivals on the same dates
as pagan ones, and with analogous ceremonies, made it easy for
the populace to pass over to the new faith without the loss of
the pomp and circumstance and play that were so necessary
to these materialists, however reformed.

For purposes of administration the city was then divided
into fourteen civil districts or regions, " regiones." The Christian church seems not to have followed this civil division, but
for its own organization to have adopted seven divisions, each
governed by a deacon. Within these divisions were the parish
churches, of which the number finally adopted at this time
was twenty-five. These churches were called *tituli*, and have
continued, with a few additions, to modern times. They later
gave their titles to the most important group of the college of
cardinals. These *tituli* were the earliest churches within the
walls of Rome.

Parish Churches. — These parish churches during the fifth
century seem to have been the following : —

Reg. I (1) S. Xysti (= T. Crescentianæ ?)

Reg. II (2) Bizanti or Pammachii (= mod. SS. Giovanni
and Paolo); (3) Æmilianæ (= SS. Quattro Coronati ?)

Reg. III (4) Clementis (= S. Clemente); (5) SS. Marcellini

et Petri; (6) Apostolorum (= Eudoxiæ = S. Pietro in Vincoli); (7) Equitii (= Silvestri = S. Martino ai Monti).

Reg. V (8) Praxedis (= S. Prassede); (9) Pudentis (= S. Pudenziana); (10) Eusebii (= S. Eusebio).

Reg. VI (11) Vestinæ (= S. Vitale); (12) Gai (= S. Susanna); (13) Cyriaci.

Reg. VIII (14) Marcelli (= S. Marcello).

Reg. IX (15) Lucinæ (= S. Lorenzo in Lucina); (16) Damasi (= S. Lorenzo in Damaso); (17) Marci (= in Pallacinis = S. Marco)

Reg. XI (18) Anastasiæ (= S. Anastasia).

Reg. XII (19) Fasciolæ (= SS. Nereo ed Achilleo); (20) Balbinæ (= S. Balbina).

Reg. XIII (21) Sabinæ (= S. Sabina); (22) Priscæ (= S. Prisca).

Reg. XIV (23) Julii (= Callixtus = S. Maria in Trastevere); (24) Caeciliæ (= S. Cecilia); (25) Chrysogoni (= S. Crisogono).

To each of these parish churches was attached a Catacomb outside the walls for the burial of its church-members, and above or in the bowels of this Catacomb were one or more basilicas dedicated to the principal martyrs buried there. The religious services in these suburban basilicas were at first in charge of the clergy of its parish church in the city, and only later was it found necessary to establish monasteries at the main suburban churches to relieve the parish priests of this duty.

It was an old Roman law that forbade burial within the city wall, and, as in everything else, Christianity never abruptly broke with Roman custom, so that throughout the fourth and fifth centuries burials continued outside the walls. The only known exception is that of SS. John and Paul, martyred under Julian the Apostate in their own house on the Cœlian, whose bodies were left in the house itself and the church built there a half century later. A number of the *tituli* were built on the site of the house of some wealthy convert which had been used for worship in the era of persecution. S. Cecilia was the house of the Cæcilii; S. Lorenzo in Lucina was the house of Lucina. Or else the church was called from the person who gave the land; thus the church built by Pope Sylvester was called the *titulus Equitii,* from a priest who gave the site, and those of Vestina under Innocent I, of Crescentiana under Anastasius and of Sabina under Celestine were named for the same reason. The city churches originally, then, were not called by the names of saints and martyrs; this was a later transformation.

The ecclesiastical organization of the Christian population very closely affected the distribution and number of the

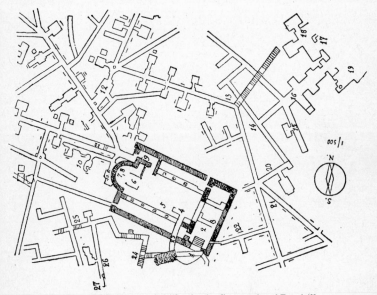

Basilica of SS. Nereo e Achilleo in the Catacombs of Domitilla.

churches. We can study it at the close of the fifth century, when its formative period was over, and documentary evidence is more exact. It was at these twenty-five parish churches in which services were regularly held that the poor were fed and clothed. Only later, after the Gothic wars (end VI c.), was the special class of diaconal churches organized for the distribution of charity, which the diminished civic and ecclesiastical wealth henceforth sadly reduced.

There were, of course, many other churches in the city besides these parish churches, and an even larger number strung along all the main roads leading from the city. In fact, these suburban basilicas, erected at the tombs of the apostles and martyrs, were ordinarily of greater magnificence than the parish churches; such were the basilicas of S. Peter, S. Paul, S. Lorenzo, S. Agnese and others. To neither class belonged such superb monuments as the Lateran, the Cathedral of Christendom, and S. Maria Maggiore, the greatest church of the Virgin.

Viewing the city in its monuments of all kinds, pagan, Christian and civil, it is certain that at any time before the sacks of Alaric (410) and Genseric (455) we may think of Rome as a great pleasure-seeking centre, surrounded by a wonderful garden of immense extent, not, as now, interrupted by a malarial *Campagna*, but extending far away to the hills and the sea in a bewildering labyrinth of beautiful villas, of Christian sanctuaries and rural shrines, filled with works of art, still cared for by a well-organized multitude of slaves and dependants, and enjoyed by a careless horde of masters or a tolerant class of ecclesiastics, quite unconscious of the rude awakening and the coming drop of the curtain upon all this gorgeousness.

Art under the Popes after Constantine.— To study the details of the Christian art of the fourth century, we must return on our footsteps and follow the lives of the Popes after Constantine, chronicling the monuments under each one of them.

There was no surcease of activity after the death of his contemporary, Pope Sylvester. Even the brief pontificate of about a year of his immediate successor, Marc, saw the construction of two basilicas: S. Balbina, a small cemeterial church near the Via Ardeatina, where this Pope was buried, and a larger church within the city, called, after him, the basilica of Marc as well as *basilicam in Pallacinis*, which became one of the twenty-five titular churches.[1]

In connection with S. Balbina was one of the earliest of those

---

[1] Hic fecit duas basilicas unam via Ardeatina ubi requiescit et aliam in urbe Roma iuxta Pallacinis.

cemeteries for burial *sub dio* (above ground), which were used
throughout the fourth century, besides the traditional burials in
the subterranean galleries of the Catacombs, together with the
others at S. Agnese, S. Peter, etc.

Julius and Basilica of S. Valentinus. — The longer pontificate
of Julius (337–352) was artistically most active. Even the
text of the *Liber Pontificalis* notes this fact, as it enumerates
his principal structures.[1] He favored the extramural region
of the Catacombs even more than the city itself. His greatest
work seems to have been the basilica of Valentinus, the main
centre of worship and pilgrimage on the Via Flaminia, two
miles beyond the city gate, from which it got its name *Porta S.
Valentini.* The keen policy of the church, in transmuting
pagan into Christian anniversaries, was illustrated in this basilica. For the old procession along the Flaminian Way on
April 25, called the *Robigalia*, by which all the people sought
to propitiate the elements and secure good crops, was continued
on that day, and the basilica of S. Valentinus was made its
bourne. This church was apparently worthy of taking its
place beside the now better-known suburban basilicas. Its ruins
were excavated in 1888. The atrium, facing the Roman road,
was immense, to receive the great crowd of processionists and
pilgrims, but has not yet been excavated. The church itself,
some forty m. long, had three aisles, the central one as much
as twelve m. wide, with Ionic columns of gray granite.
In one peculiarity the practice here was unique. In all other
suburban basilicas, erected at the tombs of the principal martyrs, everything was sacrificed in order to leave the remains of
the martyr untouched and *in situ.* The disinclination to change
was absolute. In order to set the altar in its right relation to
the tomb of the martyr, several basilicas had to be sunk so deep
into the ground as to become almost subterranean, as was the
case at S. Agnese, S. Lorenzo, S. Petronilla and S. Alessandro.[2]

[1] Hic multas fabricas fecit: basilicam in Via Portuense miliario III, basilicam in Via Flaminia, mil. II, quae appelatur Valentini, basilicam Juliam quae
est regione VII iuxta Forum divi Traiani, basilicam transtiberim, regione
XIIII, iuxta Callistum, basilicam in Via Aurelia, mil. III, ad Callistum.

[2] Sometimes, even, the basilica was entirely subterranean, like that of
S. Ippolito.

But in the case of the Catacomb of S. Valentino the hill made such a scheme impossible, and the basilica was backed against the hill, between it and the road; and the body of the saint was actually transferred from the Catacomb to the church. Around the new tomb an ambulacrum or corridor was constructed, communicating with the side aisles, but below the level of the church, in imitation of the galleries of the Catacombs, — probably the first example of a custom that became current many centuries later, at S. Prassede, for example, when the violation of the sacred remains in the Catacombs by Lombards and Saracens forced the Popes of the eighth and ninth centuries to remove the bodies of the martyrs to the churches within the walls. The arrangement had been copied even earlier, at S. Pancrazio, on the Via Aurelia, in the time of Pope Honorius (625–638).

Of the other basilicas built by Julius nothing remains of his time, though two are still famous — the urban basilica of the Apostles (= bas. Iulia) and that of S. Maria in Trastevere (= bas. Transtiberim, etc.), which have undergone many transformations. Of the other two suburban basilicas, that on the Via Portuensis seems to be the basilica of Felix, of which no trace has yet been found, while that on the Via Aurelia connected with the Catacomb of Callixtus was selected by Pope Julius as his burial place.

Liberius and S. Maria Maggiore. — The days of Pope Liberius (352–366) were rather dark for Rome and Orthodoxy. The Emperor Constantius had violently constituted himself the apostle of Arianism. The withdrawal of the financial help of the imperial Treasury combined with the exile of Liberius himself to reduce artistic activity in Rome, especially in the ecclesiastical field. The Pope's life merely tells us that he made a basilica that was called by his name next to the Macellum Liviæ.[1] This basilica, rebuilt or restored by Sixtus III in the following century, is the famous church of S. Maria Maggiore. It is a matter of some doubt how much of the church structure and its mosaic decoration belong to the time of Liberius. It has been most improbably suggested that the

[1] Fecit basilicam nomine suo iuxta macellum Libiæ.

main walls and windows are earlier, and belong to a hall of the
second century, a *basilica Sicinini*, which formed part of a
large private palace. The theory that attributes to the time
of Liberius the original structure and the mosaic pictures of
the nave, with their Old Testament histories, seems the more
probable.[1]

Damasus and the Revival. — The eighteen years of Pope
Damasus (366–384) were not only remarkable for an increasing
intensity in religious art and cult, but for the renewed interest
taken by the Emperors themselves in the monumental welfare
of the city. The immediate successors of Constantine, — Constantius, Constans, Julian, — far from adding new buildings,
hardly provided for necessary repairs, and it was only after
Gratian had become sole ruler (378) that the imperial ex-
chequer was again opened for the benefit of the orthodox
Church in Rome.

The latest historian of the Papacy regards Damasus as the
greatest Pope of the fourth century ; and this because he was
no opportunist, but a man with clear and far-reaching aims in
Church policy ; a successful opponent of heresy ; a promoter of
unity and of the supremacy of Rome ; a standard-bearer of the
Church's independence of imperial interference. But there is
a phase of this Pope's career that is of vivid interest for the
internal history of Rome as a city, if we bear in mind the fact
that it seemed rapidly sinking into such a slough of spiritual
decrepitude as to call forth cries of warning from the principal
leaders of the Church. Like his great contemporaries, Augustine
and Jerome, he was keenly sensitive to the growing worldliness
of the Christian community of Rome and the contaminating influence both of the superior culture of pagan society and of the
very apathy due to Christian success. He seems to have felt
that, besides the weapons of theological controversy, of monastic example, of moral exhortation, there was another of great
power — that of example of the past.

[1] Meanwhile the anti-pope Felix (355–358), during his period of possession,
had built a basilica called after him *basilica Felicis*, on the Via Aurelia. It
was a structure of considerable age and magnificence, restored by Hadrian I,
but of which even the site is now unknown.

To steep his flock in the blood of the martyrs, Damasus devoted himself to the work of seeking out their tombs in the various Catacombs, of establishing their centres of pilgrimage and worship, setting up at each tomb superb metrical memorial inscriptions, with the history and praises of the dead. All the Catacombs seem to have been carefully searched and their most sacred centres thus fixed and commemorated. For several centuries they served as the finger-post to pilgrims who have left us copies of some forty of these poetic inscriptions, copies that have enabled modern explorers to identify many a tomb through the discovery of a small fragment of one of them. We even know the name of the secretary of Damasus, Furius Dionysius Filocalus, to whom the peculiar beauty of the Damasian inscriptions is due. Damasus thus constituted himself, in a way, the historian of the martyrs, drawing his material largely from the archives of the Roman Church, of which he was librarian before being Pope. But for him the modern world would know far less of early Christian Rome.

In fact, the basilica in Rome, which was called after him S. Lorenzo in Damaso,[1] was a building of peculiar interest, flanked on either side by porticos in which were lodged the archives and libraries of the Roman Church, and where they seem to have been kept until they were transferred, perhaps in the following century, to the palace of the Lateran. Nothing remains above ground of this unique building, but excavations in the Cancelleria Palace have made an interesting reconstruction of its arrangement possible. As for his basilica on the Via Ardeatina, where he was buried, with his mother and sister, near the Catacombs of Domitilla, it has completely disappeared.

The basilica of S. Sebastiano, which Damasus built in connection with the famous Platonia, where the bodies of Peter and Paul had rested for a time in the era of persecution, has

[1] The life of Damasus thus describes his artistic activity: "Hic fecit basilicas duas: una beato Laurentio iuxta theatrum et alia Via Ardeatina ubi requiescit; et in catacumbas ubi iacuerunt corpora SS. Apostolorum Petri et Pauli . . . platoniam . . . versibus exornavit. Hic multa corpora sanctorum requisivit et invenit, quod et versibus declaravit. Hic constituit titulum in urbe Roma basilicam quam ipse construxit."

for many centuries preserved but slight traces of its Damasian form. To Damasus other sources attribute the completion of the basilica of Rufina and Secunda on the Via Cornelia, begun by Pope Julius; the building in the Catacomb of Generosa of the basilica of SS. Simplicius, Faustinus and Beatrix, of the basilica of SS. Petronilla, Nereus and Achilleus in the cemetery of Domitilla.

Perhaps to his pontificate belongs also the primitive basilica of S. Clemente. The fate of S. Clemente has been curious.

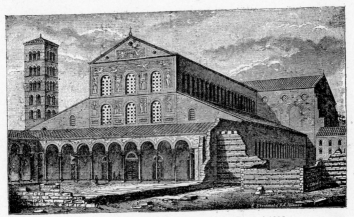

S. Paul in the Middle Ages, before the Fire of 1823.

The primitive church, redecorated early in the sixth century, subsisted until the fire of Guiscard in 1084, and when it was rebuilt, some thirty years later, its ruined decorations were used in constructing and decorating the new basilica. The old church was left as the crypt of the new, and so we can see that, as was so often the case, the early Christian Church was considerably larger than the mediæval. I will also mention here the house of the martyrs John and Paul, on the Cœlian; its unique frescos will be described elsewhere.

Siricius and S. Paul's. — A curious injustice was done to Pope Siricius (384–399) in the official annals. Not a single monument is credited to his pontificate. The new basilica of S. Paul was, however, built at this time and dedicated by him. His name is still to be seen on a column saved from the fire of 1823, *Siricius episcopus tota mente devotus*, while on the base the date of Nov. 18, 390, is given as that of the consecration of the church by the Pope. In the imperial letter addressed in 386 to the prefect of Rome, Sallust, ordering the construction of the church, the Emperors, while placing the

Ruins of S. Paul, after the Fire of 1823.

architect (probably Cyriades) at the orders of the prefect, according to immemorial custom, advised the prefect to consult the Pope in everything. The new basilica was faced in the opposite direction from the Constantinian building, and was so much larger that its transept alone was larger than the entire old church.

To Siricius should also be given the credit of completing some of the buildings commenced by Damasus, for instance, the basilica of S. Petronilla. He doubtless also encouraged the wealthy proconsul and senator, Pammachius, the devout friend of S. Jerome, to build in 398 his famous hospital and basilica at Porto, and to erect a parish church over the house of the martyrs John and Paul on the Cœlian.

The excavations on the site of the hospital at Porto have disclosed the plan and arrangements of this only building of its kind. It centres around a quadriportico or atrium and a basilica exactly like the contemporary churches, and it seems certain that this building was for religious and not civil purposes. The rooms and halls for the sick and poor were grouped around it. The only peculiarity about the basilica was that its aisles were separated not by columns, but by piers; but as this peculiarity also appears at S. Sinforosa on the Via Tiburtina and S. Petronilla, which are certainly early churches, it is no argument against this building at Porto being a church.

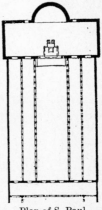

Plan of S. Paul.

His most valuable remaining artistic record is the church of S. Pudentiana and its mosaic. This church is connected

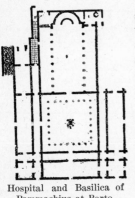

Hospital and Basilica of Pammachius at Porto.

with the family of Pudens and with some of the earliest Christian traditions of Rome. Its peculiar wide apse seems to indicate a pre-Constantinian hall church. It became as early as the fourth century one of the parish churches with three aisles. Formerly it had mosaics and inscriptions of this time that have perished, and among these was one which read: *Salvo Siricio episcopo ecclesiæ sanctæ et Ilicio Leopardo et Maximo presbb.* The three priests here mentioned had charge of the construction or decoration of the church, and two of them receive the credit in another lost inscription which gives the dates 387–398 for the work:—

E

FVND. A. LEOPARDO. ET. ILICIO . . .

VALENT(INIANO) AVG ET (387–390)

PERFECTA HONORIO AVGVSTO IIII ET

EVTYCIANO COS (398)

Another suburban Constantinian basilica, that of S. Lorenzo, — was restored by Leopardus, this time at his own expense and perhaps because the church, being sunk so deeply in the bowels of the Catacomb, was flooded with water.

The coöperation of these same priests of the *ecclesia Pudentiana* with the civil authorities, and especially with the prefect, is a most interesting instance of what we may conclude to have been quite a common occurrence. The Prefect Messala embellished the long street on which the church stood, the *Vicus Patricius*, with a colonnade, doubtless to connect it with the general network of colonnades throughout the city. But it was not done entirely at the expense either of the Emperor's or the city's treasury. A certain section, apparently on either side of S. Pudentiana, and beginning at the oratory of S. Hippolytus, was done by the priest Ilicius at his own expense. He recorded this in an inscription: *Omnia quæ videntur / a memoria sancti martyris Yppoliti usque huc / surgere tecta Ilicius / presb. sumptu proprio fecit.*

These two priests, — Leopardus and Ilicius, — must have been extremely wealthy members of the clergy, for we shall find Leopardus engaged in extensive building operations at his own expense under the successors of Siricius, and they may also be regarded as superintending architects with technical knowledge.

Anastasius. — It is impossible to identify even the site of the one basilica — the titulus Crescentianæ[1] — attributed to the brief pontificate of Anastasius (399–401), who was buried on the Via Portuensis, not far from the great basilica of Abdon and Sennen, built at about this time, if not earlier, over the cemetery of Pontianus.

[1] Fecit . . . basilicam quæ dicitur crescentiana, in regione II, via Mamurtini.

Innocent. — The sixteen years of Pope Innocent (401–417) were full of stress and pathos, of artistic production and destruction. They saw the reconstruction of the walls and gates of Rome, to protect her against the expected invasions, and the erection of the last triumphal imperial monuments. They saw the flight of a large part of the population, both rich and poor, and the terrible blow of the capture of Rome in 410, which meant for all nations throughout the empire, East and West, the shattering of her inviolability, of the ideal of the *Roma Dea.* They witnessed the bitter controversy between pagans and Christians as to the responsibility for the catastrophe, and they also saw the courageous attempts to rebuild the ruined buildings, bring back the exiles and restore public confidence.

II. ROME FROM ALARIC TO THEODORIC THE GOTH

If all the deterioration and decay thus far described happened as early as the fourth century, when Rome was still prosperous and happy, what was to happen when the flood of barbarian invasion broke all barriers in the fifth century and Rome was sacked three times?

For some time before Alaric actually entered Rome in 410 fear had driven away a large part of the population. Sicily, Africa, Constantinople, Sardinia, Dalmatia, Gaul and many other parts of the Empire received thousands of fugitives. They were of all classes, but we hear principally of the two that particularly interest the history of art — the patricians and the artisans.

When the scourge had passed, special legislation was found necessary to force the artisans of the corporations to return. They must have emigrated *en masse.* We can easily imagine that the hunt throughout the provinces for these unwilling fugitives from Rome, who mostly hated the yoke of their occupation, must have been largely futile. The majority of the aristocracy also never returned, but helped to make the Constantinople of Honorius several times as large as that of Constantine and to fill it with monuments that far surpassed those that had been built in Rome since the days of Diocletian.

Now indeed the ruin of the great estates around Rome was almost consummated; the backbone of public art in Rome finally broken. It is true that the efforts of the imperial police and the influx of refugees, mostly poor, from other parts of Italy, especially from the country districts that were more exposed to the ravages of barbarian hordes, again raised the number of the inhabitants of Rome to such an extent that in 417 the prefect of the city asked for an increase in the amount of the imperial dole or largesse to the poor. But this was rather a source of weakness than of revival, a further step in the pauperization and degradation of the city, consummated by the sack of Genseric in 455.

And it was not only Constantinople and other cities outside of Italy that acted as lodestars for aristocrats, artists and artisans. Ravenna, which rivalled and finally succeeded Milan as the centre of imperial power in Italy, was growing into a monumental city, the link between East and West. This growth, which began in the last decade of the fourth century, continued uninterrupted. Undoubtedly many corporation artisans who fled there from Rome in 410 never returned, and joined the local organizations, which were so largely Hellenic. Hence sprang up almost at once a fruitful composite art, an art specifically Christian. It has been noticed that with the year 410 there seems to have been an absolute break in the production of sculpture in Rome, particularly in the branch of sarcophagi with reliefs, of which the Roman school was so prolific in superb examples throughout the fourth century. Not a single example in Rome can be dated after 410. It would seem as if the whole Roman corporation of stone-carvers had left and never returned. Did many of them go to Southern Gaul, that last and most brilliant refuge of Roman culture, where, especially at Arles, there was at this time a wealth of such sarcophagi? Did they go to Spain, to Milan, to Trier, where such sarcophagi are found? At all events it seems as if some of them went to Ravenna and bent their art to suit the spirit of the place, for suddenly, after complete sculptural silence, the Ravenna of the years immediately after Alaric blooms with a school of sculptured sarcophagi that continues to develop uninterruptedly for two centuries as the logical successor of the Roman school, though transformed by the special artistic spirit that was so potent in Ravenna from the beginning.

But was there no reflex action, very soon, of Ravenna upon Rome? When the Empress Galla Placidia and her son Valentinian, children of Byzantium, who turned their capital and residence, Ravenna, into a great centre of Christian art, began to devote large sums to the beautifying of Rome, they must have been forced to supply the better class of artists as well as the funds. That the imperial court at Ravenna had under its control a considerable body of artists is evident. Agnellus, the chronicler of Ravenna, says, for example, that Galla Placidia placed thirteen builders at the disposal of the Princess Sigelgaita for the construction of a church. Honorius had a court architect, Lauricius, whom he sent to Ravenna to superintend the building of S. Lorenzo in Cæsarea.

Between 420 and 450 we meet in Rome with a new art, in monuments of the greatest interest; foremost of which are the wooden doors of S. Sabina and the mosaics of the triumphal arch of S. Maria Maggiore. We can hardly explain this art on the basis of the simple Catacomb frescos or the reliefs of the sarcophagi. It shows the mark of Ravenna on Rome, which preceded and prepared the mark of Constantinople. The winged angels; the white-robed apostles, prophets and saints, marked with the sign of the Lamb; the abode of the blessed as a city, not a garden; the emphasis laid on the King-Christ instead of the Christ as miracle-worker and teacher: these are some of the elements that seem to have been introduced or fostered by the artists of Ravenna. We see the final act of this influence in the mosaic of SS. Cosma and Damiano and the frescos of the cemetery of Commodilla.

Reviewing the various elements of the situation up to this time, the impression we gain is that there was no interruption in the monumental life of the city until the close of the reign of Honorius; that even after the sack and fire of 410 the work of reconstruction was resumed along the old lines as far as the limited financial and artistic means allowed. Ancient Rome was not yet completely fossilized. Its corporations still held to the old methods and orders and ornaments. The city prefects still had charge of public monuments, with the growing assistance of leading ecclesiastics such as Leopardus. For instance, Pope Innocent placed in charge of the ubiquitous Leopardus and his colleague Paulinus the basilica of S. Agnese, which had evidently suffered severely from Alaric's hordes, being outside the city. They were to roof it and decorate it (*gubernari et tegi et ornari*) as well as administer it. As the same Leopardus was also put in charge of the construction of the new parish church of Vestina, it is natural that this basilica should use the cemetery of S. Agnese for the burial of its members.

In fact, there is an interesting passage in the *Liber Pontificalis*, showing how churches were then sometimes built, relating to this parish church called from its founder *basilica* or *titulus Vestinæ*. The Pope's life says that "he dedicated the basilica of SS. Gervasius and Protasius, built at the expense of an illustrious woman named Vestina, under the direction of the priests Ursicinus and Leopardus and the deacon Livianus." By a clause in her will this woman ordered that this basilica should be built from the proceeds of the sale of her ornaments and pearls, etc. It also appears that she specified that these two priests should have charge of the work. The Pope gave rich ornaments to the church, which corresponds to the present church of S. Vitale.

Boniface and S. Felicitas. — The next two pontificates, of Zozimus (417–418) and Boniface (418–422), were too short and agitated to have left monumental records of interest. The papal authority and prosperity were still temporarily undermined by the capture of Rome by Alaric, and hardly able to withstand the assaults of the Pelagian and Nestorian heresies.

We may connect with Boniface a work of art not only interesting in itself, but as an artistic landmark — the chapel of S. Felicitas with its frescos near the baths of Trajan. Boniface, when opposed by the antipope Eulalius, had received an imperial order to leave Rome and had sought refuge in the buildings above the cemetery of Felicitas on the Via Salaria. He attributed to her protection his triumphant return to Rome, and built and decorated an oratory to her at the Catacomb,[1] where he directed that he should be buried. There still exists in Rome an oratory of this saint, thought to have been built in her house and place of captivity, decorated with

---

[1] Hic fecit oratorium in cymeterio S. Felicitatis, iuxta corpus eius et ornavit sepulchrum S. martyris Felicitatis et Sancti Silvani.

frescos like those at the Catacomb, representing Felicitas and
her seven sons, all martyred as in heaven, crowned by the

S. Felicitas and her Children, Martyrs.
Fresco in her chapel.

hand of Christ. This painting is a last echo of the purely
Latin style of Catacomb fresco, before the advent of the first

breath of foreign influence, whether Hellenic or Oriental, that was to add spiritual and poetic elements to the art of Rome even before transforming it into its own image. The art of Boniface was still simply Roman; that of Sixtus III was impregnated with a new spirit.

Celestine and Galla Placidia. — Shortly after Celestine (422–432) became Pope, the Emperor Honorius died (423), and the Empire was ridded of a worse than incapable incumbrance, of a futile and chicken-hearted fool to whom more than to any

Incrusted Marble Decoration of Nave of S. Sabina.

other man the downfall of the Western Empire was due. His much-tried sister Galla Placidia became Empress of the West as guardian of her young son Valentinian III. Whatever her capacity as a ruler, she was a great patron of art. Established at Ravenna she helped to Byzantinize its art with artists from Constantinople. A comparison of the earlier virile and realistic mosaics of the baptistery of the cathedral of Ravenna with the more Hellenic and poetic mosaics of the mausoleum of Placidia illustrates the change wrought in little more than a decade. That Placidia had a large part in the activity among all branches of religious art that set in at Rome is proved by the famous inscription of the mosaic on the triumphal arch of S. Paul's, stating that it had been commenced by Theodosius, finished by Honorius, and that under Pope Leo it was restored and decorated by Placidia. Then again, the construction of the larger basilica of S. Lorenzo, "basilica maior," under Sixtus, is attributed by the *Liber Pontificalis* to Valentinian; but as he was then a mere youth of fifteen or twenty, he was certainly only his mother's puppet in these works.

Once more, then, imperial gifts were poured into the coffers of the church at Rome, and the days of Constantine seemed

Interior of S. Sabina.
(Early fifth century.)

renewed. The treasuries of the churches were again filled with superb works of the goldsmith's art. Though the political capital of the West continued to be Ravenna, the imperial family — Placidia, Valentinian and then his wife Eudoxia — lived for a large part of the time in Rome. The connection between the two cities became extremely intimate.

In the life of Celestine we read one of the few distinct

records of the damage done to Roman monuments by the sack of 410. He restored and enriched the basilica Julia, now S. Maria in Trastevere *post ignem geticum*, "after the Gothic fire." The important series of paintings or mosaics which he placed on its walls are cited by Pope Hadrian more than three centuries and a half later in his letter to Charlemagne.

Completely a monument of this age is the basilica of S. Sabina, commenced under Celestine and finished under Sixtus. The *Liber Pontificalis* refers it entirely to the reign of Sixtus : " *Et huius temporibus fecit Petrus episcopus basilicam in urbe Roma sanctæ Savinæ ubi et fontem construxit.*" But from the dedicatory inscription it was founded under his predecessor, and its columns are supposed to have been taken from the near-by temple of Juno Regina ruined by Alaric. Its decoration in mosaic and *opus sectile* of rich marbles, its unique carved doors and the excellence of its design, are proofs of the persistence of a high quality of workmanship.

Sixtus. — The pontificate of Sixtus (432–440) is monumentally famous for the basilica of S. Maria Maggiore which the *L. P.* attributes to him : *hic fecit basilicam S. Mariæ quæ ab antiquis Liberii cognominabatur, iuxta macellum Libiae;* though we suspect that he merely restored it and decorated it with some of its mosaics. More certainly his work was a basilica which he built to S. Lawrence next to that erected by Constantine and rebuilt by Leopardus over the martyr's tomb. The *L. P.* says : *fecit basilicam sancto Laurentio quod Valentinus Augustus concessit.* Evidently the Emperor supplied the funds. The apse of this basilica backed against that of the earlier sanctuary and it was called *maior*, the larger, to distinguish it from the earlier one, which was called *ad corpus*, *i.e.* built over the martyr's grave itself. He also enlarged the Lateran baptistery, placing there the eight porphyry columns still remaining : *constituit columnas in baptisterium basilicæ Constantinianæ, quas a tempore Constantini Augusti fuerunt congregatas ex metallo purphyretico numero VIII, quas erexit cum epistolis suis et versibus exornavit.*

At S. Sebastiano he built a monastery, one of the earliest if not the earliest in Rome, the forerunner of the many that were soon to be established next to all the suburban basilicas in order to insure the continuous religious services which could not possibly be supplied by the parish clergy of the city church with which each basilica outside the walls was connected.

This Pope was industrious in continuing to repair the damage done by Alaric, not only in restoring churches, but in replacing the sacred vessels and sculptures in metal that had been de-

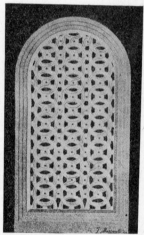

Pierced Marble Windows of the Fifth Century.

stroyed. More such precious objects are enumerated as his gifts than are attributed to any Pope since Sylvester; in this he was helped by imperial munificence. The confession and ciborium of S. Lorenzo *ad corpus* are described in detail, including a silver statue of the martyr, as well as numerous vessels. The Constantinian ciborium at the Lateran basilica, destroyed by Alaric, was replaced by the Emperor Valentinian: *fecit autem Valentinianus Augustus ex rogatu Xysti Episcopi fastidium argenteum in basilica Constantiniana; quod a bar-*

baris sublatum fuerat. It was of silver, weighed two thousand pounds and was decorated with figures of Christ and the apostles.

More plainly than any previous Pope did Sixtus III wield art and inscriptions in defence of dogma. He dedicated his mosaics at S. Maria Maggiore to the people: *Sixtus Episcopus*

Interior of S. Pietro in Vincoli.
(Fifth century, from antique materials, and Barocco.)

plebi dei; and selected the themes of his mosaics so as to illustrate the dogma of the divine motherhood of the Virgin, just proclaimed by the Council of Ephesus. His great inscription at the Lateran baptistery is so worded as officially to proclaim the orthodox doctrine of original sin against the dangerous heresy of Pelagianism, then current.

Not mentioned in the Papal Chronicles is another church — that of S. Pietro in Vincoli — whose construction was due, according to tradition, to the munificence of another imperial lady, Eudoxia, daughter of Theodosius II and wife of Valentinian, one

of those tragic female figures of the last days of the struggle
with the barbarians, so full of epic contrasts. Years before she
was carried off to Africa as Genseric's prisoner, after the sack
of Rome in 455, she had built this church in the time of Sixtus III, and it was later called, after her, *basilica Eudoxiana*.
It contained the famous relic of the chains of S. Peter, and so
its final name became S. Peter *ad Vincula*. Though often
restored, it retains its original plan and columns, and is not
only one of the most important remaining churches of the
pre-Gothic age, but is unique in Rome in having columns of
the Doric order, whose effect is almost obliterated by the
barbarous Barocco superstructure.

Leo. — In Leo the Great (440–461) the Church found its
greatest leader. His times were big with both glory and disaster : the glory of the deliverance from Attila and his Huns
through Leo's personal genius in 452 ; the disaster of the sack
of Rome by Genseric and his Vandals in 455. Leo's lament
that, after the city had been saved from Attila, the citizens
showed their joy by flocking not to the churches, but to the
games of the circus, is a fit counterpart to the absolute lack of
resistance to the Vandal raid in 455. Genseric carried off or
destroyed not only the bulk of works of both pagan and Christian art in bronze and the precious metals, but a large number of
illustrious captives. Rome was depleted of most of its remaining wealthy families. Their great estates in various parts of
Italy had been mostly destroyed. The theory of Rome's inviolability, already shattered by Alaric, was destroyed. The
Roman Empire had been still represented at the beginning of
Leo's reign by powerful individualities like the Empress Galla
Placidia. The murder of Ætius in 455 removed from the political scene the last heroic figure; the murder of Valentinian,
shortly after, removed the last male representative of the dynasty of the great Theodosius. Then came Genseric.

Artistic Atrophy. — Civic art, even now, was not quite dead,
though atrophied by the decay and flight of the art corporations.
Statues in bronze and marble were still erected, especially in
the Forum of Trajan. Maximus, before he became Emperor in
455, had been honored by a bronze statue in this Forum ; so

was the famous Gallic writer, Sidonius Apollinaris, in 456, by vote of the Senate.

Majorian, himself, took vigorous steps to check the decay of the city's monuments, and issued a decree which was embodied in Justinian's code and is a real landmark. He says : —

" We, the rulers of the State, with a view to restoring the beauty of our venerable city, desire to put an end to the abuses which have already long excited our indignation. It is well known that in several instances public buildings, in which all the ornament of the city consisted, have been destroyed with the criminal permission of the authorities, on the pretext that the materials were necessary for public works, etc."

This last effort to heal the wounds of the city by Majorian, who had been made Emperor in 457 by the will of the barbarian leader of mercenaries, Ricimer, failed because Ricimer aimed at being the real ruler, like a Merovingian mayor of the palace. Finding Majorian lacking in subservience and filled with antique Roman pride, Ricimer assassinated him in 461.

In the field of Christian art, Leo was extremely active, although his monuments have left but few traces. One of the bevy of pious Roman women, Demetrias, of the house of the Anicii, pupil and friend of S. Augustine and S. Jerome, left her fortune for the construction of a basilica on the Via Latina, dedicated to S. Stephen. Leo, who was made her executor, made the priest Tigrinus building-superintendent of the

Capitals at S. Stefano on the Via Latina.

new church. It was not built until the end of Leo's pontificate (460–461), and its ruins show the crude workmanship of the decades following the sack of Genseric.

This was not the only work done by testamentary funds.

The façade mosaic of S. Peter was given by the ex-pretorian prefect Marinianus and his wife Anastasia.

The *L. P.* proves the extent of Leo's energy in repairing the damages of 455. He renewed the ceilings of all three of the greatest basilicas, — the Lateran, S. Peter and S. Paul, — and he replaced by others all the stolen sacred utensils of the Roman churches: *renovavit post cladem Wandalicam omnia ministeria sacrata argentea per omnes titulos.*

The only work that has survived is the mosaic of the triumphal arch of S. Paul, and that is so badly restored as to have hardly more than the form of the original. It was completed in the early part of Leo's reign, with the help of the Empress Galla Placidia.

Of his basilica to S. Cornelius over the cemetery of Callixtus nothing remains. He built the first monastery attached to the basilica of S. Peter (SS. John and Paul) to supply clergy for continuous service, thus popularizing a series that was being continually enlarged, which became indispensable in church organization, and an important source of art production.

Hilary's Revival. — It is almost inexplicable how the pontificate of Hilary (461–468) could furnish such a mass of artistic

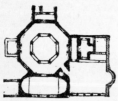
Baptistry of the Lateran.

matter. His group of annexes to the Constantinian baptistery was certainly one of the most interesting in Rome — the oratory of the Cross with its court, and those of John the Baptist and John the Evangelist with their mosaics and bronze doors.[1] A part of them are among the few surviving relics of the primitive group of buildings at the Lateran, including the baptistery itself which he reconstructed. Its wooden roof contrasted with the dome of S. Costantia marks the decay of architecture since Constantine.

His favorite basilica, however, seems to have been S. Lorenzo, where he was buried. He added to it a monastery,

---

[1] Fecit oraturia III in baptisterio basilicæ Constantinianæ, Sancti Johannis Baptistæ et Sancti Johannis Evangelistæ et S. Crucis, omnia ex argento et lapidibus pretiosis.

and a Papal palace or villa with hot and cold baths, quarters for pilgrims and a library for both Greek and Latin books. He built a similar palace at S. Paul.

The bare enumeration of his numerous gifts to the churches suggests the immense wealth of the Church, due partly to the successful policy of Leo the Great. We can only doubt whether the quality of their art equalled their number and material.

Simplicius and Barbarian Rule. — In the times of Pope Simplicius (468–483) the pale travesty of an Empire of the West ceased to be even a stage property. Ricimer, after allowing the incompetence of the puppet Emperor, Anthemius, whom he had grudgingly accepted from Byzantium, to become thoroughly evident in the futile expedition against the Vandals, made selection of Olybrius as his successor. When Anthemius dared to resist him in Rome, Ricimer besieged and captured it in 472. Except that the city was given over to pillage, we are in the dark as to the extent of the disaster. Four years of anarchy followed, until, in 476, Odoacer, after obtaining the leadership of the barbarian mercenaries, abolished even the title of Emperor of the West, and frankly assumed to rule in Italy as king. The Eastern Emperor, Zeno, was content to let him govern it under the sophism that he was a Byzantine official, a "patricius," and that Italy thus became a province of the Eastern Empire — a figment at which Odoacer was well content to wink.

The following thirteen years under Olybrius were politically peaceful. But what was their effect upon the art and monuments of Rome? For the first time Rome was under the direct yoke of the barbarian. With the seat of government at Ravenna, with the financial aid of the Eastern Emperor withdrawn, with the cessation of the *frumentatio* for the people, Rome must have felt economically pinched and incapable of recuperating from the last pillage. There was also, for a time, at least, an interregnum in the upper magistracy, as the illiterate barbarian cared nothing for the mechanism of civil administration. We must imagine that there was a complete lapse in the care of public monuments — both in appropriations and officials — and

F

that in these years before the advent of Theodoric, great progress in disintegration was made.

The appropriation of several public buildings by the Church is not only a proof of this but also of the lapse of those strict imperial regulations that had guarded ancient monuments. We may well imagine that Pope Simplicius did not feel it necessary to ask permission of the Emperor Zeno, who had abandoned Rome and Italy to their fate, or of the barbarian leader, who was probably entirely ignorant of the governmental ownership of public buildings.

At all events, the *Liber Pontificalis* is authority for the fact, authenticated by a dedicatory inscription, that the Pope transformed the beautiful public hall of Junius Bassus, already described as one of the most interesting works of the time of Constantine, into a church of S. Andrew. An apse was added and decorated with a mosaic, but otherwise there was little change. The elliptical vestibule was used as a narthex, no colonnades were added in the interior to divide it into nave

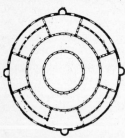

and aisles, and the superb marble incrustations were left to decorate the walls. It was not directly, but through the munificence of the Gothic chieftain Valila, that the Pope obtained possession of the building.

Here enters also upon the scene the "sphynx of the Cœlian," the circular church of San Stefano Rotondo, dedicated, as the *Liber Pontificalis* tells us, by Simplicius.[1] It is the most

S. Stefano Rotondo.

peculiarly shaped church: an enormous central tower-like drum supported on 20 columns and surrounded by a second row of 28 columns intersected by four colonnaded wings.

[1] This is the passage in the life of Simplicius that concerns his buildings: "Hic dedicavit basilicam Sancti Stephani in Celio monte, in urbe Roma, et basilicam beati apostoli Andreæ iuxta basilicam Sanctæ Mariæ, et aliam basilicam Sancti Stefani iuxta basilicam Sancti Laurenti, et aliam basilicam intra urbe Roma, iuxta palatium Licinianum, beatæ martyris Bibianæ, ubi corpus eius requiescit." . . . Hic fecit in ecclesia Romana scyphum aureum, pens. lib. V; canthara argentea ad beatum Petrum XVI, pens. sing. lib. XII.

Though shorn of some of its size at the Renaissance, it is impressive and mysterious. Some of its capitals are antique: most are contemporary. According to most modern critics this building would be another example of the ease with which public civil structures were then annexed by the Church, but no such secular building can be shown to have existed then

Interior of S. Stefano Rotondo.
(Fifth century.)

nor can it be traced in the present church. Most of its decoration is posterior even to Simplicius. It was a religious structure from the beginning.

Two mosaics of this time, in the apses of S. Andrea in Catabarbara and S. Agata in Suburra, represented Christ among the apostles, and, though destroyed, the drawings made by Renaissance students show heavy realistic types of statuesque character. The artists who worked between 460 and 475 in painting were still of the same school, therefore, as the mosaicists of S. Sabina.

The three ensuing reigns of Felix III (483–492), Gelasius (492–496) and Anastasius II (496–498) appear to have been artistically sterile. The confused and insecure political condition to which this was partly due came to an end with the advent of Theodoric the Goth.

III. ROME UNDER THEODORIC

AFTER a brief surcease the influence of Ravenna on Roman art was once more intensified under Theodoric, who brought the two cities into the closest connection by placing the civil administration of Rome so completely in the hands of his own appointees and by overseeing so closely from Ravenna the details of the restoration, care and construction of monuments. He even appointed the architects and engineers in charge of Roman monuments. It is during the forty years between his

Corinthian Capitals of Sixth Century.
(1) S. Martino ai Monti
(c. 500).
    (2) Palatine
(c. 500).
    (3) S. Lorenzo
(578–590).

advent and the coming of Belisarius that Roman art was more generally affected than before in all its branches by the Ravenna school. This is particularly evident in architecture, in the decorative details and the treatment of capitals. In the time of Popes Hilary and Simplicius, in the calamitous times after Genseric's sack, the handling of such work had been deplorably crude and helplessly inefficient. Only the intention remained classic. How can we explain, then, except by the advent of artists from Ravenna, the sudden change that is evident in all the works of Theodoric's age in Rome ? The church of S. Martino ai Monti, for example, has work that is

69

superb, equal to the best of the age of Constantine, but of a totally different type, analogous to that in the churches of Ravenna itself, such as S. Apollinare Nuovo, S. Spirito and S. Agata, though even superior in handling.

In one branch, however, Rome still held supremacy, that of surface revetments in various marbles cut into patterns, such as we have seen at the basilica of Junius Bassus and at S. Sabina. For there is a letter written c. 508 by Theodoric to

Interior of S. Martino ai Monti.
(c. 500 and Barocco.)

the prefect of Rome, Agapitus, asking him to send to Ravenna skilled *marmorarii*, marble-workers, for the decoration of the basilica of Hercules with " pictures in many-colored marble incrustations."

Among the interesting documents preserved in the collection of Theodoric's learned secretary Cassiodorus, we find a number bearing on the architecture of Rome, the restoration of the Circus Maximus, the theatre of Pompey, the city walls, the palace of the Cæsars, the public storehouse for grain, the aqueducts, etc. The Senate was sharply reproved by him for lack of vigilance, the prefect was reminded of his duties, Symmachus praised for his architectural enterprises. Officials were appointed to oversee the aqueducts and sewers, the government manufactory of bricks, the restoration and care of the imperial palaces on the Palatine, the preparation of cement and mortar. Most interesting is the oath of office taken before the prefect by whoever was made city inspecting architect.

Symmachus. — Notwithstanding his long and bloody controversy with the antipope Laurentius, Pope Symmachus (498–514) was fortunate in living under King Theodoric. The churches as well as the civil buildings of Rome were thoroughly repaired. Everywhere we find the bricks and tiles of Theodoric. Symmachus himself had the oversight of such work for ecclesiastical buildings, while profiting by the materials, such as bricks, supplied free by the manufactories of the State and probably also making use of stone-cutters and other artists from Ravenna. The most important of his early works were at S. Peter, while Laurentius, his rival, still had possession of the Lateran and of S. Paul. He was the first Pope to make a Papal residence at S. Peter, for he built a palace, symmetrically, on either side of the atrium in front of the basilica, decorating the centre of the square with the famous fountain of the bronze Pine-cone (Pigna), widening the staircase of approach to the basilica and decorating the atrium with mosaics. He also built or restored a number of other annexes to the basilica, including the beautiful circular church of S. Andrew, S. Peter's brother, to whom Simplicius had already built a small basilica.

The ever increasing grasp of the Church in matters that in imperial times had been civil, as well as the development of the Christian idea of charity, so foreign to the old paganism, is shown by the group of hospitals and hospices which Symmachus built in connection with the great suburban basilicas — at S. Peter, and S. Paul and S. Lorenzo, — besides that at Portus, where the previous hospital of Pammachius was probably insufficient to provide for the seafaring population.

For four years in the early part of the pontificate of Symmachus (501–505) the antipope Laurentius had practical possession of all the churches of Rome, with the exception of S. Peter, and an interesting memorial of his ephemeral rule is a part of the series of portrait busts of the Popes painted in medallions on the two walls of the main nave, one of the last works of painting in which the Roman school showed its independence.

Hormisdas and John. — Under Hormisdas (514–523), the peaceful course of events continued, and was even accentuated by the reëstablishment, in 519, amid universal rejoicing, of the union with the Eastern Church, which healed the schism of thirty-five years. But the good effects of this reconciliation were more than nullified by the sudden development of the enmity of

Choir-screen of Hormisdas at S. Clemente (restored).

Theodoric, which began under Pope John I (523–526), perhaps out of Arian jealousy of this very reconciliation with Constantinople, at a time when Justin issued his famous decree of persecution against the Arians (523). Foreseeing, perhaps, the Byzantine attempt to wrest Italy from the Goths, the aging king enveloped in his fatal suspicions the last eminent Romans — Boethius and Symmachus — and his reign ended in acts of suspicious tyranny and violence recalling the days of Domitian. His plan was not only to extinguish any desire for political intrigues with Byzantium on the part of the Senate, but to make of the Papacy a political slave and tool. He obliged Pope John I to make the long journey to Constantinople to ask for the cessation of the Arian persecution and on his return threw him into prison at Ravenna, where he died. Theodoric then

forced on the clergy his candidate for the Papacy, Felix IV
(526–530). This led to a clearer definition between the two
hostile currents in Rome — the Gothic and the Byzantine —
which at once showed itself in the party of the Greek antipope,
Dioscorus.

These two currents are evident, I believe, in contemporary
art. The most characteristic example of each are, on the
Byzantine side, the decorations of S. Clemente by the Presbyter

Apsidal Mosaic of SS. Cosma e Damiano.

Mercurius, who afterwards became Pope John II (533–535);
and on the Gothic side, the mosaics of SS. Cosma e Damiano,
done under Felix IV, the Gothic partisan, while a middle
ground is held by some of the recently discovered frescos in
the cemetery of Commodilla, which seem to be those mentioned in the *Liber Pontificalis* as being ordered by Pope John
I (523–526).

I am aware that, in the unanimous opinion of critics, the
superb apsidal mosaic in SS. Cosma e Damiano is the last

effort of pure Roman art, before the advent of Byzantinism; but I cannot find in any other contemporary or previous work of the Roman school the element of barbaric intensity, of almost ferocious energy, so well embodied in thick-set bodies and harsh, heavy features. It stands alone, the work of a man who, if not himself a barbarian pupil of the school of Rome or Ravenna, represented the Gothic spirit violently divorced from Byzantium. Yet the elements already assimilated could not be thrown off. Hovering over these militant figures in the hemicycle are the angels with ideal faces and outspread wings on the face of the apse!

Capital of Old Basilica of S. Clemente.
(Early sixth century.)

Without any admixture of Roman or barbaric are the frescos of the subterranean chapel in the cemetery of Commodilla, for which the closest analogies must be sought in Ravenna, at S. Apollinare Nuovo and S. Vitale.

The present *schola cantorum* at S. Clemente, with its marble screen and pilasters and its ambones, is reconstructed largely from those with which the presbyter of the basilica— Mercurius — decorated it under Pope Hormisdas, completing it after he became Pope as John II in 533. Part of the epistyle and two of the columns of his ciborium are also preserved. Their basket-work capitals are purely Byzantine, of the type that was adopted also by the schools of Ravenna and the other cities on the Adriatic at this time, such as Parenzo, Pola and Grado. Equally foreign to classic Roman tradition is the decoration in low relief of circles and crosses on the panels of the *schola cantorum* and the schematic vines of its pilasters, an importation direct from Constantinople rather than through Ravenna.

Rome still the Antique City. — The impression we receive of the Rome of Theodoric is precisely that expressed by the sentence *laus Gothorum est civilitas custodita.* Theodoric's preoccupation to keep intact the antique tradition was carried out in the most trivial details. All outward life moved in the old grooves. The Senate met; the consuls presided over the games ; the Circus, the public baths and the theatre were still the great resorts of the masses to whom *panem et circenses,* though with reduced munificence, were still freely offered; the Forum of Trajan still received honorary statues and was the resort of the literary.

The city was still fundamentally antique in its appearance and in its daily life. The dissensions due to the aggressive Arianism and the bloody suppression of the national party in Rome in the last years of Theodoric prepared the way for the attempt to reunite Italy to the Empire under his weak successors, an attempt that was encouraged by the Byzantine party formed in Rome itself. Had the fatal result been foreseen by the Italians they would have far preferred the somewhat harmless friction with an alien race to the complete ruin that resulted from their blind appeal to Byzantium.

IV. ROME AFTER THE GOTHIC WARS: THE BYZANTINE CITY

No knight-errant was ever sent by his lady-love on an apparently more hopeless mission than Belisarius received from Justinian when he was charged with the recovery of Italy and Africa from the Goths and Vandals and its reunion to the Empire. What his weaker predecessors had acquiesced in seemed a weakness to Justinian, who, though far from a warrior himself, planned a reconstruction of the Roman Empire — religious, legal and political — that involved extensive wars and conquests.

In Belisarius he found a perfect instrument, a disinterested, unworldly, unambitious genius, whose exploits read like fantastic fairy tales. How this man, with a handful of hybrid soldiers, never over twenty-five thousand, first put an end to the Vandal kingdom in Africa, and then, landing in Sicily in 532, marched northward, occupied Rome and fought the Goths repeatedly to a standstill, to leave their final subjugation to his successor, Narses, in 553, is a page of almost pure romance. But these wars of over a quarter of a century were more destructive at the beginning of the Middle Ages in Italy than the plague was to be at its close in the fifteenth century. Two-thirds of the population is said to have perished in the life-and-death struggle of the heroic Goths. Procopius reckoned the loss at about fifteen millions. From one end of Italy to the other the waves of battle surged; yet of all the districts, Rome and the Campagna were by far the severest sufferers.

Depopulation of Rome. — During and between its sieges Rome was left practically without inhabitants. Its aqueducts were cut; its country-side made desolate. Ancient and modern villas, up to this time retaining a shadow of the beauty of the days of Cicero and Horace, were thoroughly gutted. The rows of ancient statues cast down upon the enemy from the parapets of Hadrian's tomb are the symbol of the final descent of the gods and emperors even from being a harmless decoration to the city.

When the war ended in the annihilation of the Goth, there was no vitality to repair damages. To make doubly sure a vindictive nemesis soon sent the plague stalking from one end of Italy to the other. And with it came the uncouth Lombards, who took possession of the entire north and of a large part of the central and southern sections of the peninsula, leaving Venice, Naples and the extreme south in the weak grasp of Byzantium.

In Rome itself the population never reassembled; personal ownership had largely ceased; property and prosperity had vanished; all agriculture, trade and industry were brought to a standstill. It was a total disruption of society. Ancient and early Christian Rome had actually ceased to exist as an organization. The few thousands whom we find within the walls at the close of the war were mainly a poverty-stricken herd of the lowest class of Italians or of barbarian immigrants, who huddled in hovels near the Tiber, getting their supply of water from the river or from wells, for there were no means in the impoverished city for restoring the aqueducts. There was no longer any pretence of restoring or respecting the ancient monuments. The Emperor Justinian in his Pragmatic Sanction, evidently blind to the real squalid facts, amusingly accords permission to private persons in Rome to restore ancient monuments at their own expense. The real facts are hinted at in the letters of Pope Pelagius appealing for the bare necessities of life for the people.

Under the circumstances, Justinian found that the one indigenous influence upon which he could rely to support imperial authority in that part of Italy which the Byzantine troops were able to retain, was the Church and the Papacy. With the fall of the Goths, the Arianism of which they were the champions had been definitely conquered by orthodoxy. At the same time the Popes, under tyrannical pressure at Constantinople, had been forced to agree to certain humiliating conditions in the recognition of the ecclesiastical and civil control of the Eastern Empire over Rome. In return the Church was granted extensive civil authority in Italy, and the Papacy grew very soon to be the rallying point for the public forces of social reconstruction. It is true that there grew up an elaborate system of Byzantine administration, with its centre at Ravenna in the person of an exarch, the viceroy of the Emperor in Italy; that under him were dukes who were his representatives in Rome, in Gaeta, in Naples, in Sicily; that there was a pretence of financial control and of both political and military direction. But in the general disruption this was largely nominal except in a few centres, because the old municipal organizations were dissolved.

The only living institution, then, was the Church; no longer as wealthy, to be sure, as in the time of Leo the Great, but now even more comparatively influential because it was the only refuge of the people.

Gregory. — Gregory the Great individualized this movement and led the reconstruction, not only in Rome, but in Italy. First a patrician, a worldling and an official of the Byzantine administration who then became a self-sacrificing ecclesiastic, Gregory turned his father's palace into a monastery, and was the last of the Church Fathers. Under his administration the Roman Church grew wealthy, increased its possessions in all parts of Italy, becoming the largest holder of landed property, as the Emperors used to be. Gregory established his authority more effectually over provincial bishops, keeping constantly in touch with them, reformed the clergy, raised the people from misery, encouraged commerce, industry and art, established more dignified and independent relations with the Byzantine empire, organized a Pontifical court, elevated the ritual and music of the Church, and accustomed the people to look to the Papacy for whatever of good could be brought to pass. He laid the foundation for the renewed artistic influence of Rome.

In order to carry out his work churches and monasteries were founded and endowed as well as libraries, hospitals and inns, schools for music and general teaching. Once more, in the first decade of the seventh century Rome began to reassert herself and Gregory, though fundamentally a Latin survival, ushered in the new era of Byzantine Rome.

Reorganization of the City. — The modest revival was centred in a very small quarter of the ancient city, close to the Tiber. The medley of Italians, Greeks and barbarians who gathered here viewed with a mixture of awe and contempt the deserted area of the Forums, the Palatine and the Campus Martius. They favored the low quarters, abandoning the hills, so that they could command the meagre trade of the city that came to them up the river, for the old ports of Portus and Ostia were disused, and the city quays were alone used for supplies from the coast towns, from Sicily and even from Greece and Africa.

Rome becomes Byzantine. — The majority of these newcomers were either of Greek blood or came from some part of the Byzantine domains, spoke Greek far more than Latin, and that part of the Tiber bank which was the centre of the settlement was afterwards always called *Ripa Græca*. They clubbed together in an association called *Schola Græca*, which probably served as a model for the different *scholæ*, national associations, or guilds into which the city was soon divided, the predecessors of the organization of the mediæval *rioni* or quarters.

The Byzantine invasion was not confined to the lay part of the population. It took even more complete possession of both the regular and secular clergy, of the monasteries and of the Pontifical court and the episcopacy. This was of paramount importance because in the new Rome the revival of art and literature was to be absolutely in the hands of the clergy, especially of the monks.

Greek Monks. — Thickly scattered over the Aventine and more sparsely elsewhere were numerous monasteries, the majority occupied by Greek monks who followed the rule of S. Basil. Singularly enough the great Western order of S. Benedict did not gain as strong a foothold in Rome for over two hundred years, until the Carlovingian Emperors became such sturdy patrons of Western monasticism. The *Liber Pontificalis*, or official Papal Chronicle, composed from the Papal archives at different intervals between c. 500 and 880 A.D., gives long lists of works of art produced at this time in Rome, and it is evident that the great majority were executed by artists in the Roman monasteries, especially by the Byzantine monks. Mosaic pictures and frescos, gold and silver altar canopies and altar-fronts as well as statues, embroidered and woven hangings with elaborate figured compositions, sacred vestments and vessels, are enumerated in such quantities and in such terms as to show not only the enormous productivity of these monastic schools but the Byzantine origin of a large proportion of the work. While all the objects in precious metals have disappeared, as well as the embroideries and tissues, there remains a large series of mosaics and wall paintings to show how thoroughly Byzantinized Roman art had become in the hands of Greek artists and their pupils.

A number of these monastic establishments remain, though largely reconstructed. At the central church of the Greek community, S. Maria in Cosmedin, there were monks who were reënforced in 752 by newcomers fleeing from the iconoclastic persecutions of the Byzantine Emperors. The tendency to image worship in the Greek Church, which had increased alarmingly during the seventh century, had provoked the famous reaction against the making of sacred images which was headed by the emperors and resulted in the destruction of many works of art, the temporary substitution of decorative and secular themes, the harsh treatment of artists even to the cutting off of their right hands, and the consequent flight of many of them from the East to the freedom of Italy, especially of Rome, where their services were in demand.

But while this emigration, which was almost continuous throughout the eighth century, added considerably to the Greek monastic colony in Rome, it would be a mistake to imagine that it had not flourished there for nearly two centuries before. For instance, the church and monastery of S. Saba on the Aventine were built for Greek monks who may have come from the monastery of the same name at Jerusalem at some time in the sixth century. At the same date the imperial chapel of S. Cesareo on the Palatine, where the images of the Byzantine Emperors were placed, was served by Greek monks, as was also the parish church of the Greeks, S. Anastasia. Several other

Greek monasteries were then prominent. Those of *Renas* and *Domus Arsicia* were so important as to send delegates to the Œcumenical Council held at Constantinople in 680–681.

The most significant fact of all, however, is that after Pope Gregory the Great founded the monastery of S. Andrew in his paternal house on the Cœlian, it contained Greek monks and was governed by Greek abbots. S. Erasmo and S. Maria Antiqua also belong to this early Byzantine group. To the later iconoclastic group belonged the large establishment of S. Silvestro in Capite.

Greek Popes and Clergy. — It was not long after the death of Gregory the Great that the effect of the influx of Greeks in every sphere became evident. As a majority of the Roman secular clergy seem to have been of Greek blood, it was natural that the majority of the Popes for over a century should be Greeks. This Greek series, begun with Pope Theodore in 642, is continued with Sergius (687), John VI (701), John VII (705), Sisinnius (708), Constantine (708), Gregory III (731) and finally Zacharias in 742. These Popes were not interlopers, but regular resident members of the Roman clergy.

The Papal court became a faithful reflex of this general condition. After the Gothic wars the material basis and ecclesiastical machinery of the Papacy required radical reorganization. The visits of the Popes of the sixth and seventh centuries to Constantinople had given them a thorough familiarity with the elaborate civil and ecclesiastical organization of Byzantium. It was natural that the Papacy should model its new court upon the imperial pattern, especially as provision had to be made, not as before for a purely spiritual and ecclesiastical machinery, but also for the secular organization made necessary by the new civil powers delegated to or gradually assumed by the Popes, and which they needed to harmonize and interweave with the functions of the civil officials that represented Byzantine power in Italy and Rome. For there was a Byzantine *dux* at Rome, residing in the Palace of the Cæsars; and the duties of prefect of the city, of curator of the monuments, of commander of the Roman militia, were technically within the gift of the Emperor.

G

The Greek language also invaded Rome. Religious services and music were held in both Greek and Latin; the confession of faith, the ceremonies and anniversaries, were in both languages. The people's choirs that marched in procession at religious festivals or went to meet Emperors, Popes or minor dignitaries outside the city gates sang both Greek and Latin hymns.

Foreign Colonists. — But to assist in the repeopling and resurrecting of Rome there were also distinct colonies of a different kind. Closest to the natives was the important colony from Ravenna. It was part Italian and part Greek, reflecting the cosmopolitanism of Ravenna. This colony was augmented by a multitude of refugees at the time of the capture of Ravenna by the Lombards in the eighth century, and the quarter where they settled, beyond the Tiber, was called *Urbs Ravennatum*, "the city of the Ravennates." It corresponds to the modern Trastevere.

Another group of colonies was formed, principally of the nations of the North, such as Anglo-Saxons, Franks and Lombards. Each of these was established in a separate quarter, owned certain streets, churches, hospitals, and monasteries, and organized itself into a *schola* for mutual protection and coöperation. All pilgrims coming to Rome sought the hospitality of their own colony, which was a sort of guardian of national interests. They naturally grouped themselves around the centre and starting-point for all pilgrims, the Vatican basilica, thus forming a new suburb of the city which was fortified later, in the Carlovingian age, and called the Leonine City from the Pope who built it, or the "Borgo" from "Burgus Saxonum," the Saxon Burgh.

Monuments. — The monumental history of Rome at the beginning of this period is both obscure and discouraging. Belisarius himself is said to have founded a church and a hospital, but they seem to have been of small importance. Narses put up pompous inscriptions on the insignificant bridge which he built over the Anio in 565. There was now no such thing as a civil and civic architecture or a restoration of the monuments. Only a portion of the Palace of the Cæsars was kept in repair as the seat of the Byzantine governor and his staff.

The public baths must have been abandoned, as their water supply was cut off. The only impediment to a wholesale conversion or destruction of temples and other public monuments was the fact that they were the property of the State, that is, of the Byzantine Emperor, and that it was necessary to obtain his permission to touch or use any of them. Not even the Pope had any right to them. There being no imperial funds for their repair, disintegration was not long in setting in.

A poetic lament written at this time begins thus: —

> "Oh, Rome ! built in past days by high-born masters,
> Thou fallest now to miserable ruin, subject to slaves.
> Long since thy kings have left thee.
> Thine honor and thy name are now a prey to Greeks."

Previously it had been the custom to tear down ruinous structures and to use their choicest parts in artistic fashion. But now, with practically the whole of the ancient city abandoned and at their disposal and paganism a thing of the past, a new fashion set in, of bodily adapting ancient buildings both religious and civil. Of course this had not been an unknown process even earlier, but it had been rare.

At the same time it was the day of small churches, of small monasteries, of small ambitions and undertakings, of a poor Church and a poorer population, the day of no aristocracy, no plutocracy. We find a chapel of S. Maria in Cannapara hidden in an angle of the basilica Julia; a chapel of the Virgin in the Library of Augustus; the little church of S. Maria in Foro; on the Rostra the oratory of Sergius and Bacchus. Wherever possible the whole of a structure was used and in this way the majority of ancient structures have been preserved which still exist in Rome: we owe them to the Church. The Curia or larger Senate Hall became the church of S. Adriano; the Secretarium or minor Senate Hall became S. Martina; the temple of Romulus and the City Archives had already become SS. Cosma e Damiano shortly before the Gothic wars; the temple of Antoninus and Faustina was turned into the church of S. Lorenzo in Miranda. The circular Temple of Honor near the Tiber and, above all, the magnificent Pantheon of Agrippa were preserved intact by this transfer to the Church.

From this time until the middle of the eighth century there appears to have been in Rome no school of architecture. The building done was of the most modest character when it did not consist in the transformation of an antique structure. The small church of S. Saba, still existing in part under the present basilica, the interior of S. Giorgio in Velabro, are perhaps the best instances.

This age of small things was, it is true, slightly modified by

Library of Augustus, converted into Church of S. Maria Antiqua.

Pope Honorius I, the rebuilder of S. Agnese; but aside from this interlude it continued unbroken through the series of Greek Popes and until the new and vitalizing connection with the Frankish rulers, Pepin and Charlemagne, helped the Papacy once more to a policy and an art that were worthy of the religious centre of the Western world.

Two basilicas, S. Prassede and S. Maria in Cosmedin, illustrate the mode of using ancient materials. In the first of these churches Pope Paschal (c. 817) framed the interior out of columns and architraves of the close of the fourth century, too poor and careless in workmanship even for a public building of that date, and apparently part of some street colonnade. We know that in the time of Honorius there were colonnades erected in this very region, particularly along the Vicus Patricius. This material at S. Prassede was probably taken from these poorly built colonnades — a suggestion confirmed by the very fragmentary bits of inscriptions of the period (c. 400) on the architraves. We can readily imagine that the numerous colonnades throughout the city had received no care since the Gothic wars and that those of the decadence were the first to fall.

The history of S. Maria in Cosmedin illustrates, on the other hand, the utilization and destruction of two other classes of earlier monuments — civic structures and temples. When this church was founded, probably toward the close of the sixth century, it was on a small scale and but an adaptation of the Grain Exchange. This ancient institution was now quite useless, as the imperial *largesse* to the people, by the distribution of grain imported from beyond the seas, was a thing of the past. The poor of the much-reduced population were to be provided for henceforth by distribution on a very small scale at the diaconal churches now established in the various parishes of the city, and of which this very church of S. Maria in Cosmedin was one. The church, set up in the shell of one earlier building, was closely encircled by some others — such as a temple of Ceres, another temple of "Hercules," both destroyed, and the other remaining circular temple of "Portumnus" or "Matuta." Not only columns and capitals but carved marble window screens and other details of the older structures were used. The *Liber Pontificalis* tells us that when Pope Hadrian lengthened the church beyond the precincts of the Grain Exchange, he was obliged to tear down a huge overhanging ancient structure that threatened to fall and overwhelm it — probably one of the temples.

Artistic Vicissitudes after 550. — What was the fate of the other arts can best be seen by a brief historic survey of the artistic activity of the Popes during the two centuries before the Carlovingian revival.

Popes Pelagius I (556–561), John III (561–574) and Benedict I (575–579) have left no certain monumental traces. One great church, however, was put up by Narses and the first two of these Popes as a triumphal monument to the Pyrrhic victory of Byzantium. It was the basilica of the Apostles, celebrated by Pope Hadrian, two centuries later, as one of the

Ancient Architraves, Capitals, and Shafts used in Reconstructing S. Lorenzo
(Pelagius II).

largest and most sumptuously decorated in the city. Built doubtless with imperial funds and before the Lombard invasion, it was probably the work of Byzantine engineers and artists from Ravenna. Perhaps to this time belong some of the earliest of the frescos in S. Maria Antiqua and S. Saba.

Pelagius I made a beginning also of replacing the destroyed Church treasures, for his biographer says that he distributed to all the churches of Rome gold and silver vases and vestments. John's zeal was concentrated on the restoration of the

Catacombs, where some of the early Byzantine frescos may be ascribed to him.

Pelagius II (579–590) fell upon even more evil times,—when the city was besieged by the Lombards and abandoned by the Byzantine Emperor to its fate; when (589) it was flooded by the Tiber and many buildings were destroyed, and then over-

Chair of S. Peter, in his Basilica, made partly of Antique Materials by Artist of Seventh or Eighth Century.

run by a second pestilence (590) by which the Pope himself was carried off.

Perhaps the building most characteristic of these conditions is the lower and smaller basilica of S. Lorenzo. The *L. P.* says, under Pelagius, that he built a basilica over the saint's tomb. As one had already been built by Constantine and renovated by Leopardus, after the sack of Alaric, it is clear that the work of Pelagius must have been required by the destruction of the older church, due to the Goths. Its columns were used and added to, and a gallery was erected above them, rising from a mass of architraves torn from ancient buildings that rested on the larger columns. Evidently there were no competent stone masons in Rome at this time, for these magnificent architraves are of all sizes and patterns and none of them match. There is no attempt to bring them into any sort of artistic relation. It is the acme of inartistic disorder. The Pope seems to have employed stone cutters from Ravenna to decorate the second story (gallery), for the basket capitals and the parapet slabs are thoroughly in the Byzantine manner of that school and of Parenzo and other places in the exarchate and on the Adriatic coast.

Classico-Byzantine Capital at S. Agnese
(Honorius I).

To this Pope is attributed a basilica at the cemetery of S. Hermes of which there are considerable remains, and a hospital for the poor. He appears to have had artists capable of producing bas-reliefs in silver gilt with which he decorated the confessions of the basilicas of S. Peter and S. Lorenzo, which had doubtless been despoiled of their earlier and more magnificent monuments of this sort.

Gregory the Great (590–604) seems to have cared but little for monumental art. His energies were, as we have seen, bent on husbanding the scanty resources of the Church for more practical and more vital purposes. He is credited with nothing more than a silver ciborium with its columns for S. Peter, doubtless to replace the one destroyed; with some decorations for the apostle's tomb; with the transformation of his ancestral house into a monastery; and with the decoration of the church of S. Agata in Suburra. His biographer describes some interesting frescos executed in the monastery in the lifetime of S. Gregory.

Of Sabinianus (604–606) nothing is recorded except some lamps given to S. Peter; of Boniface III (607) absolutely nothing; of Boniface IV (608–615), in whose time Rome went through a terrible experience of famine, pestilence and inundation, it is said that he turned his house into a monastery and obtained from the Emperor Phocas the permission to transform the great rotunda of the Pantheon into a church dedicated to the Virgin, to which the Emperor sent many rich gifts. Nothing is attributed to Deusdedit (615–618), under whom the popular misery continued. Boniface V (619–625) completed a small rectangular basilica at the entrance to the catacomb of S. Nicomedes on the Via Nomentana.

Honorius. — A change came with the accession of Honorius I (625–638), a fervent lover of religious art. His biographer attributes to him the construction from their foundation of a number of buildings, the majority of which it is more likely that he merely restored and decorated, so that he should be credited rather with a revival of painting and metal-work than with that of architecture, though his constructions also show good taste. I give his text as a sample of the extracts from the Papal inventories given in the *Liber Pontificalis*.[1] He contributed to

---

[1] Renovavit omnem cymiliam beati Petri apostoli et investivit confessionem beati Petri ex argento puro, qui pens. lib. CLXXXVII. Hic investivit regias in ingressu ecclesiæ maiores, qui appellatur mediana, ex argento, qui pens. lib. DCCCCLXXV; fecit et cereostatos maiores ex argento, paria duo, qui sunt ante corpus beati Petri apostoli, pens. sing. lib. LXII. Fecit et ad beatum Andream apostolum, ubi supra, ante confessionem, tabula ex argento, qui pens. lib. LXXIII. Huius temporibus levatæ sunt trabes in ecclesia beati Petri numero XVI. Hic cooperuit omnem ecclesiam eius ex tegulis æreis quas levavit de templo qui appellatur Romæ, ex concessu piissimi Heraclii imperatoris.

Eodem tempore fecit ecclesiam beatæ Agne martyris . . . a solo . . . quem undique ornavit, exquisivit, ubi posuit dona multa. Ornavit autem sepulcrum eius ex argento, qui pens. lib. CCLII; posuit desuper cyburium æreum deauratum mire magnitudinis; fecit et gavatas aureas III, pens. sing. lib. sing.; fecit abside eiusdem basilicæ ex musibo, ubi etiam et multa dona optulit. Item fecit basilicam beati Apollenaris . . . in porticum beati Petri . . . *ad Palmata*, a solo, ubi dona multa largitus est. . .

the ruin of the beautiful temple of Venus and Rome by removing its bronze tiles and using them for his new roof of the Vatican basilica. The masterpiece of his time is thought to be the basilica of S. Agnese, which certainly has one of the most delicate and well-proportioned interiors in Rome, and even if the lower part of the nave should be of Constantinian materials, the rest, including the present apse, was put together and decorated by Honorius, including the apsidal mosaic. Above the high altar he placed a large gilt-bronze ciborium. The SS. Quattro Coronati, though ruined by Guiscard's fire and rebuilt within the old shell on a smaller scale, still shows its original size and impressiveness. The other churches attributed to him are: S. Apollinare, near S. Peter; S. Ciriaco on the Via Ostiensis; SS. Marcellinus and Peter on the Via Labicana; S. Pancrazio on the Via Aurelia, which he decorated with a silver ciborium, gold candelabra and many other precious ornaments; S. Lucia near S. Silvestro. It was also he who turned the ancient Curia into the church of S. Adriano. The inlaid doors, confessions, candelabra and other works of this Pope seem to show the presence in Rome of skilful metal-workers and mosaicists, probably from the East and from Ravenna.

Fecit ecclesiam beato Cyriaco martyri a solo, via Ostiense, miliario VII, ubi et donum optulit.

Eodem tempore fecit ecclesiam beatorum martyrum Quattuor Coronatorum, quem et dedicavit et donum optulit. Fecit ecclesiam beato Severino, a solo, iuxta civitate Tiburtina ... quam ipse dedicavit, et dona multa optulit. Renovavit et cymiterium beatorum martyrum Marcellini et Petri, via Lavicana. Eodem tempore fecit basilicam beato Pancratio martyri via Aurelia, miliario secundo a solo et ornavit sepulchrum eius ex argento, qui pens. lib. CXX. [Et ibi constituit mola in murum in loco Traiani iuxta murum civitatis, et formam qui deducit aqua in lacum Sabbatinum et sub se formam qui conducit aqua Tyberis.] Fecit et cyburium super altare ex argento, qui pens. lib. CLXXXVII. Fecit arcos argenteos V, qui pens. sing. lib. XV. Fecit et candelabra aurea III qui pens. sing. libras sing., ubi multa dona simul optulit.

Fecit ecclesia beate Luciæ in urbe Roma, iuxta sanctum Silvestrum, quem et dedicavit, et dona multa optulit. Fecit ecclesiam beati Adriani in Tribus Fatis, quem et dedicavit, et dona multa optulit. [Fecit autem in domum suam iuxta Lateranis monasterium in honore beatorum apostolorum Andrea et Bartholomeo, qui appellatum Honorii, ubi prædia et dona simul obtulit.] Sed et multa alia fecit quas enumerare longum est.

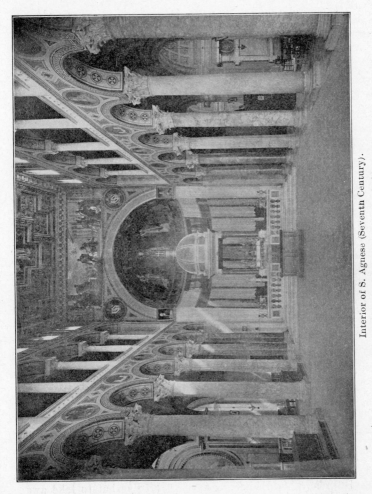

Interior of S. Agnese (Seventh Century).

Other Popes of the Seventh Century. — Severinus (640), in his one year, found time to complete the restoration of S. Peter by renovating the mosaic in its apse. John IV (640–642) will be remembered by the construction of a chapel annexed to the Lateran baptistery and dedicated to S. Venantius and to many other martyrs whose relics were brought from Dalmatia and Istria. The mosaic in the apse of this chapel is one of the best preserved in Rome, and characteristic of the prevailing Byzantinism.

Under Theodore (642–649), a Greek from Jerusalem, one of the earliest recorded transfers of relics took place. The bodies of the martyrs Primus and Felicianus were taken from their tomb on the Via Nomentana and placed in the basilica of S. Stefano Rotondo, where the Pope decorated an apse with a mosaic of these saints and where he added a number of gifts. He completed the important basilica of S. Valentinus, begun by Honorius near Ponte Molle, and built two oratories, one to S. Euplus outside the Ostian gate and one to S. Sebastian at the Lateran, where he also built a large reception hall.

To the heroic martyr and Pope, Martinus (649–653), who suffered severely from Byzantine oppression, was violently forced to go to Constantinople and then punished by exile to Cherson, the Byzantine Siberia, no works of art are credited in his life; but we know from the frescos themselves that he celebrated the triumph of Orthodoxy against the Monothelite heresy by a series of frescos at S. Maria Antiqua, which he remodelled as a Papal chapel and decorated after the Roman synod had condemned the Patriarch of Constantinople and the Eastern supporters of the heresy. The Papal painters selected the figures of a series of Church fathers representing Orthodoxy in two series to represent the East and the West, showing no desire to break with the Eastern church, but to purge it.

Nothing is attributed to his successors, Eugenius (654–657) and Vitalianus (657–672), but under the latter came the ruinous visit to Rome of Constans II, in 663, the first visit of an Emperor since the extinction of the Western Empire two centuries before. This Emperor came not to give but to take away: as an enemy of the Roman Church and Latin liberties. He stole the gilt-bronze tiles that covered the Pantheon, though it was now a church, and packed up all the bronze statues remaining in the city for shipment to Constantinople. Certainly the city must have looked to him, used to the orderly cities of the East, like a vast cemetery.

Adeodatus (672–676), though a Roman by birth, was a monk by profession and a Byzantine by education. He rebuilt, enlarged with many new buildings, endowed and filled with Greek monks the monastery of S. Erasmus on the Cœlian, where he had himself lived. He rebuilt the church of S. Peter in the *Campo di Merlo*, about seven miles on the Via Portuensis. It was almost Byzantine in the squareness of its plan (25 m. long, 24 m. wide), though it had the basilical columnar nave and aisles.

Domnus was in the chair hardly more than a year (676–678), and is merely said to have paved the court of the inner atrium of S. Peter with marble slabs and to have restored and dedicated both the church of the Apostles (Peter and Paul), near S. Sebastiano, and that of S. Euphemia on the Via Appia.

Under Agatho (678–681), the triumph of Roman ecclesiastical supremacy in the East as well as in the West, and the final defeat of Monothelitism, was more than counterbalanced in the city by the fearful pestilence of 680. Its arrest, at the supposed intercession of S. Sebastian, was the occasion of the consecration of a mosaic figure of the saint in the church of S. Martino ai Monti, where it now exists.

In the ten months' pontificate of the Sicilian Leo II (682–683), the bodies of Simplicius, Faustinus, Beatrix and other martyrs were transferred from the Catacomb of Commodilla to a church which the Pope built and dedicated to S. Paul, near S. Bibiana. It seems almost certain that some of the recently discovered frescos in this cemetery were then painted to record the places where the saints' bodies had rested, while others were of earlier date. A marginal addition to the original text of this Pope's life attributes to him the construction of S. Giorgio in Velabro; he may be the author merely of a restoration. He is said to have dedicated it to S. Sebastian, and probably it was a thank-offering for the saint's help at the time of the pestilence of 680. If the restoration of S. Teodoro is also by him, this may be the date of the mosaic of its apse, a pale adaptation of that of SS. Cosma e Damiano.

After an inexplicable interregnum of about a year, Pope Benedict II (684–685), though a Roman, intensified the closeness of the relations with the Eastern Empire by becoming godfather to Constantine Pogonatus's two sons. The Holy See seems now to be in somewhat more prosperous condition. The basilicas of S. Peter and S. Lorenzo in Lucina were restored. To S. Valentino, S. Maria ad Martyres and S. Lorenzo, the Pope gave superb textile altar covers, hangings and gold chalices.

Diaconal Churches. — He appears to have organized anew the church institutions of beneficence called *diaconies.* They had succeeded, on a far smaller scale, the imperial institutions for the distribution of free supplies of corn and oil to the poor of Rome, which had been discontinued by the Gothic wars. Already under Gregory the Great we hear of the church granaries (*horrea*) for this purpose. In the time of Pope Benedict II those charitable establishments were in charge of special monasteries quite distinct from the ordinary monasteries attached to the basilicas for song and service. They were placed, necessarily, in the heart of the city, and preferably near the Tiber. That of S. Maria in Cosmedin was on the very site of one of the imperial granaries. The large and growing estates of the Church furnished the stores, and the deacons of the church had the general supervision, while the *personnel* in charge of the details of the work consisted — in this monastic age — of Greek and native monks. There were, according to tradition, seven original diaconies. When, a century later, Hadrian I became Pope, he found sixteen of these establishments, and he about doubled this number. To each of them a church was, naturally, attached; and these old structures often remain, if not among the larger, yet among the most interesting in Rome. Such were S. Maria Antiqua, S. Maria Rotonda (Pantheon), SS. Cosma e Damiano, S. Adriano, S. Giorgio in Valabro, S. Vitale, S. Bonifacio, S. Maria in Domnica, S. Lucia in Septisolio, SS. Sergio e Bacco, S. Maria in Cosmedin, S. Maria in Porticu, S. Nicolo in Carcere, S. Angelo in Pescheria, S. Eustachio, S. Maria in Aquiro, S. Maria in Via Lata, S. Agata, etc.

One peculiarity is that they were usually built in or on

ancient temples and other Roman structures, which was naturally the case, owing to their position. They deserve much
more careful study than has been given them.

With the successor of Benedict II there commences a long
series of Greek and Oriental Popes who, while remaining faithful to Roman ecclesiastical traditions, naturally strengthened
the hold of Byzantine art upon Rome. Under John V (685–
686) and Canon (686–687) there are no records of works of art,
but quite a number under Sergius I (687–701), who restored
and endowed S. Susanna, S. Euphemia and other churches.

The Growth and Organization of People, Army and Clergy. — It
is at this time that the Papal Chronicle lays increased stress
upon the division of the Romans into three classes — the
clergy, the army and the people. The steady increase of the
population corresponded to a more thorough organization.

The Roman army was growing into an important factor;
Rome's new population was not effete but warlike. Its militia was nominally under command of the Byzantine *dux* and
his subordinate officers, but it soon outgrew any subserviency,
and represented the city itself. Its leaders actually grew into
a sort of primitive feudal lords. Together with the corresponding army or militia of Ravenna, it was to play a very important rôle in the politics of the next two centuries. Whatever there was of civil rank should be counted in the same
group as the army, in the way of imperial functionaries and
men of family.

The clergy also, in its two main branches, — regular or
monastic, and secular or parish and Papal, — was thoroughly
organized, and formed a large proportion of the population.

The third class, the people, were again marshalled into
guilds and under regions or *rioni*, with their banners and
their captains. Their organization was sufficiently close to
include *scholæ* or meeting-houses and to involve common
marching and singing on all great civil and religious occasions.
The people were again partitioning out the city, assigning
streets to each guild, and evolving some order out of the
chaos.

In so far as art is concerned, it is probable that during these

apparently fallow years there was, in any case, a continued
activity of the fresco-painters, probably from Ravenna, who
had long since introduced the Byzantine style of the age of
Justinian into Rome and whose school continued so exactly in
the same traditions that the S. Luke in the Catacomb of Commodilla, dated from the reign of Constantine Pogonatus, can
hardly be distinguished from frescos and mosaics that are
over a century earlier.

How in these years of which we know so little there had
been incubating in the Italian territories, still governed nominally by Byzantium, a spirit of national independence and a
renewal of virility, is shown by the defence of Pope Sergius
against the Emperor's plot by the armies of Ravenna and of
the Pentapolis (Marches of Ancona).

Architecturally, nothing is recorded of Sergius except an
oratory to S. Andrew on the Via Labicana, but he placed innumerable precious objects in the churches and was the author
of at least one mosaic — that of the apse of S. Euphemia.
Metal-work was extremely popular, but not entirely to the
exclusion of work in marble, as is shown by the inscription
describing the tomb to Leo the Great, which Sergius erected
in S. Peter. Still, gold and silver work, enamel work and
precious stones, characterized the gifts to the basilicas; they
were works on a smaller scale and with greater preciosity of
detail than the *ciboria*, tabernacles and sacred vessels of the
earlier periods.

John VII. — The Greek series was continued in Popes John
VI (701–705) and John VII (705–707), Sisinnius (708) and
Constantine (708–715). In architecture it still remained the
day of small things; in painting there was continued and even
increased activity, though there came a certain decadence in
style, and a loss of the classic beauty of the school of Justinian. The two most famous works of this time are due to
John VII; the more complete decoration in fresco and restoration of S. Maria Antiqua, which became more specifically the
Papal chapel, under the shadow of the imperial palace on the
Palatine; and, secondly, the chapel of the Virgin, or of Veronica, at S. Peter, which was filled with mosaics of peculiar

originality. On the other hand, a centre of Lombard influence was established at the very gates of Rome, in the monastery of Farfa. But, though governed by Lombard law, it undoubtedly served to mediate Roman culture and art to the still barbarous Lombards. An even more important agent for the Roman idea outside of the city was the monastery of Subiaco which John VII rebuilt and reorganized as a Benedictine institution.

To Pope Constantine is ascribed the restoration of S. Croce in Gerusalemme, and its transformation from a hall-church, which was substantially the unchanged hall of a Roman palace, into a typical basilica, by the addition of two lines of columns. A curious controversy now centred about a work of art, a painting representing the different Councils of the Church set up in S. Peter. Philippicus Bardanes, the heretical Emperor, undertook to change the picture in a Monothelite sense, and the Roman people rose in revolt and refused to accept or recognize his title, his coinage, his decrees or his portrait. They set up the orthodox painting of the synods in opposition to the imperial will.

The father of John VII was a Greek magnate, of the name of Plato, who held the Byzantine office of Curator of the imperial palaces in Rome, and attended to their repair and maintenance. He restored its main stairway, ascending from the Forum, and his sepulchral inscription at S. Anastasia is one of the most interesting records of Byzantine pseudo-administration. It was probably the fact that Plato lived on the Palatine which induced his son, on becoming Pope, to build a palace for himself on the edge of the Palatine near S. Maria Antiqua, thus temporarily supplanting the Lateran as the seat of the Papacy.

Gregory II and the Iconoclasts. — Gregory II (715–731) was the first Roman Pope after this series of Greeks, and reëstablishes the tradition of practical territorial extension. For some thirty years before him, it is true, the missionary spirit that had led Gregory the Great to send missionaries to England had borne practical fruit in the establishment and strengthening of the Anglo-Saxon Church and in the coming to Rome

H

itself of Anglo-Saxon kings and princes anxious to lay themselves and their treasures at the feet of the successors of S. Peter. The Anglo-Saxon quarter, with its hospice and its church, was established near the Vatican and endowed by King Ina in 728, who built both a church and a hospice. The focussing and strengthening of these Northern energies by Rome just before and after 700 resulted in the great mission of the Anglo-Saxon Boniface to the wilds of Germany, there to organize what was to become one of the most powerful branches of the Western Church. He was sent by Gregory II. Boniface founded Fulda, which became the greatest centre for theology and art in the northeast of Europe. This Pope restored several churches, such as S. Agata, and decorated with mosaics an oratory in the Lateran.

It was also under Gregory II that the greatest crisis in the history of Christian art occurred. The declaration of war against images by the Emperor Leo the Isaurian was formally issued in his edict of 726, which he attempted to enforce in Italy as well as throughout the East. The result was a general insurrection in Italy and the ending of all Byzantine authority in Rome with the slaying of the last imperial duke. The Emperor had threatened to have his emissaries go to Rome to destroy the famous image of S. Peter in his basilica. This has been erroneously referred to as the bronze statue, which still exists there, but the Pope's letter expressly refers to it as a *painting*.

The ensuing convulsion — the only revolution which ever raged about an artistic controversy — had an indelible effect upon art. In the East it radically stunted realism in the representation of the human figure in religious art. In Italy it increased the strength of the Greek element at a time when Byzantine art was entering on a period of ebb-tide. The danger to life and limb for the practising painter drove a multitude of them to Rome, which upheld the mission of art, and this not only filled to overflowing the Greek monasteries already established, but made new foundations necessary.

After having thwarted an almost successful attempt of

the Lombard king, Liutprand, to conquer Rome and make of all Italy a Lombard kingdom, Gregory II died and was succeeded by a Greek, Gregory III (731–741), who showed unusual activity in the field of art. He commenced by causing the Roman synod to excommunicate the iconoclasts, and then gave a practical illustration of his belief in the decoration of the Roman basilicas. He supplemented the large iconostasis in S. Peter by a smaller one, consisting of six onyx columns supporting an architrave, on which were figures in silver of Christ and the Apostles.

Among his works were the basilica of S. Maria in Aquiro, the monastery of S. Crisogono, the oratory of S. Maria *de cancellis* at S. Peter. He undertook a complete restoration of the city walls as a defence against the Lombards.

Zacharias and the Lombard Danger. — The last Greek Pope, Zacharias (741–752), is an example of the fact that even in the Benedictine monasteries at Rome (Lateran) there were Greek monks. He also gave proof of the most extraordinary political sagacity and magnetism in building up the Roman State and protecting the Byzantine provinces at the expense of the Lombards, and takes his place by the side of Leo the Great and S. Gregory. In his time the third great monastery in the Roman province was founded (after Subiaco and Farfa), that of S. Silvestro on Mt. Soracte, where Pope Sylvester is said by tradition to have sought refuge in an early persecution before Constantine's miraculous conversion and baptism. It was founded by a royal Frankish convert to monasticism, Carloman, son of Charles Martel.

Under Zacharias the Papal Chronicle records the lavish use of hangings and altar covers throughout the Roman churches, and enters into great detail as to their manufacture and the subjects represented on them. These details are evidently copied textually from contemporary inventories. They were probably due largely to the skilled monastic workmen from Constantinople and Syria, who fled to Rome from the persecution of Leo the Isaurian; perhaps also to Greek nuns, such as those established in 750 at the nunnery of S. Maria in Campo Marzo.

The additions which Zacharias made to the Lateran palace were for centuries among its greatest glories. Partly for defence, partly for ornament, he constructed a monumental approach, guarded by a tower, beneath which was a broad painted portico, and beyond it a large hall or throne-room — all filled with frescos, harmonizing with the world-wide ambitions and paternal charity of the Pope.

S. Maria Antiqua continued to furnish records of the pictorial activity in Rome, in both new and restored compositions.

The five years of Stephen II (752–757) were busy with the momentous political issues raised by the final success of the Lombards under Astolf in conquering Ravenna and putting an end to Byzantine dominion in Northern and Central Italy. The next logical step was their conquest of Rome, and it was to avoid this that the alliance between Stephen and King Pipin the Frank was established, which was to develop the Western Carlovingian Empire and the Papal temporal power, raising all those questions of the relations between the spiritual and temporal spheres which had remained largely in the background as long as the temporal overlord was the distant and powerless Byzantine Emperor.

Still, the Pope found time for the erection of some monuments. He will always be associated with the earliest known bell-tower or campanile in Rome, which he built in front of S. Peter, on the right side of the atrium. He also added considerably to the buildings around S. Peter, such as the monastery of S. Thecla — making the fourth of the Vatican monasteries; he redecorated the rotunda at S. Petronilla, transforming it from a mausoleum of the dynasty of Theodoric into one of the new Frankish dynasty of Pipin. Stephen also restored the basilica of S. Lorenzo, after the Lombard ravages, and built several *xenodochia* or hospices for pilgrims.

Destruction of the Catacombs. — We must here note a momentous and irretrievable loss to art in consequence of Astolf's long siege of Rome in 756. Though the Lombards did not capture Rome, they completely devastated its neighborhood, including all the suburban churches and monasteries except the apostolic basilicas of S. Peter and S. Paul. In this way all that had been done for over a century, since the days of Honorius I, to bring back prosperity to the Campagna, was obliterated, including the recently founded colonies of Zacharias. The keenest blow was, perhaps, the violation of the Catacombs, the spoiling of their tombs and the destruction of their churches and oratories. Still, an impetus was given to church-building and decoration within the city by the wholesale transfer of relics from the Catacombs by Pope Paul, after the Lombards had shown their disregard for their sanctity in the time of Astolf's siege.

Paul I. — With Paul I (757–767) the political relations with Byzantium were definitely severed. This had perhaps an effect on Roman art — or rather on Roman painting — in that it stopped the influx of Greeks to Rome and turned the Roman school into a local institution trained by Greek teachers, but consisting more and more of native practitioners. This is illustrated by the series of frescos in the apse, chapels and presbytery of S. Maria Antiqua, with which the painters of the time of Paul I seem to have overlaid the series of John VII.

His brother, Pope Stephen, had founded a monastery in his own house to SS. Stephen and Sylvester, which became the famous S. Silvestro in Capite. It was completed by Paul I and given to Greek monks. Its mosaics and frescos, its rich gifts and large possessions, placed it at once among the most important Roman monuments.

Stephen III (768–772) came to the throne in the midst of atrocious scenes of confusion, barbarism and murder. The danger from the Lombards continued; the help of Pipin and his Franks had been desultory and ineffective; the disorders at the Papal election necessitated changes in its method, including the exclusion of the laity from participation. Among the few architectural works of his time was the reconstruction of the diaconal church of S. Angelo in Pescheria by Theodotus, uncle of the coming Pope Hadrian, who had already decorated S. Maria Antiqua.

We now reach the time when Rome is to meet new issues, and to be pitted against the Northern races instead of against the

East in questions of religious and artistic supremacy as well as in politics and diplomacy. Will she bring these new races within her orbit? Will she show the elasticity, fertility of resource and psychological insight required to understand and dominate these formidable factors?

V. THE CARLOVINGIAN CITY AND THE DARK AGE

Hadrian, Temporal Power and the Western Empire. — Pope Hadrian I (772–795) marks a new era, through the new church policy which he developed and which resulted in the establishment of the patrimony of the states of the Church, in the alliance with Charlemagne and the foundation by Papal initiative of the new Frankish Empire of the West. The Lombard kingdom, always a menace at the door of Rome, was destroyed; the dangers of the overlordship of Byzantium, fatal to the life and honor of more than one Pope, were abolished. The territorial influence of the Papacy in Italy, its material wealth and opportunities, backed by the resources of the new Empire, were immensely increased. New fields of missionary work in Northern and Eastern Europe were opened up, and the episcopal and monastic hierarchies, largely on the increase, were brought into closer connection with Rome. In music, literature, liturgy, art, the Roman school found itself called upon to plough in virgin, or semi-fertilized fields, and this acted as a stimulus on Rome itself, which entered upon almost a century of extremely active production, though of diminishing artistic skill.

Under this stimulus, art became more national. While the Byzantine element was still strong, a much smaller percentage of actual production can be credited to Greek hands, and more to Romans, who still felt the spell of their antique traditions.

Restoration of Monuments. — The twenty-four years of the pontificate of Hadrian were artistically the most fruitful since the fourth century. He was the greatest restorer and lover of Early Christian Rome since Pope Damasus, and he accomplished a more extensive work than Damasus, for he had far deeper wounds to heal, a far longer stretch of centuries to reconstruct. He was a man intensely of his age, so that we must not expect of him the work of an archæologist seeking to give back the exact physiognomy of the past.   With the artists at his command, quite alien to the earliest stage of Christian art, such an attempt, had it been made, would have been an impossible feat.

But Hadrian was, at all events, a thorough master of the artistic traditions and history of Rome, and a thorough believer in the great mission of art.   He showed it in his defence of the use of images, in his vindication of the right of the Church to

Iconostasis Choir-screen of S. Maria in Cosmedin, restored, illustrating
Marble Decoration of Age of Hadrian I.

teach the truth through art.   His famous letter to Charlemagne gives a list of the principal mosaics and frescos placed by the Popes in Roman churches from the time of Constantine and Sylvester.

Hadrian's work was not confined to any one part of the city or any one class of monument.   He restored the aqueducts, strengthened and rebuilt the city walls and towers; was impartial in the restoration of churches and monasteries both within and without the walls.

It was largely through the financial aid of Charlemagne that Hadrian must have been able to spend such enormous sums in Rome. The imperial coöperation is attested, somewhat later, for instance, in the church of S. Susanna, where Hadrian's successor, Leo III, is represented in the apse mosaic on one side and Charlemagne on the other. Immense crowds of laborers were called in from every part of the Roman province for work on the walls and the aqueducts, of which the four restored were the *Traiana, Claudia, Jovia* and *Virgo*. Equally extensive and carried out largely by the help of the same unskilled labor was the restoration of the many miles of colonnaded streets that connected the city proper with the settlements that had grown about the great suburban shrines — S. Peter, S. Paul and S. Lorenzo. The chronicler reports that twelve thousand blocks of stone were used in the foundations alone of the colonnades to S. Peter.

The principal architect of Hadrian was Januarius, and probably to him is due the work at S. Maria in Cosmedin, which included the dangerous engineering feat of tearing down an immense ancient ruin before extending the church. The triple apse which Hadrian added to the church is the earliest departure in Rome from the single apse termination, and was not popular. It is probable that the Greek frescos recently uncovered are of his time. The church itself was not fundamentally modified in the twelfth century, except for the changes required by the closing of its galleries.

The *Liber Pontificalis* allows us to follow the trace of his healing hand among the Catacombs and the early cemeterial basilicas that encircled the city, restoring, rebuilding, redecorating, effacing the ravages of time and of the Goths and Lombards. On the Via Portuensis the large basilica of Abdon and Sennen, and those of Candida and Felix ; on the Aurelia, those of S. Pancratius and S. Victor, etc.

Among the monasteries he restored was that of SS. Vincenzo ed Anastasio at the Tre Fontane. He found it in a state of decay and rebuilt from the foundations the basilica, baptistery, monastic structures and annexes, decorating them with frescos, of which faint remnants appear in the ancient gateway, while the decadent masonry of this age is still seen in parts of church and monastery.

Leo III (795–816) had an even greater political genius than Hadrian; it was more concrete. The imperial support was pledged to him even more thoroughly. He continued the work of restoring the basilicas and monasteries of Rome. While Hadrian had extended his activity to the Catacombs and cemeterial basilicas, Leo III went further and restored the churches of neighboring towns, especially those in the Alban Hills and on the coast line — Palestrina and Velletri, Ostia, etc. He continued to improve the two greatest groups of Papal buildings, adding a triclinium or throne room, and a chapel to the Lateran; a triclinium, a palace and a hospice for pilgrims at S. Peter.

Marble Decoration. — In decoration the eighth century was in some ways a turning-point. Until then the precious metals and bronze had had all the honors, but since the previous two centuries marble had begun to compete, particularly in such classes as choir-screens and parapets. Under Leo III this tendency became quite general, coinciding with the development of the decorative designs in low relief, elsewhere described. When we reach the reign of Paschal I (817–824), it is evident, from the *Liber Pontificalis*, that the art of casting and hammering metal was a thing of the past, and that marble had definitely taken possession of the fields of altar-ciboria and altar-fronts, pulpits and candelabra, confessions and their varied forms of decoration and accessories. Leo III still had paschal candlesticks made of silver. Leo IV ordered a marble ciborium. This style of design was to rule in art until the beginning of the twelfth century in Rome and a large part of Italy. It was based largely on classic patterns, as we shall see, handled in a way foreshadowed by some Byzantine work of the sixth century. The effect is partly due to the shallow and unskilful style of marble cutting, and is the least artistic of all mediæval styles of ornament except certain forms of Anglo-Saxon and Lombard animal creations.

Not entirely without influence on this universal use of the same ornamental system may have been the fact that in consequence of the donations of Pipin and Charlemagne, between

754 and 784 a large part of Italy, especially in the eastern and central sections, was handed over to the Popes as a territorial possession. In most of the cities of Emilia and the Pentapolis, the chiefs of the civil and military administration were sent from Rome. The Pope's permission was asked by Charlemagne, even, when he wished to dismantle the palace of Theodoric at Ravenna to use its material in the construction and decoration of his imperial church at Aix-la-Chapelle. It is in this region, including Bologna and Ravenna and their subordinate cities, far more than in Lombardy that we find this ornamentation in use, and we are forced to attribute its origin to either Byzantium or Rome.

Finding it in Byzantine Greece, in Byzantine Egypt, in Dalmatia and in other parts of the Eastern Empire, it seems natural to conclude that it came straight to Rome from the East and thence spread over the parts of Italy most subject to Roman influence.

It has been quite commonly said of late that the new and strong Carlovingian culture of the North revivified effete Rome; that it was inspired in part directly from Byzantium, through Marseilles. This contention is on its face illogical and strained. The great and only sources of Carlovingian culture, besides the small imperial school, were the large monasteries. I will select two of the most important and early of these northern monasteries — Centula and Fontanella. An examination of the original documents illustrating their early history shows that at Fontanella (S. Wandrille) the best models for the manuscripts in its superb library either came from Rome or were written and illuminated in the Roman style. Codexes written *romana litera* are twice mentioned in the eighth century. Of a gospel codex it is said: *codicem illum evangelicum ut scriptura eius insinerat in Romulea urbe scriptum constat* (Chron. Fontan.). One of its most famous monks, Harduin (811), went to Rome and wrote a manuscript of the gospels *romana litera*, probably also teaching it to his fellow-monks, for we find that the great Abbot Ansegisius ordered one of those superb manuscripts in purple and gold to be executed *romana litera*, of which only three of the four gospels were

finished. The same Roman origin is attributed to several of
the finest textiles in these monastic sacristies. That Rome
was and had been for over a century a great centre for the
manufacture of sacred textiles, hangings, altar-fronts and
vestments, covered with religious themes, is shown by the
Papal Chronicle. The church music of both the Anglo-
Saxon and the Frankish churches of Pipin and Charlemagne
was of Roman origin and taught by Roman masters. If these
great Carlovingian monasteries were then free to acknowledge
their debt to Rome,
why should we, at
this distance of time,
pretend to dispute it?

Dalmatic of "Charlemagne" at S. Peter.
Example of Byzantine models for Roman textile-makers.

Paschal I (817–824)
was almost as active
artistically as his two
more glorious prede-
cessors, though his
artists were inferior
to theirs. He patron-
ized both the native
and the Byzantine
types of art in mosaic,
painting and textiles.
As he increased the
number of Greek
monasteries, it is evi-
dent that he did
everything to encour-
age the production of
works of art in these establishments, so that we may conclude
that until the very downfall of art, toward the close of the
ninth century, the Roman churches were supplied with these
products of their native looms and needles after the time-
honored Byzantine models (cf. p. 380).

The most important work of Paschal has always been considered to be S. Prassede. An amusing error has attributed
to his age the great transverse arches of the interior, instead of

to the restorations of the late Renaissance. Also the colonnade, aside from these transverse arches and their piers, has little to do with the age of Pope Paschal, perhaps put together out of fourth-century material at some period after the Gothic wars, and merely remodelled by him. This church was decorated, however, by Paschal with mosaics, and received also the addition of the chapel of S. Zeno. We are reminded in these colonnades of the hasty methods of Pelagius at S. Lorenzo, while the mosaics are a travesty, rich but lifeless, of the purer Greek works of Leo III.

S. Maria in Domnica is the only building of Pope Paschal I which clearly shows the handiwork of his workmen in the treatment of capitals. In fact its series of capitals is the most interesting in Rome for the Carlovingian period. At the same time one must be careful to distinguish between Paschal's capitals and those of the earlier church which he restored. The *Liber Pontificalis* says that Paschal rebuilt, enlarged and decorated a church which was here *olim constructa*. The inscription under the mosaic in the apse begins also: *ista domus pridem fuerat confracta ruinis nunc rutilat . . . metallis.*

In the restoration or reconstruction the old columns and some of the former capitals were used. These are of a design very similar to that of the capitals at S. Martino ai Monti and probably also belong to the age of King Theodoric.

Gradual Artistic Decay. — Notwithstanding the wealth lavished on art by these three Popes, Hadrian, Leo and Paschal, it must be confessed that the results were not correspondingly important. It was a fictitious revival, due to a material prosperity, which multiplied the mediocre products of a decaying art. Not a single basilica of artistic beauty or of imposing dimensions belongs to this age, which was one of greater luxury than taste and skill. The ever decreasing strength of the Byzantine element weakened the Roman school and left it represented by third-rate practitioners.

Under Gregory IV (827–844) the abyss of ineptitude, into which art and culture had been gradually sinking during half a century, is exemplified by the mosaic in the apse of S. Marco, with its bloodless and vapid silhouettes of meagre and lifeless puppets, the perpetrator of which — we cannot call him artist — succeeded, as a French critic has keenly said, in showing himself an innovator in the science of petrifaction. Fragments of the sculptured decoration of pulpits, choir-screens and ciboria, scattered in Roman churches, show the same inanity in decorative sculpture.

It is well that Rome should allow dead silence to brood henceforth over its churches and its streets and should wait for nearly two centuries for a new dawn in the field of art.

This silence could not, of course, be absolute; yet it was almost so. And by a curious fatality hardly one of the few monuments of this period remains to contradict the sentence of decadence. Stephen V (885–891) rebuilt the basilica of the Apostles; Formosus (891–896) restored and filled with frescos the basilica of S. Peter; Sergius III (904–911) rebuilt from its foundations the Lateran basilica. We are also told that the famous and infamous men and women of the house of Alberic, Marozia and their brood were prominent benefactors of churches and monasteries.

There were, however, some fine works of military engineering. One of the last great enterprises of the Carlovingian Papacy was the construction and fortification of the Leonine City, the new quarter (Borgo) across the Tiber, between Hadrian's mausoleum and S. Peter. This had been for some time needed in order to prevent any repetition of the pillaging of the basilica, such as had happened not long before. Pope Leo IV wrote in 848 to the Emperor Lothair that he wished for his help and advice in the construction of this city which had not only been planned, but begun by his predecessor Leo III. The Emperor immediately sent a liberal sum and the new suburb was dedicated June 27, 852. The engineer who planned and built the fortifications was Agatho, presumably a Greek versed in the advanced methods of Byzantine military science.

Political Decay and Poverty. — The disintegration of the Carlovingian dynasty had brought back the old political chaos, general insecurity and impoverishment. The climax of Rome's sad plight was reached under Pope John VIII (872–882). In a letter to the Emperor Charles the Bald in 877 he paints the situation and urgently asks for help : " for the (Roman) Campagna is entirely depopulated ; we have nothing, nor does there remain anything wherewithal either we, or the venerable monasteries and other sacred places, or the Roman Senate, can find bodily sustenance. All the suburban district of Rome has been so pillaged that it no longer seems to contain a single inhabitant."

When the bare necessities of life were lacking, the arts could not flourish. The same Pope John VIII wrote to King Louis of Germany to send him an organ with a skilled artist (*artifex*) to work it and to give instruction in it. We are far indeed from the time, a century before, when Rome gave religious music to the national churches of the North !

Still, the very year of the Pope's letter to Charles the Bald (877) there happened the famous battle of Cape Circeii in which the Papal militia and the imperial troops saved Rome from capture by the Saracen invaders, who completed the destruction of whatever had been left about Rome by the Lombard raiders of the two previous centuries. It was probably with the financial help of Charles the Bald that the Pope did on a smaller scale for the basilica of S. Paul outside the walls what Leo IV had done for the protection of S. Peter. He surrounded with a circuit of walls, with battlements and towers, the basilica and the suburb that had grown up around it, calling the new annex to Rome by his own name, Johannipolis.

Then was inaugurated the era of fortification that was to characterize the rest of the Middle Ages in Rome and its province.

The material and artistic prosperity, so rapidly on the wane, was destroyed by the final success of the Saracen raids in the latter part of the ninth century. For some thirty years, until their final defeat in 916 by John X, these Mohammedan invaders — northernmost representatives of the conquerors of Sicily — had terrorized the entire territory about Rome, burning the principal monasteries such as Farfa, Subiaco, S. Elia, Cassino, Soracte.

In this general devastation the *domus cultœ*, the colony

farms established by the Popes, had also disappeared, and all villages in the plains had been abandoned for new fortified towns on rocky hills. This cut off a large source of revenue for the maintenance, restoration and decoration of the churches in Rome itself.

Nothing better shows the completeness of the decadence than the fact that when the greatest of all basilicas, the Lateran, had

Interior of Basilica of S. Elia, near Nepi.
(Tenth century.)

fallen in 897 from old age and decay, it was allowed to lie, a shapeless mass of ruins, for seven years, though it was the cathedral church of the Papacy. When Sergius III (904–911) and John X (914–928) began and completed the reconstruction, it was, however, on a large scale, and the interior was covered with mosaics and frescos.

Some of the monasteries ruined by the Saracens were rebuilt. One of these, S. Elia near Nepi, was given in 939 to Abbot Odo, famous head of the Benedictine order of Cluny, then the foremost monastic body in the world, and the present church with its frescos, appears to date from the reconstruction that shortly followed. It is almost unique as dating from an age that produced so little and that little so poorly calculated to endure.

Still, it must be confessed that there was a certain vigorous recrudescence among the monasteries, even though art flourished but little in Papal circles. A passage in the interesting contemporary chronicle of Benedict of Mt. Soracte is very suggestive. He says : " The glorious prince Alberic . . . built the monastery of S. Lorenzo in Agro Verano and that of S. Paul (both in Rome), and restored to the monasteries the property that had been taken from them by evil men. He heard of the desolate condition of the monasteries of S. Andrea (in Flumine, near Soracte) and of S. Silvestro on Mt. Soracte, which had been captured by the Saracens, etc." Alberic then restored them under the direction of Abbot Leo and gave them property and gifts. At S. Andrea were then built three towers to defend the gate of the monastery and a castle on each side of it, and later a church, which is probably the one still existing, with frescos so similar to those of S. Elia.

Darkest Age. — One might call the period from the death of Pope Formosus in 896 to the accession of Pope Leo IX in 1049 the dark interregnum. *Thirty-nine* popes in only a century and a half ! Most of them were incapable or ignorant, some of them were mere tools ; one of them a depraved youth ; one a mere layman. The destructive raids of Saracen and Hungarian hordes, the disruption of the political forces, the decay of education, morality and spiritual force, sapped both the material and intellectual patrimony of Rome so seriously that it was bankrupted almost as completely as after the Gothic wars. The clergy had become hopelessly corrupt and barbarous ; there was no longer any learning, even in the monasteries, but here at least morality was not as lax, and art found a last refuge.

Our ignorance of the historic and monumental facts of the tenth century is increased by the lacuna at this point in the Papal Chronicles. Only in the twelfth century was the thread dropped in the ninth century worthily picked up again.

I

Artistically we miss but little.   The fragments that can be approximately dated between c. 875 and 1050, like some ornamental pieces at S. Lorenzo and the Lateran, or at Soracte; the well-head at S. Marco and S. Giovanni a Porta Latina and other similar pieces show a complete lack of taste and technique.

It seems difficult to attribute to Roman artists the only mosaic of this age, that which surmounted the tomb of the Emperor Otho III (983) at S. Peter's.   But the two branches of painting

Interior of S. Maria in Capitolio or Aracœli.

appear to have remained in far better condition than either architecture or decoration, and Rome's supremacy in this art was not interrupted.

Latest remaining monument of this decadence before the dawn is the church of Santa Maria in Aracœli.   Standing on the highest of the two Capitoline peaks, on the site of the ancient *arx* or citadel of the Capitol, its ancient name was S. Maria in Capitolio.   It belonged in the tenth century to a monastery called *monasterium Capitolii*.   This church inherited the aureole of the ancient Capitol, became the principal meeting-place of the mediæval Senate of Rome, the courthouse from which its laws were proclaimed, the national church of the Roman oligarchy, whose numerous tombs made of it their West-minster Abbey. Though Pius IV and other Renaissance van-dals did their best to obliterate its interest by destroying most of the mediæval monuments and church furniture, its shell and colonnades remain.

Now begins the golden age of frowning feudal architecture. The older peaceful palaces, inherited from classic and luxu-rious Rome are no longer in harmony with the furious feuds of the storm-tossed city. They are either transformed, like Al-beric's palace, into monasteries, or into fortresses with heavy towers. A new use is thus found for the ancient ruins : a tower rises on the foundation of a triumphal arch (Circus Maxi-mus and Septimius Severus) ; soon entire quarters of the city will be recognized as the camping-ground of one of the great feudal families.

The mention of Alberic recalls many other proofs that this extraordinary man, " tyrant " of Rome, and other members of his family, like the famous woman Marozia, were liberal bene-factors and builders of monasteries in and around Rome. That of S. Maria in Pallara on the Palatine, with its still remaining frescos, belongs to this time. Another feudal magnate, Cre-scentius, built and endowed a basilica of considerable size, S. Tripho. There still exists in Rome a part of an immense for-tified palace and castle, variously called house of Pilate, house of Crescentius, or of Rienzi. Originally it was of great extent and centred around a tower which is partly preserved. It stood near the entrance to the Quattro Capi bridge. It is like nothing else in Rome and the only relic of its earliest feudalism.

VI. ROME BEFORE AND AFTER THE GUISCARD FIRE

WE now approach the time when the face of almost the entire city is to be first obliterated, through the fire kindled by the Norman army of Robert Guiscard in 1084, and then transformed by the Popes, prelates and nobles of the twelfth century. Let us imagine what it looked like before this catastrophe which changed the levels and the lines of the streets so radically as to necessitate the complete reconstruction of many quarters.

The City before 1084. — Until then we have no record of any considerable fire sweeping the city in Christian times, — none equal to the two or three greater ones of imperial times. The lines of the city's streets were still practically those of the Rome of Constantine and Honorius. This is hardly too daring a conclusion to draw from the interesting topographical document of the age of Charlemagne called the Einsiedeln Itinerary. Its author enumerates the monuments, both pagan and Christian, according to some map which he had before him. He follows the principal streets and sets down the buildings on both sides, proceeding as far as the city walls, and even beyond. He reads the inscriptions on the monuments and identifies them; he also enumerates the churches.

He is far from following the erroneous identifications of ancient buildings that were current in the later Middle Ages, and his work shows a scholarly acquaintance with the Constantinian *Notitia*. The main street of Rome, the *Via Lata*, still had its colonnades; he knows the names of the Circus Maximus and Flaminius, the theatre of Pompey, the Septizonium, etc. The walls of Aurelian were still intact. Benedict of Soracte, somewhat later (c. 860), enumerates fifteen gates, six thousand eight hundred battlements, forty-six castles or bastions and three hundred and eighty-one towers.

The main change in the conformation of the city had been caused by the new fortified suburb around S. Peter — the Leonine City. The colony of Jews was settled in the region of the Ponte Quattro Capi; the larger Greek colony still occupied the quarter near the church of S. Maria in Cosmedin, further along the river up to the foot of the Palatine. The foreign colonies, especially of the northerners, occupied the "Borgo"; and the Trastevere was still filled with the descendants of the emigrants from Ravenna. The Cœlian and Aventine hills were owned mainly by the large monastic establishments, with an occasional palace or fortress. The Palatine itself was too thickly crowded with the ponderous ruins of the imperial palaces to do more than give room for an occasional monastery or church, such as S. Maria in Pallara and S. Cesareo. In the same way the Roman Forum was only sparsely populated and given over mainly to religious establishments and to lime-kilns and workshops established in some of the principal ruins, while others were turned into fortresses and surmounted by towers and battlements.

The great mass of the population was grouped in the Campus Martius and along the river banks, breaking away up the Quirinal slope. The lack of water continued to prevent a denser population on the heights.

The city was, therefore, characterized by the following groups of buildings: (1) the prominent antique structures, overlooking a mass of Roman monuments which still formed the main groundwork of the city; (2) the larger monasteries, often fortified and forming, with their annexes and grounds, quite a prominent feature; (3) the fortresses and palaces of the recently arisen nobility, either entirely mediæval, like the palaces of Alberic, of Marozia and of Crescentius; or formed by the adaptation of Roman buildings, such as the theatre of Marcellus, the Circus Maximus, Hadrian's mausoleum, the mausoleum of Augustus; (4) the principal basilicas with their annexes, hospitals, small monasteries, courts and towers.

Connecting these groups, partly hiding the gaping rents in the antique structures, were the lines of colonnades and arcades, the best of which were a classic heritage renovated by

Pope Hadrian and supplemented in every century, so that practically every street was flanked by them on both sides. One thing certainly did not yet exist: a mediæval domestic form of architecture of artistic character, except in the case of the larger feudal palaces.

The historic events that led up to the great fire are well-known. The degradation of the Papacy, become the mere puppet of warring feudal factions of the Crescentii or the Counts of Tusculum, the licentiousness of a Benedict IX, the loss of public order and safety, the simony and immorality of the clergy, which characterized the first half of the eleventh century, had led the people and the clergy to place themselves unreservedly in the power of the German Emperors. Though the ensuing peace made it possible to initiate the much-needed religious and moral reform of the clergy, the rights over the Church and over Rome, that Emperor Henry III arrogated to himself, inevitably led to the conflict that broke out when Gregory VII, Hildebrand, became Pope. The struggle is historic.

Struggle between Hildebrand and the German Emperors. — Already in the preliminary contest of 1063 between the Hildebrand party under Alexander II and the German Feudal party under the antipope Cadalus, the fortress and basilica of S. Paul, the Lateran palace, and S. Peter had all suffered from the continuous street fights. The city saw more feudal towers rising at every point of vantage, at the entrances of the bridges, on the triumphal arches.

The excommunication of the Emperor Henry IV by Gregory in 1076 — their mutual dethronements — cleared the ground for a death-struggle that ended temporarily at Canossa with a Papal victory. When the struggle was renewed in 1080, the Pope had the Norman, Robert Guiscard, as his ally. The Normans had been for half a century establishing a great kingdom in Southern Italy and Sicily, and by trading on their piety and astuteness the Papacy had legalized their conquest by receiving their allegiance as temporal sovereign, thus storing up a claim to these provinces for the States of the Church. But for three successive years the German Emperor besieged Rome unsuccess-

fully and laid the country waste without the Norman's moving
to Gregory's assistance. Henry's final capture of the Leonine
City and S. Peter, the siege of Gregory in the castle of S.
Angelo, the successive capture of the fortresses in the city
held by Papal followers — the Septizonium, the Island of the
Tiber, the Capitol — did immense damage in 1083 and 1084.
This finally brought Robert Guiscard to relieve the Pope, who
still resisted in S. Angelo.

Ruin of the City. — His soldiery entered through the Flaminian gate. Their barbarous sacking of the city led to a revolt of
the Romans, to quell which the Normans set fire to the city at
several points. The flames swept everything away, from the
Lateran to the Flaminian gate; the city was a mass of black-
ened walls. The inhabitants were sold into slavery by the
thousands, — even the most illustrious, — and many were carried off to Southern Italy.

A few years after, a French visitor, lamenting its ruin, says
of it: *Roma fuit.* Truly, this must have seemed the end. As
this prelate says: "So much still stands, so much has fallen,
that what stands cannot be levelled and what has fallen cannot be rebuilt." To rebuild the impoverished city, with empty
treasury, seemed impossible. Rome was now hardly habitable.
The great arteries of colonnades framing the highways as far
as S. Paul, S. Peter and S. Lawrence were in ruins and block-
ing the roads. The Lateran palace, the basilicas of S. Clemente, SS. Quattro Coronati and all the other churches between
the Lateran and the Forum, were badly injured or destroyed.
The Island of the Tiber, the Trastevere and Borgo, the Campus
Martius were almost wiped out. Certain regions, such as the
Cœlian and Aventine hills, have never recovered to the present
day and remain largely even now in picturesque ruin, a curious *pendant* to the modern city.

The condition of the city may be imagined from the fact
that the Vatican basilica and its enclosure was used as a fortress and regularly besieged in the years following Gregory's
death, when there was a conflict between his successor, Victor
III (1086–1087) and the antipope Clement III. This Pope
dreaded the ruined city and fled from it three times. Greatest

patron of art of his age, establisher of a school of art in Monte
Cassino, partly trained by Byzantine and partly by Lombard
artists, as abbot of this great monastery before he became
Pope, he exercised an imperishable influence on the æsthetics
of his age in architecture, painting, mosaics — but so far as
Rome herself is concerned he is known only to have profited
by her ruin to the extent of carrying off her columns and marbles for his new buildings at Monte Cassino.

Urban II (1088–1099) began his reign as possessor of merely
a small section of the city, and the street fights were wild and

S. Saba, on the Aventine, in Process of Excavation.
Below, single-nave church of sixth century.
Above, basilica of twelfth century, built after Guiscard fire.

bitter. Life in Rome was one of hellish disorder and extreme
poverty. This Pope, the preacher of the first crusade and a
Frenchman, never had a moment's peace in the city, and
only toward the close of his life was able even to enter the
palace of the Lateran. It was so ruinous that he did not live
there but in one of the fortified palaces of the Pierleone family,
then one of the greatest among the rough feudal nobles. At

this time contemporary writers lay especial stress on the unhealthiness and poverty of the city, ravaged by malarial fevers. Still, S. Maria in Cappella was due to him (1090).

Paschal II and Reconstruction. — In 1099 there came to the Papal throne Paschal II (1099–1118), a monk of the order of Cluny, who, after a long fight, like that of a secular lord, succeeded in subduing the barons who infested Rome and the Campagna. For years the city was still ravaged by street fights. The Corsi, the Normanni, the Baruncii, the Pierleoni, the Frangipani, were among the Roman nobles prominent in this warring. Paschal was to commence the work of reconstructing Rome, but not until after 1112, when he made peace within the Church by repudiating his concession to Emperor Henry V. It was in 1111 that the Pope, captured and ill-treated by the Emperor, had given up the struggle of Gregory VII and had granted to the Emperors the right of investiture by which the bishops and abbots were made subject in their selection to the Emperor and not to the Pope. But Paschal abjured the concession wrung from him before a council of the Church the following year. Then followed about five peaceful years before the last two years of martyrdom, when he was finally hounded to his death by the imperialists.

It was during these five years that Paschal made the first efforts to rebuild the city that had been made since the fire of 1084 — nearly thirty years before. Modern researches are continually enlarging the scope of this brief activity. S. Lorenzo in Lucina, S. Maria in Monticelli, S. Bartolommeo all' Isola, S. Clemente, S. Maria in Cosmedin, were then rebuilt and partly decorated.

But before discussing these works and their style, a few words must be said of the brief art movement in the generation before the fire, under Hildebrand, because it explains how Paschal found artists to carry out his plans. Even before Hildebrand's time there had been a beginning of artistic activity, shown in the rebuilding of S. Valentino on the Via Flaminia, with frescos, porticos, campanile and monastic buildings. While the Papal treasury was then at a low ebb, it seems as if in certain branches art began to show improvement,

especially painting.   The frescos of S. Clemente are certainly
the foundation stone of the revival of painting, and they date
from Hildebrand's time; so do those in S. Pudentiana, which
he restored, and those in the Cappella del Martirologio at S.
Paul.   In fact, Hildebrand undertook a radical restoration of
this basilica and its annexes, of which he was titular cardinal; and its famous bronze doors were made in Constantinople
by his orders.   His great friend was Desiderius, Abbot of
Monte Cassino, the famous importer of Byzantine artists and
artisans from Constantinople for the decoration of his new

Capitals of Propylon of S. Maria in Cosmedin (capital on r. antique;
crude capital on l. c. 1121).

monastic buildings, then the greatest in Italy.   It is even
thought that the present monastic buildings and cloister at
S. Prassede are the work of Hildebrand.

    There were, therefore, artists of a kind at the disposal of
Paschal II when he began to attack his problem of renovation,
to tear down the half-ruined buildings, establish new levels
and new lines of streets and lay the foundations of modern
Rome as it was until its dismemberment by the Renaissance
Popes and its disruption by the Italians after the annexation
in 1870.   We know the names of a few of these artists:
Paulus, chief among his architects and decorators; Guido and
Petrolinus among his painters.

The new style arose through a direct study of the antique combined with an infusion of Oriental color sense. The debased decorative work in low relief sculpture was abandoned for plain moulded marbles and simple classic details. Gradually there was added to this simplicity an ever increasing element of color through the insetting of disks and slabs of rich antique marbles, porphyry, serpentine, rosso antico, granite,

Slab of Choir-screen at S. Maria in Cosmedin, discarded in Twelfth Century (c. 780).

cippolino; also by geometric patterns of small cubes of these and other marbles. Sparingly used at first, the whole century elapsed before full richness was attained and the splendor of perfect mastery of moulded and carved detail. In this the Roman school marched side by side with that of Campania and Sicily. Applied to architecture and to all manner of church furniture and detail, this style has commonly been dubbed "Cosmati" or "Cosmatesque," from the name of one of its prominent exponents.

In carrying out their new ideas these artists of Paschal II

and his successors in the twelfth century showed themselves pitiless toward the work of the previous five centuries. Every few years, in the course of restorations in the churches in and near Rome, some slabs are found covered with the low relief work of the Byzantine period, which were at this time turned around and either used as mere building material and paving slabs, or decorated on the other side with the new style of inlaid mosaic work. The choir-screens, altar-fronts, pulpits and ciboria were torn away to make room for their successors. Not a single Roman church has preserved its internal decoration in this style. It must be reconstructed out of fragments by the special student, as has been done so interestingly by the late architect, Professor Mazzanti.

Political circumstances hardly gave a fair opportunity to the Popes and to Rome to develop this art, after the death of Paschal II. One of the great voids to fill was due to the sacking of the churches by the Normans, who looted the works in precious metals which had been accumulated during the Byzantine and early Carlovingian periods. Of these confessions, choir-rails, groups of statuary, ciboria, altar-fronts, of gold and silver gilt, it is hardly probable that a single one remained. What the fire spared the soldiers stole. It took two centuries to recoup the treasuries and churches.

A figure now looms up even larger in death than in life, that of the great Countess Matilda. She had inherited enor-

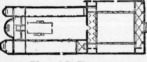

Plan of S. Clemente.

mously extensive fiefs and estates, extending through a part of Lombardy, nearly the whole of Emilia and Tuscany, large sections of Umbria and the Abruzzo. Her territory comprised about a third of the entire peninsula. During her lifetime she was the stanch supporter of the Church and especially the friend of Hildebrand, who persuaded her to will all her possessions to the Church. She died in 1115. Her donation was the most epoch-making in the history of the temporal power. It is true that the flourishing communes already organized in these regions, such as Pisa, Siena, Florence, Lucca and Brescia, paid no attention to the Papal claims, and that the Emperors as well as the free cities disputed the right of Matilda to dispose of the territory in this way; but it is also true that the bequest not only gave a basis of law for the organization of the States of the Church, but proved to be an increasing source of revenue as the estates were occupied by the successors of Pope Paschal. It has a distinct bearing upon the artistic fortunes of the city, for it was partly in this way that the means were provided for its reconstruction.

Still, no immediate improvement followed the accession of Pope Gelasius (1118–1119), who was forced to leave Rome for France by the bloody fights of the Frangipani and the Pierleoni and the strength of Antipope Burdinus. His successor, Calixtus II (1119–1124), a Frenchman, was elected in France, at Cluny, and in 1120 came to Rome, which he was able to occupy entirely. His triumphal entrance foreshadowed the yielding of the Empire to the Papal claims which culminated in the Concordat of Worms, in 1122.

This date marks a distinct advance. We find that for some years the Roman population had been recovering. The twelve regions into which the city was administratively divided were all on the north bank, and were supplemented by the Island and by the Trastevere (*Urbs Ravennatum*), as well as by the purely Papal district of the Borgo, between S. Peter and Hadrian's mausoleum. The twelve regions had their senators, their captains and their militia. The entire organization was under the Senate and the prefect of the city, whose appointment rested with the Pope, though for a long time the Emperor dictated or approved it. Gradually Rome began once again to take shape and slightly to resemble a city rather than a series of fortified oases in the desert of crumbling ruins. The display of the people in receiving Calixtus in 1120 already shows a certain return of well-being.

An important step taken at once by Calixtus was to forbid the fortification of churches; but that he did not deprive S. Peter of its defences is shown by subsequent events. The Lateran had been uninhabitable ever since the fire; he began to restore it — both church and palace. He also repaired the

aqueducts and brought water to the Lateran. In the palace
he built a Papal chapel, dedicated to S. Nicholas, and two halls,
a dining and a throne room, though he was not able to com-

S. Clemente, restored as it was in the Twelfth Century.

plete their decoration. Under him was completed the reconstruction of S. Clemente, S. Maria in Cosmedin and other
churches.

The days of Honorius II (1124–1130) were passed in an absolute tranquillity that gave the best opportunity for artistic

activity. The Roman school of art was now constituting itself anew. Hand in hand with the Pope it was even beginning to reach out to conquer the neighboring cities æsthetically, as he was temporally. S. Clemente was completed and dedicated; S. Niccolo in Carcere and S. Crisogono were completed.

Artistic Revival. — The schism between Innocent II (1130–1143) and Anaclete did not check the growing prosperity. Both men were Trasteverines and during their joint rule the Trastevere arose to great magnificence. Anaclete, of the famous and wealthy Pierleone family, was previously cardinal of S. Maria in Trastevere, while John of Crema, the wealthy and

Bird's-eye View of the Lateran Basilica, Palace and Annexes, restored
as it was in the Middle Ages.

able leader of the Innocent II faction, was cardinal of S. Crisogono in Trastevere. So we find a galaxy of large and small new buildings: S. Crisogono, S. Cecilia, S. Maria in Trastevere, S. Cosimato, S. Tommaso in Parione, etc. There were not only churches built, but usually monastic buildings attached to them.

In such a superb structure as S. Maria in Trastevere we hail once more a perfect art, as perfect as that which created S. Maria Maggiore in the fourth and fifth centuries. There is no more patchwork, no "crazy quilts" of undigested antique fragments. The buildings are on a large scale and of an art harmonious and complete, with its system of decoration and furniture.

Innocent II. — In fact under Innocent II greater strides were made in reconstructing and adorning the city and in forming a style of architecture and decoration than under any Pope since Paschal. The crudeness still evident at S. Lorenzo in Lucina, finished in the year of his accession, has quite disappeared in the great basilicas that now arose, especially S. Calixtus and S. Maria in Trastevere. He continued work at the Lateran, reroofing the basilica, rebuilding the campanile, completing certain halls in the Papal palace and decorating them with historic and other frescos, such as the scene of the coronation of Lothair.

Lucius II in the single year of his pontificate (1144–1145) is said to have rebuilt S. Croce in Gerusalemme. As he gave to the Lateran the church of S. Giovanni a Porta Latina, it is to this time that we may attribute its early Cosmatesque details.

Great Monasteries. — With Eugenius III (1146), a great friend and pupil of S. Bernard, a member of the Cistercian order and abbot of its monastery of SS. Vincenzo and Anastasio, outside the walls, the monastic movement in the Papacy reached its climax. He completed the work of Lucius II at S. Croce. The Popes were leaning more and more on the monasteries, and the multiplication of cloisters recalls the similar wave that passed over Rome in the seventh and eighth centuries.

The City. — The movement to rebuild and beautify was by no means confined to sacred structures. The entire city arose from its ashes; burghers and nobles created a new civic architecture which seems to have been more important in relation to the religious structures than had been previously the case since early Christian times.

We infer this not only from remaining houses but from an amusing and interesting diatribe of a contemporary German ecclesiastic, Gerol of Reichersperg, who, writing to Eugenius III, is especially indignant at the building of the new communal palace or senate house on the Capitol, as a sign of the civic and antipapal pride of the Roman republic. "For behold," he says, "some are now daring to rebuild the accursed city . . . out of which only the house of Rahab, that is the Church, had been saved. Its civil structures destroyed, it had

grown up both in morals and in structures to be a holy temple
to the Lord. A plain spectacle to all . . . its imperial palaces
and many other wonderful buildings in sad ruin represent
Jericho, while the religious structures, every day increasing
and shining with brilliant images, prove clearly through the
daily increase and beautifying of morals and structures that
this is indeed the saved house of Rahab. Thus in our own
days the church of the Lateran, and the church of S. Croce,

Interior of S. Maria in Trastevere (c. 1140).

and the church of S. Maria Nova were amplified both in religious use and in size of walls. The house also of the blessed
apostle Paul, repaired by Gregory VII, shines now with
monastic fervor, which also has been made to flourish at the
monasteries of SS. Quattro Coronati and S. Anastasio, as well
as in the other churches and monasteries in the city of Rome
belonging to the regular clergy.

"Hence we are not unduly afflicted to see that the abom-
ination of desolation still remains in the house of S. Peter,

K

prince of the apostles, where battlements and warlike apparatus are placed in the upper part of the church, above the body of the blessed Peter. . . .

" If these rebels were more shrewdly attacked by the Church . . . they would not be able to rebuild Jericho or Babylon, as they are doing in Rome, where the Capitoline, once destroyed, is now rebuilt over against the house of God, the house of Rahab."

The bitterness of these words can be understood only after studying the movement by which the Roman people showed the growing consciousness of its power and sought to become a free city, as the majority of the other great cities of Italy had already done or were preparing to do. They succeeded, in the teeth of both Popes and Emperors, in establishing a Senate, a republic ruled under a constitution, and in wresting almost complete autonomy. For forty-four years the Popes suffered every imaginable ill from this revolutionary movement before the Papacy returned in 1188 with Clement III. Meanwhile five popes — Eugenius III, Alexander III, Lucius III, Urban III and Gregory VIII — lived in exile from Rome.

Necessarily, during this half century the Popes themselves had but a small part in directing the artistic destinies of the city, which were left to the wealthy clergy, burghers and nobles. The building activity of the new Republic showed itself in the restoration of the city walls. An inscription on the Porta Metrovia of 1157 reads, after the date, *S.P.Q.R. haec menia vetustate dilapsa restauravit* (!), *senatores,* followed by the names of the senators then ruling.

With the name of Anastasius (1153), who occupied the chair for only a few months, we associate the completion of that series of political anti-imperial frescos in the Lateran, begun by Calixtus, that created such a sensation in Europe. His equally short-lived successor, Hadrian IV, built a fortress at Radicofani and the fine porch and campanile were added to SS. Giovanni e Paolo in the city.

Alexander III. — During the long and heroic pontificate of Alexander III (1159–1181) the chronicler Boso records only the consecration of the church of S. Maria Nova (1161) in the

Forum, probably marking the completion of its apse mosaic and of the destroyed mosaic and porch of its façade, begun under Lucius II or Eugenius III. But it was really under this great Pope, the strenuous adversary of Emperor Frederick II, that the Roman school attained to complete mastery in the handling of its peculiar style. The little city of Ninfa, where he was consecrated, contains numerous structures of about his time and was abandoned in the following century, its

Ninfa, Ruins of the Mediæval Town and Monasteries.

ruined towers and churches with faded and crumbling frescos still rising among the head waters of the stream at the foot of Norba mountain. Everywhere in the Roman territory construction and decoration on a large scale was commenced. The superb cathedral of Terracina was built, that of Anagni was completed (1179) and that of Civita Castellana partly constructed, entirely or in part by artists of the Roman school.

We cannot associate his successors, Lucius III (1181–1185), Urban III (1185–1187) or Gregory VIII (1187), very closely with Roman monuments, for the Romans kept them in exile, and the war of the Romans with Tusculum and the raids of the imperialists prevented any close artistic relations between Rome and the Campagna, where these Popes largely resided.

Spread of Roman Art. — Still, the very political vicissitudes of the Papacy really helped to spread Roman art. During a great part of the twelfth and thirteenth centuries the Popes were absent from Rome, in an exile voluntary or forced. Except for their journeys to France, they spent the greater part of this time in the various cities of the province, such as Viterbo, Orvieto, Sutri, Nepi, Civita Castellana, Perugia, on the north; Palestrina, Tivoli, Tusculum, Albano, on the east; Velletri, Terracina, Gaeta, Segni, Anagni, Veroli, on the south. Of all these cities the two favored by the longest sojourns were also the most important, Viterbo and Anagni. In these peregrinations they were accompanied by the bulk of the college of cardinals and the rest of the Curia. Whether there were also artists included in their following we cannot be certain, but we can in some cases trace a connection between Papal visits and the activity of Roman art in the same place. I shall describe in special chapters how this took place.

VII. ROME UNDER THE GREAT MEDIÆVAL POPES

It is, therefore, in the second half of the twelfth century that a consistent artistic expansion brings the cities of the province into close connection with Rome. The continuous wars made the work sporadic, it is true, but gradually the new mosaic decorative system became almost as much the prevalent and only style in the churches of these cities as in the metropolis, superseding the old system of low relief sculpture. In such epoch-making buildings as S. Maria di Castello at Corneto (1143–1166), the cathedrals of Sutri (1170) and Nepi, the monastery of Falleri, the cathedrals of Civita Castellana, Terracina, Fondi, Anagni and Segni, practically the entire decorative work, the church furniture and even parts of the structure were placed in the hands of artists from Rome.

As for Rome itself, the common notion that attributes to the personal initiative and financial aid of the Popes the production of the works of art is evidently to a certain extent an error. There is plenty of negative evidence in the prolonged absence of so many Popes; in the fact that several of them never set foot in Rome; in the extreme poverty under which several of them labored. There is also plenty of positive evidence in inscriptions that the works were due largely to the wealthy clergy and nobles. This was in line with Roman traditions from the very first. In the fifth century Severus and his wife Cassia had decorated S. Anastasia with mosaics, and Leopardus, the deacon, had restored S. Lorenzo at his own expense. This custom had never been discontinued, and had been exemplified even in the darkest ages by Alberic, Crescentius and their ilk. Among typical noble benefactors were the Paparone family, shortly before and after 1200. An inscription of

1201 at S. Pantaleo attributes its reconstruction to Aldruda, widow of Scotto Paparone. This Scotto was consul and senator of Rome in 1198 when Innocent III on ascending the throne persuaded him to abdicate. He and his son Giovanni Paparone gave its magnificent mosaic pavement to the basilica of S. Maria Maggiore, where these two were represented on the central slab as knights in full armor, carrying bannered lances and shields and sitting on caparisoned horses. They,

Detail of Main Portal, Cathedral of Civita Castellana, with Mosaic Inlay.
(Signed by Laurentius, c. 1180, and one of the most artistic works of the school.)

or two knights exactly like them, appear again in the pavement of S. Lorenzo-fuori-le-mura, which apparently was also made at their expense. To give a list of patrons of art during these two centuries would practically mean the enumeration of members of the principal historic families — Colonna, Orsini, Conti, Savelli, etc.

Sometimes the expense was divided between the different wealthy families of the parish, who were buried in the church, and each one paid for one or more bays of the interior, or for a section of the pavement.

But the majority of church benefactors were the members of the upper clergy. The right-hand man of Paschal II in his reconstruction of the city was the famous Papal chamberlain Alphanus, whose tomb is at S. Maria in Cosmedin. John of Crema under Innocent II bore all the cost of the erection, decoration and endowment of the church and monastery of S. Crisogono. Cardinal Raniero Capocci and later in the thirteenth century Senator Bertoldo, his brother Cardinal Stefaneschi and Cardinal Colonna were energetic and generous patrons of art and artists, and for them such men as Giotto, Cavallini, Gaddi, Rusutti and the latest of the Cosmati did some of their best work.

But once again the Popes seriously concerned themselves with the city. To Clement III (1188–1191), who was able to return to Rome in peace, is assigned the construction of the cloister of S. Lorenzo and a further section of the Lateran palace ; to Celestin III (1191–1198), a papal residence near S. Peter ; and to Innocent III (1198–1216), the hospital of S. Spirito in Sassia, the reconstruction of the church of S. Sisto, with its cloister and charming campanile, and the completion of the decorative work at S. Maria in Trastevere. But, as usual, the art records are absurdly incomplete in the Papal chronicles, for Innocent III was extremely active, artistically. He renewed the apse mosaic at S. Peter, by the hand of mosaicists from Venice, enlarged SS. Sergius and Bacchus, adding its portico, and built the porch and bell-tower of S. Silvestro in Capite. In his gifts of sacred vestments and objects in precious metals and manuscripts he was supremely generous.

Innocent III was in every way one of the greatest of mediæval popes. The fact that he belonged to the ancient Conti family, the greatest in Latium, with preponderating interest in its principal cities — Segni, Anagni and Ferentino — helped to fuse the art of this region with that of Rome ; helped him also to coerce the city with his famous family fortress, the Torre de Conti, then reputed the highest in the world. Curtailing the republican liberties of Rome to almost a shadow and establishing his authority firmly over an extensive part of Latium, Sabina and Tuscany, he inaugurated an era of powerful Popes in the same way as Hildebrand had previously done, and with far greater results in the domain of art and monuments. Not the least of these triumphs was the peaceful one over the Emperor Otho, by which earlier conditions were reversed and

S. Lorenzo, Main Basilica.

the Empire acknowledged itself the vassal of the Papacy. Rome was then truly the arbiter of the world.

To **Honorius III** (1216–1226) his life attributes the reconstruction of S. Lorenzo and of the Papal chapel of the Sancta Sanctorum at the Lateran, the restoration and decoration of the apse and façade of S. Paul and the reconstruction of S. Bibiana. The greater basilica of S. Lorenzo will always be associated with him as one of the foremost achievements of mediæval Rome, though its decoration of frescos and inlaid furniture was not completed until the middle of the century. It was under this Pope that the two new orders of S. Francis and S. Dominic, which were to become the mainstays of religion and the Papacy and the great sources of religious art, began to emerge. They had been founded under Innocent III, and their value, as suited to the democratic spirit, the emotionalism and the intellectual curiosity of the age, was recognized at once. Perhaps Rome itself was the latest of any great Italian city to be affected by them, owing to the force of its historic traditions.

The greatest artistic gems of this generation were the cloisters of S. Paul and the Lateran, in which the Roman school reached the most perfect known combination of architecture and color, between 1205 and 1230. In their awakened color-sense, showing itself in decorative work, in mosaics and frescos, the Roman artists were now to anticipate the Venetians, and for the same reason, for they also acted as mediators between Western art and the Byzantine schools of the East whence they derived the love and knowledge of color. To this they added the plastic sense due to their constant contact with the remains of classic art, whose forms they were reproducing with ever increasing purity.

Gregory IX. The Roman Commune and the Germans. — Under Gregory IX (1227–1241) the fierce conflict in which this inflexible old man passed his reign raged alternately with the Roman Commune and the Emperor Frederick II. The Commune was seeking again not only to establish its independence of both Pope and Emperor, but its suzerainty over the States of the Church from Tuscany to the Neapolitan border. The Romans fought against Viterbo, Anagni and the smaller cities. The Pope successfully invoked the aid of the Emperor to preserve his temporal domains, but this temporary alliance was broken by the attempt of the Emperor to subjugate the whole of Italy. In their fear of a greater enemy the Romans themselves changed their policy, and by defending the Pope caused the failure of Frederick's attempt at annexation.

The Romans had just cause for hating the Emperor, because in their defeat by the imperialists before Viterbo, in 1234, they

Cloister of S. Paolo (Early Thirteenth Century).

had lost over ten thousand men. In the midst of this great struggle of Guelfs and Ghibellines, Roman art continued to grow and be diffused over the territory claimed both by Pope and Commune. The Pope himself was of the noble Conti family of Anagni, whose palace was in that city. He resided there quite as much as in Rome; and the completion of the decoration of the cathedral of Anagni by Roman artists at this time is but another indication that some of these artists were likely to follow in the train of Pope and Curia in their travels. It is Cosmas who in 1231 directed the work in the crypt, which he paved and decorated, with the assistance of his sons Luke and James.[1]

The last days of Gregory IX and the interregnum of nearly two years that followed were not, owing to raids and wars, auspicious for art either in Rome or the province. The greatest disaster was the destruction by the Emperor Frederick's Saracens of the city of Albano in 1243. With Innocent IV (1243–1254) came a truce and better times. He had personally but little to do with the rapid and splendid development of art in the city unless we attribute to him — though he was a Genoese, not a Frenchman — the introduction of what has been regarded as a French specialty: the charming engraved tombstones, in which the figure of the deceased is given in incised outline. He lived at Lyons for a considerable part of his reign, helping to build its cathedral and the great bridge over the Rhone. He added many and influential Frenchmen to the ranks of the Roman clergy, and his Francophile tendencies may have affected the Roman school to the extent also of introducing the pointed arch in its decorative system, in place of the architrave; an innovation which certainly did not occur much later.

Dying shortly after he had in a few weeks won and then partly lost the kingdom of Southern Italy, Innocent IV was succeeded by another Pope of the Conti family — Alexander IV (1254–1261). It was at this time that the Roman Commune, under the government of the Bolognese dictator, Senator Brancaleone, was truly governed as a democratic republic, and well governed until the conflict between the clergy and nobility on one side — inimical to Brancaleone — and the guilds of the people on the other, after leading to the temporary downfall of Brancaleone and to the old anarchy, ended by his recall and

---

[1] It was from the prominence of the work of this artist and his family that all this Roman style of artistic work was called "Cosmatesque."

Detail of Choir Seats, Cathedral of Civita Castellana, by Jacobus and Drudus.
Examples of Roman mosaic inlay.

the initiation by him of a campaign of vengeance against his and the people's enemies, the great Guelf nobles. To them belonged the majority of the great strongholds in the city, usually based on some ancient monument, supplemented by one or more towers. These Brancaleone ordered to be destroyed, and a chronicler states that about one hundred and forty of these towered fortresses were razed to the ground, with great destruction, both of the finest buildings of antiquity and of the most palatial examples of mediæval civil architecture.

Charles of Anjou and French Influence. — For several years the Papacy was, willingly or not, strongly tinctured with French

Sacred Vestment, by Roman Artist at Cathedral of Anagni.
(Middle thirteenth century.)

influence, by the combined action of the election of several French Popes and the successful expedition of the adventurous French prince Charles of Anjou, who was called by the Papacy to oppose the German Emperor Henry and who founded the Angevin dynasty in Southern Italy. Alexander's successor, the Frenchman, Urban IV (1261–1264), never was in Rome and called in Charles of Anjou to offset the selection of the Germanic Manfred as Senator of Rome; but he died before seeing the success of his scheme, which was carried forward by the election of a devotee of Charles, the Provençal Frenchman, Pope Clement IV (1265–1268).

The next few Popes were more closely connected with Viterbo and the province than with Rome. Clement IV, Hadrian V and John XXI died at Viterbo, and magnificent tombs were built there for them by Roman artists; the episcopal palace there was rebuilt to house the Popes and their court.

Fortunately for Rome, there came a change in 1277, when a great Roman was elected pope, brought back the court and once more gave to Rome its natural place. The seven years of this pontificate of Nicholas III (1277–1284) were tremendously productive of artistic works, especially in painting. Some idea of this is given by his contemporary historian, Ptolemy of Lucca. After describing the large fortified palace and garden which he made at S. Peter, as if in anticipation of the transfer of the Papal residence from the Lateran, Ptolemy says that he almost entirely restored the basilica of S. Peter. An interesting confirmation of this somewhat startling statement is a report on the dangerous condition of the building made by the master-builders to the Pope, showing how far the walls were cracked and out of plumb. He continued the restoration of the Lateran and there built the exquisite Papal chapel of the Sancta Sanctorum. He died of apoplexy at Soriano near Viterbo, where he had built a superb residence, a fortified palace and villa.

As a city, Rome had now reached quite a different stage from that of the previous century. The main masses of ruined colonnades and buildings, tottering since the Guiscard fire, had been levelled; new grades and new arteries established; the new houses with their continuous colonnades formed consecutive lines; the *disiecta membra* of antiquity had been put to use in the new structures; from the revetments and pavements of decaying buildings had been fashioned the pavements of choice marbles and the furniture of the new churches, whose interiors and porticos were reared with the antique columns and finished with details borrowed or imitated from Roman works. No longer concealed behind courts, the churches helped to decorate the street fronts, and their bell-towers in large numbers served to give picturesqueness to the city landscape, while the same purpose was more ruggedly served by the innumerable feudal towers and fortresses, no longer mere appendages to classic ruins, but often like the Conti, Anguillara, and Milizie fortresses, works of purely mediæval design. At last Rome had acquired some artistic homogeneity and the triumphal arches and temples of antiquity reared themselves amid surroundings not too incongruous.

Rome, the Source and Seat of the Revival of Painting. — It was now that Rome became the centre for the revival of Italian painting. First Cimabue came to Rome, in 1272; then Giotto and Gaddo Gaddi. The leader of the Roman school, Cavallini, became the greatest painter of the age and Giotto's teacher. When the Franciscan order intrusted the decoration of their mother church at Assisi to a large body of painters, who were to make of it the greatest museum of late mediæval painting, the lion's share fell to the Roman school, and the Florentines and Umbrians who came there fell under their influence. Here Giotto took his first steps as an independent artist, on emerging from his Roman apprenticeship.

Marble Statue of S. Peter.
Example of adaptation of the antique.[1]

Honorius IV (1285–1287), though his pontificate was but brief, is closely associated with several works of art. He belonged to the great Savelli family, munificent patrons of art, who lorded it over the Aventine, where their great feudal fortress stood,

---

[1] The statue is antique; the head and hands mediæval. It stood in front of the old basilica, and is now in the crypt.

near the older fortress-palaces of the Emperor Otho and of the Pierleoni. He immediately built, near the church of S. Sabina, in the midst of the family estate, a superb palace, where he lived. It formed the centre of numerous other residences of the court and family. His monument, placed next to that of Nicholas III at S. Peter, was dismantled, and its statue transferred by Paul III to the mausoleum of his mother at S. Maria in Aracœli.

Under Nicholas IV (1288–1292) the two noble families of Colonna and Orsini were paramount, not only politically, but as art patrons, as we see from their works at S. Maria in Aracœli, S. Maria Maggiore, and other churches. The favorite church of this Pope was S. Maria Maggiore, where he built a palace for his residence, and built the portico, campanile and other annexes, beginning also a superb decoration in fresco and mosaic, which was carried out by such artists as Torriti, Cavallini and Rusutti. The equally exquisite remodelling and supplementing of the mosaics at the Lateran and S. Maria in Trastevere was due to this Pope and these artists.

Boniface VIII (1294–1303) was more active politically than monumentally, and his works at the Lateran and Vatican were connected with his Jubilee and Papal glorification. Still, there was no interruption, as yet, in the activity of the school, though it seems to show diminished artistic skill in architecture and sculpture as clearly as it does a great advance in painting and mosaic work. It was under this Pope, however, that the crisis came which was to put an end to the artistic, as well as the political, activities of Rome as a Christian city.

VIII. ROME DURING THE PAPAL EXILE

THE transfer of the seat of the Papacy from Rome to France
on the election of a Frenchman, Clement V, as Pope in 1305,
is commonly considered to have been the signal of the downfall
of mediæval Rome. This clutching at a spectacular historic
fact, as a peg for a dramatic exit, is somewhat fallacious. The
absenteeism of the Popes for about a century merely set the seal
to a catastrophe that had been for some time brewing, which at
this most critical period in the revival was to eliminate Rome
as an artistic as well as a political factor.

The first material sign of the beginning of the downfall had
been the embitterment of the strife between Commons and
Barons which led to the destruction of the towers and palaces
of the nobility in 1257. Larger causes had their effect. The
second half of the thirteenth century saw a pitiable descent
from the inspiring and altruistic world-policy of the great Popes
who had fought the Empire for freedom until the death of Frederick II. They had stood for the cause of democracy and of
Italy, and the people were behind them. But now there was a
change. First came the short-sighted bartering of Innocent IV,
who gave away kingdoms to the highest bidder; then the un-
fortunate Papal subservience to France and Charles of Anjou,
through whom the Popes sought to rule Italy; and finally the
narrow nepotism of Nicholas III paving the way to its even
more irritating form under Boniface VIII. The Popes' influence weakened in proportion as the people of Italy saw them
abandon the championship of national interests and of the free
cities, whenever a policy of expediency seemed to dictate it.

And so, when Boniface VIII was elected in 1294, the pas-
sionate spirit of this last great mediæval Pope found itself surrounded by egotistical time-servers, and beat its wings against
the meshes of a net it had helped to set. The famous Jubilee
celebration of 1300, when Rome saw some two million of

pilgrims, was a final effort to conceal the real growing weakness. All Italy and many leaders of the rest of Europe were there; and on them Rome made an unforgettable impression, which we see reflected in Dante, who was himself one of these pilgrims. But if the pathos and grandeur of Rome still bound the spirits of men, the nearer view of the Papacy failed to rivet them. Spiritual weapons without a spiritual force and a conviction of right to back them were but weapons of straw against sceptical flesh and blood. Even France turned against the Pope; and the scene at Anagni of the final humiliation of Boniface at the mercy of a low-minded notary of Philip le Bel and of a leader of a band of mercenaries, is one of the unforgettable facts of history. Its date, September, 1303, is the antithesis of the triumph of the great Hildebrand over the Empire at Canossa.

Exodus of 1305. — The withdrawal of the Papacy in 1305 from Rome, to become a tool of French politics, was therefore not by any means the beginning of the decadence of Roman art. The prosperity of the city between 1257 and 1303 had been periodically endangered by anarchy, by the open warfare between Commons and nobles, by the opposition between the Popes and the Roman republic which was constantly seeking to limit the local authority of the Popes, and by bloody feuds between rival noble families, especially those of the Colonna and Orsini factions. But even the Papal departure in 1305, and the announcement of its definite character in 1306, did not cause an absolute and immediate catastrophe. The Romans were slow to recognize the fundamental difference between the previous temporary Papal absences and the present withdrawal, and that the vitality of the city as well as of the Papacy had been fatally sapped.

Destruction of the Lateran. — The difference, however, soon became apparent as a consequence of the transfer of the immense funds of the Papacy and of the wealthy college of cardinals, who were the principal private patrons of art. The noble families themselves, owing to their exhausting feuds, no longer possessed the wealth of their ancestors of the twelfth and thirteenth centuries. But the most obvious sign of the times, one to terrify popular imagination, came almost at once. It was the conflagration which in 1308 destroyed almost completely the historic seat and centre of the Papacy, the palace of the Lateran, and its church of S. John, "head and mother of all churches." As the people were just then beginning to realize the reality of the establishment of the Papal capital at Avignon, this destruction seemed like the finger of God. The city was full of processions of mourners.

Destruction of Monuments.—The impression of desolation and ruin which it was beginning then to give was increased in 1312. Then the German Emperor Henry VII, trying in vain to imitate his heroic ancestors, the Othos and Fredericks, and to attain to the Roman Empire of the West, entered Rome with his German followers, seconded by the Ghibelline party in the city. A fierce struggle with the Guelfs ensued. Every street, palace and monument was fortified and defended, and every inch of ground was contested. The Emperor sought in turn to force his way to S. Peter, to the Capitol and to S. John Lateran as a last resort, to carry out the historic ceremony of a coronation in Rome that should consecrate his claim. Whole quarters of the city were gutted by fire, towers and monuments razed to the ground as soon as captured. When the imperial whirlwind had departed peace did not follow, for the democracy of the exhausted city rose against the nobles who were the cause of the disaster and in their rage completed the work of the mob of 1257 in destroying the feudal strongholds, palaces and towers. When one realizes that almost every ancient monument was used by the nobles as a fortress, the effect on the ruins may be imagined. And almost as much to be regretted was the loss of the superb civil architecture of mediæval Rome. If we can judge by the miserable remnant of the palace which once guarded the approaches to the Ponte Rotto, with its huge tower, by the towers of the Conti and the Milizie, this civil architecture must have been one of the most original and impressive in Italy. This catastrophe of 1308 well-nigh wiped it out. There followed now a period of unrestrained disorder: assassination and robbery were unchecked by any authority. Even the younger clergy gave way to lawlessness.

In limited fashion the Popes, though absent, sought to heal these wounds. A restoration of the basilica of the Lateran was commenced, with the help of contributions from the Romans themselves — only to be partly nullified by a second fire in 1348. Work was carried on at the other great basilicas: at

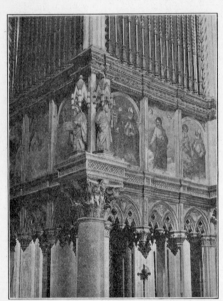

Corner of Tabernacle of Main Altar at Lateran Basilica.
(Middle fourteenth century and later.)

S. Paul the mosaic of the façade was made over by John XXII in 1324, and shortly afterward the roof of S. Peter was repaired. But only driblets from the Papal purse found their way to Rome in the fourteenth century. The bulk of the funds was applied to the erection of that pile of feudal grandeur, the immense fortress-palace at Avignon, which was to be a shield against the raids of freebooting condottieri and symbol of the temporal power. When Italian artists were called to Avignon to decorate the palace and other Papal buildings, it is significant that they did not come from Rome, but from Siena and Umbria.

Tuscans and Umbrians were superseding the native school in Rome itself. It was to the Tuscan painters, Giottino, Giovanni da Milano and the sons of Taddeo Gaddi, that the Pope turned when he ordered an important series of frescos. It was partly of Umbrian artists that the shrine and tabernacle of the restored Lateran were ordered, and later it was to a Sienese architect that Pope Urban V confided the direction of the restoration of the Lateran after the second fire.

Evidently, then, by the middle of the fourteenth century there was no school of Roman artists upon which the Popes could depend. Yet it was some time in dying and in its very dispersal scattered quite broadly the peculiar perfume of a style that was to have no morrow.

A few names of these children of exile have survived. The sculptor, Marcus Romanus, went to Venice, which in 1317 he made a remarkably dignified and impressive reclining statue of the prophet Simeon for the church of S. Simeon Grande. Ruskin was quite right in admiring it. A last scion of the family of Cosmas, the Deodatus who had done so many things for the Lateran basilica, perhaps after the fire of 1308, went in his old age as far as Teramo on the Adriatic, where he made a charming portal for the cathedral in the Roman style in 1332. Stray traces of this Roman decorative work in mosaic are to be found as far as Germany and France, probably by itinerant craftsmen.

A group of Romans appears to have entered the service of the Angevin dynasty in Naples, then one of the principal patrons of art in Italy. Here came together Tuscans and Lombards as well, to direct or coöperate with the provincial school. These Roman decorators appear to have strongly affected the style of sepulchral monuments in the South. For while the figured sculpture of the numerous royal and feudal tombs of the fourteenth century in Neapolitan churches remained largely in the hands of Tuscan artists and their pupils, the decorative scheme included in many cases columns and friezes inlaid with mosaic work evidently according to Roman models, such as we find in the Papal tombs at Viterbo and in those by Giovanni Cosmati and his contemporaries in Rome. But the most important accession was the leader of Italian painting, Pietro Cavallini, who was employed on a yearly salary of thirty gold ounces in 1308 and successive years by the Angevin King Charles II, and left in Naples, among other works, the frescos of S. Maria Donna Regina, executed before 1320.

Next in prominence among Roman painters had been Filippo Rusutti, part author of the mosaic on the façade of S. Maria Maggiore. French documents show that the court painter of Philippe le Bel had been in Rome in 1297 and secured the services of Rusutti, his son Giovanni and his other pupil Nicola di Marzo, who went to France and remained court painters until their deaths many years later, on a regular stipend. It would be interesting to trace their work in France and its effect.[1]

What would the Roman school have accomplished had the Papacy and Rome retained a leading part in Italy's changing life during the curious transitional period of the fourteenth century? What share would she have had in the Renaissance of the fifteenth century? If her artists had held the reins and had thrown off the passing Gothic incubus, it is likely that we should have had from them a more restrained and purer form of Renaissance and that the Barocco would not have afflicted the world with its monstrosities.

But it died not only too early to complete its work, but too early to insure the appreciation by posterity of its glorious accomplishments, because the literary creators of the fame of Italian art, the Vasaris, the Albertis and the Ghibertis, were sons of other centuries and ideals who despised or ignored what they could not understand or in which they had no hereditary pride, and who were also richly endowed with the local fanaticism that could easily dispose of the just claims of other schools than the Tuscan. Only now do we see that the very leaders among these Tuscans, such as Cimabue, Arnolfo and Giotto, were pupils of Rome, that the sculptors and decorators of the Pisan school, beginning with Niccola and Giovanni, were immensely influenced. Rome handed on the torch.

When the Papacy returned to Rome with full purpose of devotion, a process beginning really in the year 1377 and culminating in Pope Martin's entrance in 1420, an overwhelming

[1] The French documents spell the name with a B in place of an R, and I am inclined to accept this spelling, as the artist's signature on the mosaic has been entirely restored: his name would really be, then, Filippo Bisutti.

combination of circumstances conspired to prevent the continuation of Rome's individual monumental career, the recovery of
her grasp on the reins of artistic influence.   For over a century
the mediæval city had been going unchecked to ruin.   In
many cases, as at the Lateran and the SS. Apostoli, the ruin
was so complete as to seem irreparable, and for the inevitably
radical renovation the Papacy had but a shadow of a Roman
school to call to its aid; mostly mere practitioners without a
spark of originality.   The foreigners who were called in despised the mediæval art of the city and felt that they were
doing missionary work in helping to obliterate rather than perpetuate it.   On these Renaissance artists of Tuscany and Lombardy, and on Italy as a whole, through the Barocco age, the
influence of Rome was henceforth to be that of the antique
city alone, whom these men helped both to perpetuate and
destroy; for while theoretically idolizing it and codifying its
models, they fashioned out of its ruins their new palaces and
churches, the gigantic bronze columns and canopies of their
high altars, and even the lime of their kilns, from the fine
marble of antique statues.   The churches of Christian Rome
did not go down alone to their dissolution.

PART II

CLASSIFICATION OF THE MONUMENTS

ARCHITECTURE

PART II

CLASSIFICATION OF THE MONUMENTS

ARCHITECTURE

BASILICAS

THE vicissitudes of Christian architecture in Rome are more determined by relative amounts of artistic skill than by changes in style. We assign a building to a certain time according to the good or poor workmanship in the making and laying of the bricks, in the carving of the capitals or cornices, in the handling of the decorative details. This is because the same materials, the same architectural forms, the same constructive system were substantially in continuous use from beginning to end, and the variations were primarily in the amount of skill shown in their use and only secondarily in the variations of the decorative themes and manner. Consequently the historic divisions hold good for architecture. The first period is from Constantine to the Gothic wars ; the second lasts until the close of the eleventh century ; the third ends with the fourteenth.

I have enumerated the principal buildings in Rome in their chronological order in the course of my historic narrative and will give here a brief systematic classification. I do not treat of that superb latter-day effulgence of vaulted architecture that closed in the early years of Constantine's reign, after producing the Baths of Diocletian and Constantine and the Basilica Nova. Though it was echoed in a few structures that are counted as Christian, such as the Mausoleums of Helena and Constantia, it had no further effect upon the fortunes of Christian Rome. The few other circular or polygonal buildings, such as the Lateran Baptistery, S. Stefano Rotondo and S. Petronilla, have been already sufficiently referred to, so that nothing need here concern us but basilical architecture, which has no connection with the static or constructive forms that were the main theme of builders in the East and North.

An index-list of Roman churches will be found at the end of this volume.

Materials. — Christian architecture in Rome not being called upon to attempt any such heavy constructions as were required by the use of vaulting on a large scale, and not needing heavy walls for its wooden-roofed churches, did not patronize concrete construction. Stone was used but seldom, in the regular courses of the *opus quadratum,* in such works of engineering as the bridges of Gratian and Valentinian and in the restoration of such monuments as the Coliseum and the theatres. But even this was abandoned after the Gothic wars: its latest use being possibly in the bridge by Narses over the Anio.

In religious architecture brickwork was the rule in the body of the structure, for the walls were not heavy enough to allow of a brick facing and a concrete core. The quality of the brickwork varied at different periods. As long as the government factories continued the manufacture of bricks, up to the time of the Gothic wars, they were of excellent quality, the main change between the brick of the Antonines (second century) and those of the fifth century being a diminution in size, a change which is found early in the fourth century, though there were also variations in color and texture.

Mediæval brickwork was less perfect during the middle period. Heavy beds of mortar and careless laying, which we find as early as the fifth century, with an interlude of excellent work under Theodoric, became the rule between the seventh and eleventh centuries. But in the course of the twelfth century there was a return to better brick-making, more careful laying and thinner bedding, which helped to give a similar effect to that of the age of Constantine.

In classic architecture it had not usually been permissible to let the brickwork be seen except in works of pure utility; with Christian architecture the treatment was different. The exteriors were carelessly treated, for they were spiritually of no interest; and their brickwork was covered only sporadically, as by a mosaic on the façade. The trimmings of doorways and porches were also of stonework. It was only in the interiors that the brickwork was as absolutely concealed as in classic buildings either by facings of thin marble veneering slabs or by mosaic work.

Two other methods were occasionally used: the *opus mixtum* and the *opus saracinescum* or *a tufelli*. The former consisted of alternate layers of small stone blocks, usually tufa, and brickwork, there being at times two rows of the bricks to one course of stone. This method became popular in the time of Constantine and during the rest of the period before the Gothic war, and again came into vogue during the tenth century. The *opus saracinescum* was a "petit appareil" of small tufa blocks which is found as early as the seventh and remained popular until the eleventh century.

It was only outside of the city that local stone was substituted for brick, and here the stone was often used in so plain a fashion as to lose its natural advantages over brick, as in the basilica of S. Eli at Nepi, or the tower of S. Scholastica at Subiaco.

The Basilica. — The plan of the basilica and its annexes is too well known to require much analysis, and an important concrete example — S. Peter — has already been described under Constantine's works.

An ante-porch usually opened on the street in a long stretch of otherwise solid wall. Passing through it, one stood in one long arcade or colonnade out of four which formed a cloistered court or atrium in front of the church itself, partly screening its façade. I shall describe each part in turn.

Atrium, Porch and Portico. — These three forms of approach to the basilical churches were in use throughout the history of the Roman school and are inseparable. No other Italian school made such use of them, as this early Christian form did not appeal to the Lombard architects except occasionally.

Ante-porch. — The atrium itself was entered through a doorway that was often overhung by a *propylon*, or ante-porch, a narrow porch which had normally the form of a single projecting arch supported on a pair of columns standing free from the wall and supporting a pair of architraves which rested at their wall end on pilasters or wall-columns. The face was in the form of an arch surmounted by a gable. The small vault was either groined or a short barrel-vault. The existing examples date between the eighth and the twelfth centuries.

Propylon of S. Prassede.
(Ninth century.)

Propylon of S. Clemente.
(c. 1100.)

The finest are at S. Prassede (ninth), S. Clemente (c. 1120) and S. Cosimato (c. 1200). In the latter case the propylon was double, projecting as far within from the enclosure as without, because the court at that time had no encircling porticos: just a plain wall. At S. Prassede it ushers into a long vaulted passage through the monastic buildings. It had even, as at S. Peter, been sometimes attached to the atrium portico.

When for the early atrium a simple portico on the street was substituted, as was especially the case in some of the diaconal churches set on the busy streets, the propylon was attached directly in front of the centre of the portico, as at S. Maria in Cosmedin. It was the prototype of that finest of all porticos

Atrium and Façade of S. Clemente (c. 1100).

— that of the cathedral of Civita Castellana, where a large central arch breaks the line of the architrave.

Atrium. — The use of the quadrangular atrium intervening between the church and the street, surrounded by a high wall and insuring quiet, was quite general before the eleventh century, not only in the suburban but in the city churches, except where pressure of space forbade it. Though not required for liturgical purposes after the seventh century, when

Porch and Façade of S. Lorenzo (Thirteenth Century).

the old divisions of catechumens and penitents had fallen into disuse, tradition maintained them in most cases.

We even see in S. Clemente a case of the reconstruction of the atrium on a higher level as late as the beginning of the twelfth century. Many old atria vanished in the Guiscard fire, and in the reconstruction that followed only the façade porticos were rebuilt, as at S. Lorenzo in Lucina and S. Giorgio in Velabro. In fact S. Clemente has the only atrium that remains. In several other cases, it is true, the quadrangular area or court surrounded by walls remains, but the porticos have vanished; this has happened at S. Quattro Coronati, S. Cosimato, S. Saba, S. Cecilia, S. Prassede, S. Martino ai Monti, S. Silvestro and others. Still there are old prints and drawings to show us the appearance of such immense arcaded or colonnaded atria as those of S. Peter, S. Paul, the Lateran (p. 47).

These atria were used for meetings, recreation, fairs, feasts, ablutions and were decorated with sepulchral monuments, fountains, frescos and inscriptions. Spaces in them were hired out to venders of sacred images, relics and other religious emblems, and their walls often supplemented the contents of the interiors.

Portico. — There were two types of both atria and façade porticos, the arcaded and the architraved; the former prevailed in the earlier period, the latter after the eleventh century. S. Clemente at present has architraves on three sides and arches against the façade. Except for the short side porch at S. Sabina, the restored closed porch at S. Maria in Cosmedin and the crude ruinous porch at S. Giovanni a Porta Latina all arched examples have disappeared, but the cuts of 1588 show that even then such porches had survived at S. Balbina, S. Eusebio and S. Vitale, which may all be dated tentatively, on historic grounds, before the ninth century. That of the Vatican basilica was also arcaded.

The type of architraved portico seems to have been established at the very outset of the revival, for it appears in the time of Paschal II (c. 1100) at S. Lorenzo in Lucina, where the crude form of the Ionic capitals with volutes cut into the surface instead of projecting from it betray the infantile stage of the school of stone-cutters and designers who were to produce, later in the century, the classic porches of S. Giorgio in Velabro, S. Crisogono, S. Maria in Trastevere, S. Cecilia, † S. John Lateran, † S. Croce, † S. Maria Maggiore, † S. Maria Nuova,

M

† S. Sebastiano, SS. Giovanni e Paolo, etc. The series closes in Rome with the finest remaining example, that of Honorius III at S. Lorenzo by Vassallettus.[1]

The same artists built similar porches in some of the cities of the province; in fact those of the cathedrals of Civita Castellana and Terracina — the latter sadly mutilated — surpassed in rich beauty the existing examples in Rome itself. That of Civita Castellana is signed with the date 1210 by two Roman artists, father and son, the famous members of the "Cosmati" family, in the following mosaic inscription on the central arch:

† MAGISTER · IACOBUS · CIVIS · ROMANUS · CUM · COSMA · FILIO ·
SUO · CARISSIMO · FECIT · HOC · OPUS ANNO DNI · M · CCX.

Giacomo and his son Cosma were son and grandson of Lorenzo who had designed and built the body of the church and its façade. In default of the Lateran porch, now destroyed, where its designer Niccola d' Angelo had introduced an elaborate mosaic frieze, the Civita Castellana porch and the façade portals show the marks of the best workmanship of the Roman school, both in design and in details. The reproduction of the antique in capitals, bases and mouldings is so perfect as to produce the illusion of the originals; and yet the elements that are entirely mediæval, such as the mosaic ornamentation, are combined with the antique in charming harmony (see pp. 134, 166).

Façade. — The façades were exceedingly simple in their upper surface. There were but two types: the central gable, following usually the outline of the structure behind it, and the screen façade, with square top, usually made to overhang, for purposes of protection, by a gradual projection of the courses of brick both forward and sideways.

The surface was decorated with none of the architectural memberment so common in most other Italian schools; none of the false or real galleries of arcades, none of the vari-colored marble facings. Architecturally speaking, the plain brickwork which was invariably used was sometimes varied by the addition,

---

[1] The porches here marked † have been destroyed and are known only from drawings and cuts.

along the edge and across the base of the gable, of the usual
line of cuneiform bricks placed diagonally and by a slight
stone cornice. But in the more important churches the entire
surface was concealed by a mosaic composition extending from
summit to portico, several of which are described elsewhere.
They were found at S. John Lateran, S. Peter, S. Paul, S. Maria
Maggiore, S. Maria in Trastevere, S. Maria Nuova, S. Celso,
etc. This converted the façade above the porch into one blaze

Portico of S. Saba, by Jacobo di Lorenzo.
(c. 1200.)

of color. Still, toward the close of the Middle Ages more windows were sometimes opened in the façade. At S. Peter in
the thirteenth century, beside the wheel-window in the gable,
there were two rows of three tall mullioned windows, the lower
row being flanked by two more. Only in such an exceptional
case as S. Saba was a second story, concealing the façade,
added to the porch, and this was due to monastic influence.

The lower part of the façade was always covered by a projecting portico, which is elsewhere described, consisting either

of one side of the quadrangular atrium or of an independent arcade or colonnade. The wall space underneath was usually broken by as many doors as there were aisles to the church, normally three, sometimes five. In the minor basilicas there was but a single door, and in exceptional cases, as at S. Peter's, there was a supplementary door for special occasions.

These doors were flat-topped, their architraves and jambs

Monastic Church of SS. Vincenzo ed Anastasio.
(c. 1140 and seventh century.)

being carved in the early Middle Ages, and decorated with mosaics after the twelfth century, though the richest doors are those made up of antique carved fragments. Among remaining doors the earliest examples are those of the tenth century at S. Elia (Nepi) and S. Stefano, near the apse of S. Peter. Quite monumental is that of S. Silvestro in Capite; and the early use of mosaic decoration appears during the twelfth century at S. Giovanni a Porta Latina and SS. Giovanni e Paolo. Compared

with the Romanesque and Gothic doorways of other schools
these Roman doors seem extremely simple and classic, except
where there is quite an exceptionally rich combination of
mosaics and classic decoration, as in the main portal of Civita
Castellana cathedral. Only in a few cases in Rome itself, at S.
Pudentiana and S. Marta, was the scheme of northern decorative sculpture adopted, between the eleventh and thirteenth

Doorway at Church of S. Elia,
near Nepi.
(Ninth and tenth centuries.)

Doorway at S. Marta.
(Twelfth century.)

centuries. Sometimes, as at S. Elia for the early mediæval
period and Civita Castellana for the middle period, the
architrave was surmounted by an arch.

Interior. — The interior of a typical basilica consisted of a
very wide central nave flanked usually by one aisle on each
side and terminating in a semicircular apse. There were
three ways in which this plan was varied. In the larger
basilicas there were sometimes two aisles on each side instead
of one, and there was interposed sometimes also a cross-nave

between nave and apse, called transept. This was entered from the nave under a great spanning arch called the triumphal arch. The third variation did not occur until late, when, in the eighth century, the apse was flanked by two apses opposite the aisles (S. Maria in Cosmedin). They seem to have

been a development out of the sacristies that often stood here, but it never became as popular in Rome as elsewhere.

So much for the plan. The elevation was quite as simple. The wall separating nave from aisles was upheld by a row of monolithic columns connected either by an arcade or a colonnade. This wall was absolutely flat and merely pierced by a single line of round-

Main Doorway of Cathedral, Civita Castellana.

headed windows forming a plain clerestory. No heavy cornices gave any horizontal play of light and shade.

It was only very exceptionally, as at S. Marco and S. Lorenzo, that the high choir, which became so common in the north during the Carlovingian era, was adopted in Roman churches. Even when confessions and crypts of some size were built under transept and apse, the rise at the apse was only of a few steps above the level of the nave, so that the sweep of the entire pavement was hardly interrupted. Neither

were there in the nave any vertical interruptions in the form
of piers or engaged shafts or pilasters, such as would have
occurred had the school adopted vaulting, which it only
occasionally used in the side-aisles. The most interesting
crypt in Rome is the post-Carlovingian one at S. Alessio.

Neither was there any relief to the flatness of effect above
the main arcades or colonnades through the use of galleries, so
common in nearly all other Italian Schools. The exceptional
galleries of the sixth and seventh centuries at S. Lorenzo and
S. Agnese were due, we found, to the low level to which it
was necessary in these cases to sink the church in order to
place it in the right relation to the cemeterial tomb of the
titular martyr. In the later (c. 1100) gallery at the SS. Quattro
Coronati there was an equally special reason, for the three
aisles of the new church, being crowded into the central nave
of the older structure, the galleries were required so that the
old outer walls could be used, with their windows.

In view, then, of this plain flatness of the Roman interior, a
pictorial decoration was absolutely necessary. Under *Frescos*
and *Mosaics* this is described. It was arranged so as to cover
the entire surface. Immediately under the roof, and between
the windows, were single figures of angels, prophets or saints.
Then below was usually a double line of oblong scenes, like
those still remaining in mosaic at S. Maria Maggiore, forming
an uninterrupted series from façade to transept and apse. In
the larger basilicas there was sometimes added, beneath them
and immediately over the columns, a series of medallion portraits. This was the case at S. Peter, S. Paul and S. John
Lateran.

The richness of the color scheme was increased by the lavish
use of large hangings woven with religious scenes or heraldic
animals, emblems and ornaments. They were hung between
the columns on rods and were among the most sumptuous
Papal gifts to the churches, supplemented by numerous lamps.

This decoration in color was supplemented by a rich cycle
of church furniture and accessories. Sometimes a line of
superb columns marked the transept or confession. Always
the upper part of the interior was partly filled by an elaborate

group of structural furniture: an enclosing rail, about the width of the central nave and of considerably greater length; within it the choir-seats, the ambones or pulpits and the paschal candlestick; at its further end the altar, often at the top of a low line of steps, with its confession, its canopy or ciborium and its decorative accessories; beyond, in the apse, the seats for the higher clergy.

The columns were, as a rule, placed very close, — far closer than was the case in other mediæval schools that used the

Interior of S. Maria Maggiore.
(Fourth and fifth centuries, with Renaissance ceiling.)

column. The shafts were monoliths, of course; not constructed in courses, as had been the Greek custom and as was to be the mediæval custom in other schools. The aisles were so much lower and narrower than the nave and so much less brilliantly lighted as to concentrate all the effects in the central section which was alone richly decorated.

In the use of the orders we notice certain peculiarities. The Tuscan-Doric is found but once, in S. Pietro in Vincoli. The rich Corinthian and Composite ruled almost exclusively, with occasional use of the Ionic (*e.g.* S. Maria Maggiore), from the time of Constantine to the eleventh century; but with the neo-antique revival of the twelfth century the palm went to the Ionic order. There are a number of forms that cannot

Rear Basilica of S. Lorenzo.
(Sixth century with Ciborium of c. 1150.)

be strictly reckoned into these orders, such as the Egyptianizing capitals at S. Pudentiana and the pseudo-Ionic cubes at S. Stefano.

This is hardly the place to discuss the question of how far at different times the ancient capitals and bases were used, how far they were imitated. In a majority of cases there is a mixture of antique and contemporary work, and the imitations vary from the crude work in the porches of S. Maria in

Cosmedin and S. Lorenzo in Lucina, to the superb work at Civita Castellana and S. Lorenzo fuori le Mura. There was no period, from the fourth to the fourteenth centuries, when antique material ceased to be used, but it was done with greater or less artistic skill, in the same way as the imitations themselves varied. At S. Sabina, for example, the entire series seems taken from a single monument, giving unity to the effect; but

Interior of S. Clemente.

(Showing choir-precinct, ambones and ciborium of twelfth century, incorporating sixth-century fragments.)

what was possible then, at the beginning of the spoliation of antique buildings, was later impossible, and capitals of all sizes, styles and workmanship were combined and eked out by contemporary works.

The columns were surmounted more frequently by arcades than by a continuous architrave. Where the architrave appears, it is sometimes, as at S. Lorenzo (rear basilica) and S. Prassede, antique material used without much change. But the influence of the large architraved interior of S. Maria Maggiore (fourth century) seems to have been very strong with the artists of the revival and to have inspired such interiors as S. Maria in Trastevere (twelfth century) and the even earlier charming, though small, S. Maria ad Pineam (1090). The ceilings were flat and coffered, hiding the beams.

Pavements. — In no school of Christian art are the pavements of such importance as in the Roman. Nowhere else in an

From Architrave of S. Maria in Trastevere.
(Showing use in twelfth century of antique fragments for corbels.)

early Christian or mediæval church does the eye instinctively seek the ground for a design and material that shall harmonize with and enrich the effect of the interior. The exceptions that come to mind instinctively at Venice (San Marco, Murano, Torcello), Florence (Baptistery), Siena (Cathedral), and in Southern Italy and Sicily (Salerno, Palermo, etc.), only serve to accentuate the richness of the Roman school, which can furnish a list of over a hundred churches with characteristic mosaic pavements in geometric patterns.

The type with which we are familiar appears fully formed

as early as the eleventh century and was used henceforth
without radical change until the sixteenth century. But how
was the type created? Some years ago I expressed the
opinion that it was adopted bodily by the Roman school from
Byzantine art. Recent discoveries and studies have led me
to modify this view and to see in the Byzantine influence a
less radical element acting upon a native substratum that was
by no means obliterated. In fact there is in Roman designs
room for a common origin, and pavements of the age of Con-

Mosaic Pavement of Nave, S. Clemente.

stantine probably served as a point of departure for both the
eastern and western schools. Among the more gifted artists
of Byzantium progress was made in two directions: in the man-
agement of colors; and in the adjustment and harmony of the
design. The descriptions of the pavements in the imperial
palaces and in S. Sophia, at Constantinople, make it quite clear
that the exquisitely fine gradations of color and symmetry of
composition in the Venetian pavements are qualities derived
from the Byzantine school, even if not due to the direct work
of Byzantine hands. If in these works we can trace the influence of the Oriental color sense in the central school at Con-

stantinople, we can see that not all Byzantine work was so rich in color, but that the more western branches (such as the school of Mt. Athos), which were the principal source of the Byzantine element in Sicilian art, used less color and more line, very much after the fashion of the Roman school. There is far greater similarity between the Roman pavements and those of Sicily and Mt. Athos, than between those of Rome and Venice.

If, then, Byzantine artists were called to the Roman province in the eleventh century to make such pavements as those of Monte Cassino and Grottaferrata, and if the earliest pavements of Roman churches in this style cannot be dated before the close of this century, it would seem natural to conclude that in their final form the Roman pavements were a Byzantine derivative.

Still, the difference is not fundamental between this type and that of the chapel of San Zeno at Santa Prassede, which appears to be of the late Carlovingian age (Paschal I). Even earlier work in the choirs of S. Giorgio in Velabro and S. Maria Antiqua appears to be a connecting link, with patterns more broken up and less elaborate, materials less carefully prepared and less varied.

In their final form the pavements consist of a succession of large porphyry or serpentine slabs, either circular or quadrangular, framed by small marble cubes of various colors set in a white marble ground and arranged in geometrical patterns. These big central disks had a symbolic meaning and were named in some of the Papal ceremonial documents describing such great affairs as the imperial coronations at S. Peter.

These pavements appear to have been the source for the later development of similar geometric ornamentation in church furniture and on vertical surfaces, where it was possible to use frailer materials than solid marble and so produce more delicate and varied effects.

The most exquisite of all is that of the Papal chapel of the Lateran, the *Sancta Sanctorum*, which is as delicate as the best vertical ornamentation.

The Renaissance period saw at first no change in this method of paving churches, as is proved by the work at S. John Lateran and the Sistine chapel in the Vatican. It was the last branch of art belonging to the mediæval Roman school to be discarded.

No description of a Roman basilica would be complete without that of its stable furniture or furnishings. Of the sepulchral monuments I shall speak under Sculpture; the rest are more completely a part of architectural decoration.

Pulpit or Ambone and Choir-screen. — Rome has preserved no examples of the ambones or pulpits of the early Christian

Carved Pulpit of Cathedral of Ferentino (reconstruction).
(c. 1110.)

or early mediæval periods, though a few fragments remain, such as that at S. Maria Antiqua (John VII). Only in Ravenna and Thessalonica can this early type be studied. In Rome and its neighborhood there is nothing intact earlier than the eleventh century.

After the time of Paschal II they are numerous and increasingly decorative. Liturgy seems to have required two in every church, placed in the upper part of the main nave on opposite sides, and in connection with the choir-screen. Often the seats for the choir-singers were run along at the foot of the ambones, forming their basement and bringing them into the general design. The Popes and prelates of the Renaissance bore a particular grudge against this part of the mediæval liturgical scheme and ruthlessly destroyed the entire choral structure including the ambones, so that it can now be seen only in S. Clemente in its original state and in a modern restoration from the old material at S. Maria in Cosmedin, both of the twelfth century, with earlier fragments.

The front of the choir-screen often had a second story or

Ambone at S. Maria in Cosmedin.
(c. 1120.)

iconostasic screen, like the English wood screens, formed of colonnettes supporting an architrave which extended across the entire nave. It served to support the hangings that screened the altar during part of the service. It has been charmingly reconstructed at S. Maria in Cosmedin. An earlier example, in the style not of mosaic inlay but of Byzantine relief work, can still be seen at Leprignano (tenth century) near Rome, but none so early exist in the city itself.

The main type of ambone or pulpit consisted of two stair-cases leading to a central raised platform. Where a different, boxlike, form appears, as at S. Maria in Aracœli and S. Cesareo, the old pulpits have been reconstructed in the Renaissance. Those of S. Clemente, S. Lorenzo and Alba Fucense represent three successive stages of increasing richness from c. 1120 to c. 1225. The second pulpit, standing directly op-

Ambone in S. Pietro at Alba Fucense, by two Roman Artists
(Pietro and Andrica.)

posite the first, was often of the simpler type with a single staircase, of which an early form appears in the restored ambone of Ferentino. At S. Lorenzo they are transposed.

Paschal Candlestick. — The earlier paschal candlesticks which stood beside an ambone were probably of metal, and shared the fate of the rest of this class of church furniture. Of existing examples none antedate the *marmorarii* of the twelfth century.

They were placed near the right-hand ambone in the *schola*

cantorum or choir, and there was only one in each church, used mainly for the Easter ceremonies; hence its name.

The normal type was a large twisted column, its spirals filled with mosaic patterns. Sole remnant of a foreign influence on the school is the candlestick at S. Paolo, which two Roman sculptors, Nicolo di Angelo and Pietro Vassaletto, carved in marble in the second half of the twelfth century, and which may be compared to some of those by the south Italian schools, at Gaeta, Palermo, Capua, etc.

None of those remaining in Roman churches are among the most conspicuous of their class, probably because those of the larger basilicas have all perished. It is to the cities of the province that we must turn for the largest examples, standing from fifteen to twenty-five feet high. Such are those of the cathedrals of Ferentino, Terracina and Anagni. The earliest of all seems also to be in the province, at Cori.

The Anagni candelabrum is crowned by a fascinating boy caryatid and is signed by one of the Vassaletti. That of Ferentino, most colossal of all, has a bewildering variety of mosaic patterns; its twelve ascending spirals, each of different design, all change their patterns at short intervals as they ascend.

Several of those in the churches of Rome itself are remarkable for beauty if not for size. Such are those at S. Cecilia, probably by Arnolfo, at S. Lorenzo and S. Clemente,— all of the thirteenth century.

Mosaic Paschal Candlestick of Cathedral, Terracina.
(Twelfth century.)

The base is often formed of a plinth resting on a couple of sphinxes, crouching side by side, or of a similar couple of lions; at other times the base is simply architectural.

The Southern school, especially in Campania, produced candlesticks of very similar type, except that they used the straight more frequently than the spiral shaft, and married the mosaic work usually to a certain amount of carving.

N

There are superb examples in the cathedrals of Salerno, Sessa and Palermo.

Altar Canopies or Ciboria. — The *Liber Pontificalis* describes some of the early ciboria of gold or silver so specifically that it is possible to reproduce them, even though none survive. Those given by the Emperors from Constantine to Honorius to the great basilicas were par-

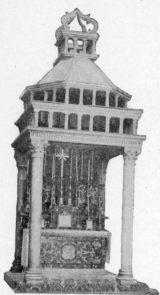

Ciborium of High Altar, Cathedral Ferentino, by Drudo.

ticularly superb, and were referred to in the historical survey.

When metal work was abandoned for marble in the seventh century, the more modest works of this age of poor art followed the style of surface geometrical decoration in low relief, and the ciborium was usually a low pyramid with four arcades supported on as many colonnettes. Early Roman examples can be reconstructed from such fragments as those of S. Alessio and the Lateran Museum; a late one, that of S. Giovanni in Argentella (eleventh century) is by some Roman artist.

Then, in the eleventh century, with the adoption of the more classic architrave in place of the arch, there came a change in the design of the ciborium, whose corner columns upheld four architraves. The simplest form appears at S. Gregorio in Rome; the next stage at the Benedictine church of Nepi, both earlier than 1100 and with a gable roof. The type of the early twelfth century, with retreating stories and pyramid above the lower architrave, was crystallized in the ciboria made by the family school of Paulus and his sons, of which that in S. Lorenzo in Rome survives, and the later one of Ponzano. In these there was at first no decorative work on the surface of the white marble except an occasional cross or simple band; but the ornamentation was constantly on the increase, until in the thirteenth century it blossomed into such superb works as the ciboria at Anagni by the Cosmati and that of Ferentino by Drudo, their associate.

The designers of the early thirteenth century also planned for the larger churches an altar canopy of heavier design, which

Angle of Ciborium at Cathedral, Ferentino, by Drudo.

served as a transition to the still more elaborate Gothic tabernacles. The architrave is made far wider and more elaborate, including a central frieze, and it supports, not a row of slender shafts on which rests another architrave, but a series of round-headed arcades from which rise an octagonal roof and lantern similar to the earlier pattern.

The final type was evolved by Arnolfo and continued by

his pupil Adeodato, and in its substitution of the pointed trefoil arch strikes a note foreign to the genuine character of the Roman school, although it is of exquisite beauty. Its best remaining examples are described elsewhere ("Sculpture").

Altar. — The form, accessories and material of the altar in the church were fundamentally modified by the cult of saints' relics, by the theory that no church could be duly consecrated

Inside of Choir Precinct of S. Maria in Cosmedin, reconstructed, with Ambones and Inconostasis and the Ciborium of Adeodato.
(Twelfth to thirteenth centuries.)

unless it was provided with such relics. They were always connected with the altar and were placed either inside or immediately beneath it. This led to the change from an open to a solid altar, from a table to a box-like structure. It was necessary to have access to the relics by means of an opening in the side of the altar facing the church; this was called the *fenestrella confessionis*, and became the decorative centre of this face which often extended downward toward the confession or merely broke the line of steps leading to the apse. In the later Roman school the altar, which had earlier been a plain structure hung with woven frontals or ante-pendia of gold or silver gilt, became decorated structurally with the mosaic patterns that were lavished everywhere.

Apse. — The apse remained extremely simple, both within and without, more consistently so than in any other school.

Ciborium of High Altar at S. Elia, near Nepi.
(Tenth or eleventh century.)

The single termination was the rule until the eighth century, when the sacristies on either side were first changed into side apses. The earliest triple apse recorded is that of S. Maria in Cosmedin, probably due to Hadrian I (c. 790). But the innovation never became popular. At Ravenna, the outside wall of the apse had become polygonal; in Rome it never varied from the simple curved outline. Neither was there any invasion from Lombardy or Tuscany of the use of real or false galleries and arcades. The one exception is SS. Giovanni e Paolo, where the twelfth-century apse has a Lombard gallery to which there originally corresponded one on the inside wall.

The only variation from this type was an early one, and all traces of it have now disappeared. This was the open apse: a form in which the lower part was opened up by a line of

Altar and Confessio of Relics at S. Alessandro.
(Fourth century.)

arcades into a surrounding portico or adjoining structure, in which it was often the custom to place the matrons of the congregation, who thus were at the opposite end of the church from the rest of the congregation, beyond the clergy in the apse and transept This arrangement existed at S. John Lateran, S. Maria Maggiore, SS. Cosma e Damiano, S. Sebastiano and perhaps at S. Lorenzo to connect with the second basilica.

There were never any radiating chapels from the apse; nor

was there ever any prolongation of the apsidal wall beyond the semicircle.

The only relief to the plain, unadorned brick surface was the frieze of bricks in the form of pointed ovoids and the row of consols or brackets of stone often carved, as at S. Martino (sixth century) and S. Bartolommeo (eleventh century).

One sporadic attempt at least was made to relieve this monotony. It was at S. Maria Maggiore, where a series of mosaic pictures were placed on the outside of the apse when the mosaics of façade and inner apse were executed, c. 1300. They were destroyed during the Renaissance.

Altar and Confessio of S. Giorgio in Velabro.
(Seventh to twelfth centuries.)

Principal Existing Basilicas. — The churches have been in nearly every case mentioned in their chronological order in Part I. The finest early group is that of S. Maria Maggiore (fourth century), S. Sabina (fifth century), S. Pietro in Vincoli and S. Martino (V–VI centuries). The lesser counterpart to this for the twelfth and thirteenth centuries is S. Clemente, S. Lorenzo, S. Maria in Trastevere and S. Crisogono. Nearly all those which preserve mediæval features are enumerated at the end of this volume.

Their interiors must not be judged by their modern condition, even where they have been least changed, because the destruction of their rich furniture has afflicted them with unnatural nudity.

At the same time it may be as well frankly to acknowledge what may be considered the shortcomings of the building as a work of art, especially as regards the exterior, which lacks

SS. Giovanni e Paolo (apse) with Roman House and Street on Cælian.

picturesqueness and impressive height. The use of brick without even the help of moulded terra-cotta bars out the rich effects of heavy mouldings in windows and doors. The church is low and plain in outline, without those central and grouped towers, without the lofty vaulting, that make such churches as the Rhenish cathedrals and those of Central and Northern France so striking.

Architectural Puzzles. — An interesting and intricate architectural puzzle is S. Maria in Cosmedin. Originally a hall church in the ancient *Statio Annonæ*, or grain market, transformed for that purpose, with many columns and considerable late Roman decoration untouched ; it was changed by Hadrian I (771–795) into a three-aisled church with three apses. As a concession to its Greek congregation a *matroneum* or women's gallery was built over the side-aisles, for with the Greeks it was not the custom to place the women below with the men. The columns then supported architraves. But when Calixtus II (1119–1124) remodelled the church, the Greek congregation with its special needs had vanished, so the gallery was closed up and the mechanical feat was performed of substituting arcades for the architraves of the nave. The irregularities of the arcade spacings and the piers are part of the penalty for the use of an old building. The choir precinct has recently been reconstructed as it was in the twelfth century, and is extremely rich and charming, as our illustration shows (p. 180).

An even more interesting puzzle is the double basilica of S. Lorenzo. It is too intricate to unravel here. I shall merely mention the great probability that the supposedly early architraves of the nave are not of the *fifth* century, nor yet of the *thirteenth* century, but were substituted for mediæval arcades, by a Barocco prelate. Its capitals are *not* antique, but are works of the thirteenth century, as is the cornice with its corbels, — all by Vassallettus, who built the porch. The subject of the mosaic on the triumphal arch, reproduced on p. 280, is one that is invariably confined to the apse, and its unique presence here proves that the two basilicas were thrown together, not as has been universally believed, in the thirteenth century by Honorius III, but 650 years before under Pelagius II.

At S. Prassede the great arcades spanning the nave and their piers, instead of being, as generally supposed, a part of the ninth-century church, were not added until the seventeenth or eighteenth century.

Another class of peculiarities is that relating to irregulari-

ties of plan and structure. Quite often the two side-aisles
vary very considerably in width and the lines of columns are
not parallel, giving a greater width at one end than the other.
It is difficult to say whether this is ever done by design or
always through carelessness.

Architectural Anomalies. — There are also in Rome a few
architectural anomalies. Some of these are due, quite natu-

Interior of SS. Vincenzo ed Anastasio.
(Seventh to twelfth centuries.)

rally, to the use of ancient buildings. At S. Croce in Gerusalemme the very wide apse is due to the fact that it was originally a hall, and that the two rows of columns were late additions.
S. Balbina has always remained quite unique as a hall church.

More interesting, because free and intentional, are the few

cases of the use of square piers instead of columns as internal supports. They appear in three very early buildings, the basilicas of Pammachius at Porto (c. 398 A.D.), of S. Petronilla and of S. Sinforosa on the Via Tiburtina, of about the same period. But the only important use of the pier is at SS. Vincenzo ed Anastasio. It was built by Honorius I, c. 625; restored or rebuilt by Hadrian I and Leo III in 782–796; again

Interior of S. Maria sopra Minerva.

rebuilt by Innocent II in 1128 for S. Bernard and decorated and consecrated by Honorius III in 1221. I should attribute the use of the piers and the severe simplicity of the interior to the influence of S. Bernard's Burgundian Cistercian monks, who were placed in charge of the monastery. This would account for its un-Roman character.

A final anomaly appears at the very close of the Middle Ages, when Gothic design was breaking into Rome. The charming chapel at the Lateran, the Sancta Sanctorum, I have

Campanile of S. Maria in Cosmedin.
(Beginning of twelfth century.)

already referred to, but the only church which shows a perfectly consistent interior of pointed architecture, is S. Maria sopra Minerva. Here are the high pointed arches, the grouped piers, the ribbed pointed vaults, such as we see at this time throughout Italy. So we are not surprised to find that it was not built by Roman artists, but by two Tuscan Dominican monks who came down from Florence to supervise its construction for their monastic order, beginning it in 1280. The way in which it was built is a striking instance of the generosity of the great Roman families to whom I have alluded as patrons of art. The Savelli built the choir; the Gaetani, the great arch; Cardinal Torrecremata, the nave; the Orsini, the façade; and others divided up the transept and aisles.

The rival order of St. Francis introduced quite timidly some Gothic features in their main sanctuary of S. Maria in Aracoeli and other minor structures, but they were not fundamental.

Until the close of the Middle Ages, Rome retained, therefore, her basilical style for church architecture, almost totally unaffected by the changes that were being introduced everywhere else, even in her own province.

CAMPANILI OR BELL-TOWERS

EACH Italian school of art affixed its particular seal to its church towers, and Rome stands in the front rank, by the side of the Lombard and the Tuscan schools, for the number and beauty of its towers. It is not derived from either.

Roman towers have the usual Italian peculiarity of position. They are independent structures, not woven into the general design of the church, as in the architecture of Central and Northern Europe, but standing aloof or resting against the outer wall of the church. They follow no rule. Sometimes they are planted squarely in front of the façade, as at the cathedral of Anagni and SS. Giovanni e Paolo in Rome. They more ordinarily stand against the wall of the nave, flush with the façade; either on the left, as at S. Giorgio in Vela-bro, or on the right, as at S. Cecilia, S. Maria in Cosmedin and S. Alessio. In one case, at the SS. Quattro Coronati, the tower even surmounted the centre of the portal leading into the atrium in front of the church, while in S. Maria ad Pineam it forms part of the right side of the façade.

There was never more than a single tower. Such exceptions as the two towers flanking the transept of S. John Lateran seem the work of foreign architects and mere accidents.

This Roman single tower has something compelling and attractive in its symmetry and simplicity. It has not the rugged heaviness of Lombard campanili. As a rule it is of brick and only occasionally and outside of Rome itself is stone substituted. It is not surmounted by battlements as in Tuscany, nor by spires as in some parts of Lombardy, but by a low peaked roof hardly apparent from below. When an occasional spire appears, as at S. Maria Maggiore and S. John Lateran, it is late and due to foreign influence. Slenderer in its proportions than those of these two schools, it has neither the sombre and heavy impressiveness of Lombardy nor the brilliant coloring of Tuscany.

There are critics who date some of the existing campanili to a period before the revival of the eleventh century. There were certainly towers during the Carlovingian era and even earlier; witness that built by Pope Stephen in the eighth century in the atrium of S. Peter's. But, in my opinion, no campanile is earlier than the middle of the eleventh century.

One of the earliest of which there is an authentic record is not in Rome itself, but at the monastery of Subiaco, where all the art was that of the Roman school. Here both a contemporary inscription and an early chronicle attribute to Abbot Humbert (1052) the building of the campanile at S. Scolastica, which while in stone is of the orthodox Roman type, and was doubtless by no means the earliest example of it. A number of the Roman campanili can be dated with certainty or probability, and I will here give a partial list of them: —

S. Prassede	c. 1080
S. Maria ad Pineam	c. 1090
SS. Quattro Coronati, Paschal II	c. 1113
S. Maria in Cosmedin, Calixtus II	c. 1123
S. Crisogono, Calixtus II	c. 1125
S. Giorgio in Velabro (?)	early XII
S. Maria in Trastevere, Innocent II	c. 1139
S. Croce in Gerusalemme, Lucius II	c. 1144
SS. Giovanni e Paolo, Hadrian IV	c. 1157
S. Francesca Romana, (= S. Maria Nuova)	c. 1140–1160
S. Pudentiana	mid. XII
S. Eustachio	c. 1190
S. Lorenzo f. le m. Clement III	c. 1190
S. Silvestro in Capite, Celestine III	c. 1195
S. Maria Maggiore	c. 1125 and 1376
S. John Lateran	c. 1360

The most symmetrical and slender of early Roman campanili are those of S. Pudentiana and S. Maria in Cosmedin, both perfect examples of brick construction. Close to

them in point of beauty are those of SS. Giovanni e Paolo,
S. Cecilia, S. Croce in Gerusalemme, S. Alessio and S. Francesca Romana.   Particularly heavy in its proportions is
S. Giorgio in Velabro.   The crudest workmanship is shown
in SS. Quattro Coronati.

S. Giorgio in Velabro.
(Twelfth century.)

In the matter of openings there was not much difference
between this school and those of other Italian provinces except
in the greater proportion of voids to solids which helped the
effect of lightness.   The lower story or two had a one-light
opening; the next a two-light window usually divided by a
square brick pier; then followed stories of either one three-
light window or two two-light windows, with marble shafts.

The capitals of these shafts do not ordinarily belong to any order, but are of simple cubic form — mere plinths. The division between the stories is made by a cornice of simple mouldings above a row of the customary diagonal cuneiform bricks and with sometimes a row of dentils. In a few cases the trimmings and mouldings are of stone, as at S. Cosimato, where there is a moulded travertine cornice.

Campanili of Cathedral, Terracina.

An attempt at further decorative effects is often made by the insertion in the masonry, at intervals, above the windows, of disks of porphyry or serpentine such as were used in the pavements and church furniture, and occasionally, even, of the brilliantly glazed Moorish plates, which were more common farther East and on the Adriatic. Such disks are used at SS. Giovanni e Paolo very effectively. It is a custom found in other schools, *e.g.* in Romagna (Pomposa).

The area of diffusion of this style of campanili was less wide and general than that of the internal decorative work. It was a peculiarity common, as we have seen, to most of the architectural features of the school which were based on brick construction and which were consequently modified in those parts of the Roman province where brick was replaced by stone. In towns as near as Tivoli, Albano and Velletri, the resemblance is maintained well-nigh intact. The campanile of S. Maria del Trivio at Velletri is a superb example of a late date. But already at Anagni considerable independence is shown, and at the southernmost boundary, Terracina, while the porch and furni-

o

ture of the cathedral are strictly Roman, the tower is of a special type, which I have not seen duplicated elsewhere, with a rich facing of false pointed arches. Plain early examples are at S. Elia, Nepi, and the cathedral of Civita Castellana. In the Sabina are the campanili of S. Giovanni in Argentella at Palombara, and S. Pietro at Montebono, of pure Roman type. Among these out-of-town works the campanile of S. Maria del Trivio is isolated, and was finished in 1353. It is 35 m. high, and is built in alternate courses of tufa, of *selce* and of bricks, giving it a polychromatic effect. The windows are round-headed below and pointed above.

The even higher cathedral tower of Viterbo (40 m.) is also polychromatic, but by different means, by alternate light and dark courses of travertine and peperino stone. The Gothic details of this part are of the thirteenth century, but the lower part of the tower, entirely of peperino, is earlier.

Of the campanili in Rome itself, one typical of the average sort is that of S. Maria in Trastevere. It is 36 m. high, and built entirely of brick, even to the cornices. Only the coupled columns and their plinths and the cornice brackets are of white marble.

The tower of the cathedral of Gaeta (1158) is a signed masterpiece by the Roman Niccolo d' Angelo.

CLOISTERS

The school showed even greater originality in the development of a new type of cloister. This was natural because its strong point was not construction, but outline, proportion and decorative effectiveness; and these qualities can be made to shine nowhere more brilliantly than in such a structure as the cloister.

Beginning with examples that are not radically different from those in other parts of Italy, the type was fully evolved in Rome before the middle of the thirteenth century, and was recognized in other parts of Italy as a Roman invention. When such a cloister was erected in 1229 at Sassovivo, in Umbria, it was called an *opus romanum*. Travel as we will over Italy, we can find none like them, even though some points of similarity seem to appear in such cloisters as that of Monreale near Palermo.

The characteristics of the cloisters of the developed type were : the retention of the round arch, when the pointed arch was invading architecture quite generally ; the use of an exceeding variety of design in the coupled shafts that sustained the arcades and in their capitals; the assimilation of classic details in the sculptured ornament and the mouldings ; the application of stuccoed ornament and of mosaic inlay to friezes, cornices, architraves, arches and colonnettes. The result was brilliant in color and delicate in design.

This exquisite type was a gradual growth. The earliest cloisters in Rome to which we can assign an approximate date stand really at the opposite pole of artistic expression, in a heavy simplicity characteristic of early Romanesque. No class of works of art in Rome is as little known as the cloisters earlier than the two spectacular examples of the Lateran and S. Paolo, though nowhere else in the world does such a group

of cloisters exist.   The universal ignorance has a good reason.
Some belong to nuns and require the special permit of the titular cardinal.   This is so at S. Cecilia.   I believe myself to
have been the first archæologist to know of its existence.
The same was until recently the case at S. Cosimato, before
its restoration.   The difficulty connected with S. Sabina is
that it is now part of a hospital for incurable diseases.
Here follows a list: —

S. Prassede	c. 1080 (?)
SS. Quattro Coronati	c. 1113
SS. Vincenzo ed Anastasio alle Tre Fontane	1130–1140
S. Francesca Romana (S. = Maria N.)	c. 1140–1160
S. Cecilia in Trastevere	c. 1150–1160
S. Lorenzo fuori le mura	1188–1191
S. Cosimato in Trastevere	c. 1190–1200
S. Paolo — Early part by Pietro di Capua	c. 1205–1210
S. Sisto	1198–1222
S. Sabina	1216–1218
S. Giovanni in Laterano	c. 1220–1228
S. Paolo — Later part by Magister Petrus	c. 1230
S. Maria in Aracœli	c. 1200–1260

Cloisters by Roman Artists Elsewhere

Subiaco — Early part by Jacobus	c. 1200
Sassovivo	c. 1228
Subiaco — Later part by Cosmas	c. 1229

The earliest of all the extant cloisters is the one at S. Prassede, where an inscription once existed stating it to be built by
Cardinal Benedict under Gregory VII (1073–1086).   It is small
and primitive.   Of greater importance is that of the SS.
Quattro Coronati, which we may consider to be part of the total
reconstruction begun by Paschal II in 1112.   It has all the
earmarks of the style of Paulus, the probable head decorator
for this Pope.   It is built of marble and is far in advance of
its age.   Notwithstanding Renaissance restorations that have
affected the basement, added retaining piers and enlarged some
openings, its condition is substantially original.   The plan

is quite oblong and the sides all curve toward the centre in plan, giving an appearance of increased length and grace. The heavy cornice is characteristic of Paschal II, and between the corbels are mosaics in the simple patterns of white and *verde antique* marble, without any admixture of artificial cubes. This is like all the work of Paulus.

The only breaks in the stretch of arcades is by means of a marble pier with pilaster strips in the centre of each short side;

Cloister of S. Lorenzo.
(Late twelfth century.)

and by a doorway framed by two marble piers with pilasters in the centre of each long side. The tunnel vaults over the galleries are Renaissance additions. What is especially remarkable is that the columns are coupled, a peculiarity that does not recur again until c. 1200 at S. Cosimato. Of course this gives a greater lightness of effect. It shows Paulus as an originator.

Not long after, Innocent II (1130–1143) rebuilt the monastery of SS. Vincenzo ed Anastasio for S. Bernard's Cistercians, and the cloister seems of this period, except the north side, where the columns are slenderer and uniform with Ionic bases. On the east side, where the second story is of mixed brick and stone, the arcades are more primitive and irregular, with the bases all different, shafts heavier and not uniform, the capitals roughly cubic with heavy oblong plinths. On all sides the columns are single, not coupled. It is barely possible that this part is considerably older, perhaps Carlovingian. The constructive scheme is to divide each group of four arcades by a heavy square pier, from which springs a high blind arcade which takes the weight of the second-story wall off of the small arcades that it encloses. There were six of these groups on each of the three sides; the fourth side of the quadrangle was formed by the church wall and was not arcaded. This alone shows a very primitive scheme. The west corridor is covered by a tunnel vault; the others by groin vaults corresponding to the piers. Nothing could be plainer and heavier than this cloister, stylistically, if not chronologically, the earliest in Rome. It is quite impressive from its size.

Attached to S. Cecilia in Trastevere is an almost unknown cloister of moderate size, which has recently undergone a painful whitewashing and restoration, but is structurally in fair preservation, and apparently contemporary with the church porch, some time after the middle of the twelfth century. The columns of white marble are not coupled, and rest directly, without bases, on a common basement or stylobate. The brick arches are narrow and low, but less heavy, and the walls are less thick than at the Tre Fontane. There is no ornamentation. The capitals are plinth-like and uncut except along the edges.

More interesting and somewhat more advanced is the large cloister attached to S. Lorenzo *fuori le mura*. One sign of progress is the use of coupled in place of single shafts to flank the central arches or doorways in each bay of the four galleries. The walls are still of plain brickwork, the arches still merely varied by plain projecting archivolts, the capitals still plain plinths, and the baseless shafts still rest directly on the continuous basement. The shape is oblong, the longer sides having three groups of arcades divided by piers; the shorter sides only two. Where not broken by doors or large arcades, each division has five supports with six arches. The long sides measure 20.45 m., the short sides 13.60 m., and the width of the corridor is 3.75. This is a fair average size. The columns are 1.65 m. high, and the intercolumniation is .71½ m. Part of the second story, with brickwork and windows in the same style as the lower story, is preserved. This is particularly valuable; practically a unique case in Rome, where the question of the second story of the different cloisters is one of controversy. The restoration of this second story might partly counterbalance the horrible vandalism that almost ruined the basilica under Pius IX, in a so-called restoration, almost as barbarous as that which under Leo XIII completed the destruction of S. John Lateran.

In about 1200 the school seems to have felt the influence of the French architects from Burgundy who had come in as members of the Cistercian order, settling in the great monasteries of the order near Rome at SS. Vincenzo ed Anastasio, Fossanuova, Casamari, Valvisciolo and elsewhere. It was natural that in so important a feature of monastic architecture as the cloister, these French monks, with their knowledge of the beautiful examples in their own country and their competence as specialists, should teach something to the Roman artists. The Cistercian cloisters in all these monasteries, as well as at Viterbo and elsewhere, show what their artistic type was between about 1175 and 1225, and how they themselves developed from Romanesque simplicity to Gothic splendor and variety. But, though Roman artists are seen to have worked with them, as when they decorated with mosaic work the portal of Fossanova, and though these Romans appear to have borrowed from the Cistercians some types of Gothic capitals, the chief debt they owe is a greater firmness of outline, an improved sense of proportion and a greater delicacy in the handling of sculptural details. They assimilated methods and principles, but did not copy. This is quite clear from a comparison of Cistercian and Roman cloisters.

A second influence was introduced from the Campanian

school by Pietro di Capua, who was both abbot of the monastery of S. Paul and first architect of its cloister, who applied some mosaic ornamentation to its surfaces and began a veritable revolution.

The first results of the advance appear in the cloisters of S. Sabina and S. Cosimato in Rome and of the monastery at Subiaco. In these works of the two decades before and after 1200, we find a return of the use of the coupled shafts under

Cloister of S. Cosimato.
(End of twelfth century.)

a single plinth, which was to be henceforth the rule throughout Italy. They were far slenderer than the early shafts at SS. Quattro Coronati and of quite a different style.

S. Cosimato had the largest cloisters in Rome, but the workmanship is careless and uneven. It marks the transition from the older style, and may still be earlier than 1200 except on the north side, which shows more careful work of the early thirteenth century. Its columns number not far from two hundred and fifty, as there are thirty-two coupled shafts on each side. On the N. and on part of the W. side the capitals are of delicate loftiform shape, the forerunners of those at S. Sabina. Inartistic restoration, both ancient and modern, has injured this cloister as much as it has that of S. Cecilia.

The monastery of S. Sabina was given by Honorius to S. Dominic as the home of his order in Rome, soon after the Papal authorization. This was in 1216. This is about the date of the cloister. Its arcades are in groups of four, separated by

Cloister at Monastery of S. Scolastica, Subiaco.

piers, the arcades being supported by shafts grouped in an unusual way, the central support in each bay being formed by two shafts flanked on each side by a single colonnette. The foliated capitals of a type similar to those at S. Cosimato, but better handled, are varied by a simpler, broader type. He also substituted marble for brick, which had still been used at S. Cosimato in the arcades and entire outsides of the galleries.

The cloister at Subiaco epitomizes the changes during this

short period that ushers in the golden age. It was the work of three generations of artists of the family of Cosmas. One side was the work of the second head of this family school, Jacobus, son of Laurentius, before the close of the twelfth century, and in careful workmanship was far superior to anything the school had yet done. He went farther than the architect of S. Lorenzo in his use of coupled shafts, alternating them with single ones, and giving each one a base. He signed himself here: —

MAGISTER IACOBUS ROMAN(US) FECIT HOC OP(US)

The three other sides of the cloister were completed, evidently many years later, c. 1225–1235, by his son and grandsons, who sign themselves: —

COSMAS ET FILII LUC(AS) ET JAC(OBUS) AL(TER)
ROMANI CIVES IN MARMORIS ARTE PERITI HOC OPUS
EXPLERUNT ABBATIS T(EMP(OR)E LANDI

In completing the work, these artists followed the paternal scheme, but in the substitution of twistéd for plain colonnettes, in the slenderer proportions, the cleaner outlines, the skilful workmanship and the freer ornament we see the influence of the change going on in the school.

The structure is oblong; the long galleries measuring 21.50 m., the short galleries 11 m.; or, including the passageways, 27.85 m. and 15.90 m. Notwithstanding the accuracy of the masonry, there is an extraordinary irregularity in the measurements. The width of the corridors varies from 2.60 m. to 4.50 m.; the same corridor measuring 3.35 m. at one end and 4.50 at the other. The arcades on the oldest side vary in their opening from .49 to .61 m. The height of the columns varies but little, from 1.22 m. to 1.25 m. on all sides.

Hardly had these cloisters just described been completed when the climax came by force of logic. Some artist of genius belonging to the school conceived the idea of applying to the details of cloistral architecture the decoration of inlaid marble and composition cubes already for a century the main decoration of church furniture, but which had been applied only in the scantiest way thus far to the broad architectural masses themselves. It had already been used, for example, on the frieze of church porticos, and in one or two cases a narrow band of the mosaic had been inserted in the frieze of a cloister. It seems really inexplicable how the Roman school could have left the cloisters so long bare and cold when they were so familiar with the decorative value of the colored cubes. Now, with a perfect burst of color mosaic-work was applied to every part of the cloister, combined with a careful and rich use of

Detail of Lateran Cloister.

relief work, both figured and ornamental, filling the arch spandrels and the under face of arches, and punctuating the richly carved cornices.

Possibly the initiator of the scheme was the foreigner, Peter of Capua, who, according to its long mosaic inscription, began, both as architect and as abbot, the cloister of S. Paul, though he did not complete it. But the credit for producing the most exquisite type should be given to Vassallettus, the architect of the cloister of the Lateran, which he built between 1220 and 1230.

These two cloisters are so much alike as to be almost indistinguishable, especially so in the case of the more advanced part of S. Paul. Both are large, the latter a trifle the larger.

The inscription proving the authorship of the Lateran cloister by Vassallettus reads : —

NOBILITER DOCTUS HAC VASSALLETTUS IN ARTE, CUM
PATRE CEPIT OPUS QUOD SOLUS PERFICIT IPSE

He began the work as his father's associate and finished it alone, perhaps after his father's death, before 1230. His father's name, judging from his signature in 1186 at Segni, was *Petrus Vassallectus.*

The plan is square, measuring 36 m. each way. Each gallery is formed of 25 arcades supported by coupled colonnettes arranged in groups of five, separated by projecting piers, with separate bases resting on a continuous basement, broken only by a single entrance in the centre of each side with an opening of 0.78 m.

The galleries are covered with their original groin vaulting corresponding to each group of arcades and supported not merely by the piers but by a group of three columns at each corner and by single columns opposite the piers with corresponding pilaster piers against the wall. All have good Ionic capitals. The columns have the greatest variety of design and of capitals. Some shafts are plain, others twisted, others spiral. Many are inlaid with mosaic patterns, especially those in the centre of each group, while the plain shafts are set near the piers, each of which has two plain engaged shafts. The columns measure 1.66 m. and the span of the arches is .66 or .67 m.

The common plinth is richly carved. It had been still plain at S. Cosimato ; there it was cut out of the same slab as the double capital beneath. The capitals also are far more deeply carved, and separated by a space ; and while they vary, the type is nearly always frankly Corinthian or a derivative.

The exterior face of the gallery is crowned by a heavy carved cornice which is 1.80 m. above the capitals. The design of this cornice is exactly like the contemporary cornice of the portico of S. Lorenzo, which would therefore seem to be also by Vassallettus. But here the cornice is broken at intervals by the piers which gave the artist an opportunity for those fascinating masks and heads described under Sculpture, to which chapter I refer also for the sphinxes and lions at the entrances and the reliefs in the spandrels, which, we learn from the long mosaic inscription of the minor frieze, were intended to impress on the monks the temptations and vanities of the flesh. Under the line of brackets is the main frieze, consisting of alternate square and circular slabs of porphyry, serpentine, granite and other marbles, set in a framework of mosaic patterns and themselves varied by inset designs. Its splendor is dimmed by many vacant spaces and by the disgusting drippings of mortar of recent workmen.

At S. Paul the scheme is exactly the same, but there is not the same unity of detail owing to the length of time consumed in the work and the change of artists. The three earlier sides are simpler; the later south side is even richer than the Lateran work. For instance, in the indrados or under surface of its arcades, the plain lines of torus mouldings are replaced by a double row of rosetted coffers, and the inner as well as the outer spandrels are carved.

The greater simplicity of the earlier part includes : the use of plain shafts throughout, as at S. Cosimato; the absence of carving in the spandrels, which appears, as in the Lateran, on the fourth side; the absence of carved corner heads, except lions, and the poor workmanship on the cornice, which, but for the lion heads, is plain. Neither are the bracket consols carved.

The mosaic inscriptions on the narrow frieze states that the cloister was commenced by Abbot Peter II of Capua (1193–1208), who also personally planned it, and was completed by Abbot John V (1208–1241). This Peter of Capua is credited, in a contemporary chronicle, with some artistic work at Salerno, and might be a connecting link between the Roman and Campanian schools. The inscription supposed to give the author of the fourth and latest side reads : —

MAGISTER. PETRUS. FECIT. HOC. OPUS.

but was cut on a small slab set into the vaulting of the gallery.

The greatest piece of vandalism perpetrated recently on a mediæval monument in Rome is the tearing down of the vaults covering the galleries of this cloister. The pilaster responds, projecting both from the piers and the walls opposite them, show that the original plan provided for vaulting; and that the destroyed vaulting was mediæval, even if not exactly coeval, has been proved by its demolition, which showed the use of hollow vases, as well as by this signature of *Petrus*. The present modern pitch roof with its wooden ceiling injures the dignity and diminishes the charm of the cloister.

In the fourth side at S. Paul's the Roman school reached the climax of its cloistral architecture between 1230 and 1240. Whatever else it may have produced later, as the upper story which crowns the earlier cloister at S. Maria in Aracœli, is in the nature of an anticlimax.

Among the many reasons for the charm of these Roman cloisters is one that has only recently been discovered. It is that here, as in so many Greek temples, there were variations from the straight line, especially in horizontals, in such a way as to give sweeps of beauty in place of purely mechanical stretches, and an illusion of greater length. This is evident to any one standing at the corner of one of the inner faces of a cloister, as he lets his eye follow the sweep of the cornice above the arcade surrounding the cloistral court. The regularity of this curve and its constant repetition show that it was not accidental, but deliberately planned. I have already noticed it in the early work at SS. Quattro Coronati, and it reappears in every later cloister that I have tested.

It is from one of the cloisters outside of Rome that we learn that this type was considered even by contemporaries as the "Roman Style." This is remarkable, because it is generally only posterity, with its historical perspective, that labels a style and provides it with a proper niche.

It is in the inscriptions of the cloister of Sassovivo that this occurs. It states that the cloister was built *romano opere et mœstria*, "in Roman workmanship and style," in 1229, by the artist Petrus de Maria. The connection between this cloister and the contemporary group by other Roman artists is perfectly evident. It is also evident why the artist took pride in stating that it was done in the Roman style: it was because Sassovivo was in Umbria, beyond the regular sphere of activity of the Roman artists. In their own province it would have been quite superfluous to use such an expression.

These are not by any means the only cloisters in the Roman province. But those of the Cistercian order at Fossanova, Casamari and Valvisciolo belong to this special monastic school, and not to Roman art. There was certainly some reciprocal influence. The other most important group is at Viterbo, where the Cistercian and the new Dominican and Franciscan orders met.

CIVIL ARCHITECTURE

It was several centuries before any change took place in the civil and private architecture of Rome. The patrician families of the fourth and fifth centuries continued to live in their ancestral city palaces and suburban villas. Early in the fifth century the palace on the Cœlian, belonging to S. Melania, the wealthiest woman of her time, included, besides the main residential quarters, a number of porticoed courts, a circus and a hippodrome set in extensive grounds. A contemporary describes the mosaics, rich marbles, frescos and statues with which both buildings and grounds were decorated. This is typical of the general condition, as we see it in the correspondence of Symmachus, Paulinus and other notables of the time. If there were any changes, it was by decay or destruction. Alaric (410), Genseric (455) and the Gothic wars were successive agents in the process of elimination. Sixty palaces on the Aventine, which was the favorite aristocratic quarter, were sacked and burned by Genseric's Vandals.

The fragments remaining from the decoration in marble slabs of the private basilica of Junius Bassus is about all the clew to what the decorative artists were then doing. But the house of John and Paul on the Cœlian embodied in a church in c. 400, while shorn of nearly all its decorative features, shows the internal arrangements, structure and a good part of the pictorial decoration of a house in which wealthy Christians of the fourth century lived. One of the few changes that we notice, besides the introduction of distinctively Christian subjects in the frescos, is the private chapel or oratory, which became so fashionable as to interfere with the public church services, so that their use was finally prohibited.

Very few of the palaces that survived the calamities of the Gothic wars remained in the hands of their original owners or were kept restored. Pope Gregory the Great, as an exception, lived at first in his family mansion, that of the Anicii, but even he finally transformed it into a monastery. In the course of the seventh and eighth centuries we must imagine that the numerous monasteries which we know to have established themselves on the Cœlian and Aventine hills where the abandoned and ruined palaces were mostly placed, settled there because they could use the broad spaces and the buildings.

A few buildings were kept in condition. The Byzantine Emperors inherited the ownership of the public civil buildings of the city, and their representatives lived in the palace of the Cæsars, a part of which was kept in repair.

The new civil and domestic architecture that arose after the seventh century was exceedingly modest and restricted. The population being concentrated on the low ground near the river, it is there that we find traces of their houses; in only one section, the Roman Forum, has anything come to light that belongs to this age. The rest of the city was too frequently built over. Such modest Byzantine residences were hidden, like the contemporary chapels, in the recesses and corners of the great monuments of antiquity, and were built of stones taken from their ruins. A number have been discovered, always to be destroyed by the excavators as of no interest until the very recent intelligent excavations under Boni. They are found in the Atrium Vestæ, the palace of Tiberius, the Regia, the Basilica Æmilia. Of these, the best preserved is the one occupying the east end of the basilica Æmilia. It is, however, hardly architecture; mere building.

Whatever art there was outside the churches, was illustrated in the annexes to these churches, in the hospitals, poorhouses, dining and reception halls, hotels for pilgrims, etc. These also have been swept away by the changes in fashion. Every large basilica was the centre of such a group of buildings. That of the Lateran, including the palace, was the most important.

Only as the Carlovingian era advanced was there a change. Now there emerged from the ruck an aristocracy of wealth and position which soon established itself upon the firm foundation of feudal possessions throughout the Roman province. They built palaces in the city and castles in the country.

P

Judging from literary sources, some of the palaces were based on the scheme of the antique courts, with halls between and around them. The life that these feudal nobles led was not wanting in a crude magnificence and pomp.

The wild feuds of the tenth century and the absolute necessity of a fortified residence for self-protection definitely eliminated all remaining traces of the type of the antique house.

When the great Alberic gave his house for a monastery, it was probably because he wished to replace it by one of the new fortified type. The counts of Tusculum had an extensive palace near the SS. Apostoli, where they held court of justice; in 1191 it passed to the Colonnas. The Emperor

Detail of Palace of Crescentius.
(Tenth and eleventh centuries.)

Otho III built himself such a palace between S. Alessio and S. Maria Aventina, of which traces still remain. But the only considerable remnant of this age is the so-called House of Crescentius, a palace built by a noble named Nicholas for himself and his son. It is an elaborate brick structure with trimmings of terra-cotta and marble, friezes and cornices that are partly classic, partly debased imitations. Even now there is enough to show that it was far in advance of the residences of the Byzantine age, and may readily have been the scene of the merry and luxurious life which the Roman nobility and clergy are accused of living in the tenth century.

The poverty of the eleventh century and the Guiscard fire proved a serious setback to civil architecture, and over a century elapsed before it recovered.

In connection with the reconstruction of the city the leaders of the Church appear to have wanted to take a sort of general " account of stock." A number of documents show that this applied not only to mediæval monuments, both religious and civil, but to the ruins of the ancient city. A guide-book to the city was drawn up which, under the name of *Mirabilia,* the Marvels of the City of Rome, had a general diffusion over Europe. It has been shown by Duchesne to have been written, c. 1130, by the monk Benedict, author of the public cere-monial book, the *Ordo.* To supplement this there was appar-ently — perhaps not till later — a bird's-eye-view plan drawn, showing the position of the principal buildings, ancient and recent. This general study was supplemented by monographs on the principal basilicas, of which the two most important, those of the Lateran and Vatican basilicas, have been preserved. Careful lists of the churches and monasteries were drawn up, with the amounts due to each from the Papal treasury, and the organization of the Roman priesthood in the general associa-tion of the *Fraternitas Romana,* with its four subdivisions, was recognized as an offset to the careful organization of the mass of citizens under their guilds and in their *rioni* or quarters.

Once more the unions, or guilds, which had never ceased to exist in Rome, became of importance in the artistic develop-ment of the city. Elsewhere I shall speak of this in con-nection with the schools of artists, and merely call attention here to the grouping of the guilds in the city. Each occupied a street or group of streets, where they lived and kept shop : here they had their guild-church or churches, where they were buried, and which they decorated and kept in repair.

Stray buildings like the old inn near the Tiber, the *Albergo*

dell' Orso, famous even in Dante's time, or the Hospital of
S. John Lateran, are types of a once numerous class.

The centre of the late mediæval city was the Capitol. At
its feet, from the Aracœli steps to S. Venanzio, was the main
market; that of the clothiers was in Via delle Botteghe Oscure,
between the arches of the Circus Flaminius; that of the
fishmongers between the columns of the portico of Octavia,
by S. Angelo in Pescheria. The thickly peopled section, along
both banks of the river, extended from the Ponte Rotto to the
Ponte Sisto. How much of this is left since the Italians began
to gut the old city after 1870? The Ghetto, which, before
being given over to the Jews by the Popes of the Renaissance,
had been one of the main quarters of the city, has been entirely
demolished. The works for the rectification of the banks of
the Tiber, in which so many millions were sunk with little
visible result, swept away nearly all the old city on both banks.
A few pitiful fragments remain, between Ponte Rotto and
Ponte Quattro Capi, keeping company with the house of Crescentius, and especially in the short tract in the Campo Marzo,
at the Trinita de Pellegrini, at the foot of the Aracœli and between Via di San Bartolommeo de' Vaccinari and S. Paolino
alla Regola. This also is threatened by the extension of the
piano regolatore. A portico of arches supported by heavy
granite shafts, crowned by Ionic capitals, remains at No. 29 of
Via San Bartolommeo, and it was originally connected with a
cross-street by a covered passage similar to the so-called *arco
de Ginnasi* and *arco de Cenci*. Farther along a larger house
forms a small square on the corner of the Via de Strengari. It
is built of brick with *tufo* trim, and is entirely surrounded by
a colonnaded portico. Its fenestration is fairly elaborate, with
double lights separated by twisted colonnettes.

It is difficult to realize that the streets of the mediæval city
were usually flanked with a double row of porticos. It was
an antique tradition which we see followed in various mediæval
and modern cities of Italy, such as Bologna, Padua and Turin —
an arrangement both artistic and salutary, a protection from
rain and sun. We have seen how the Rome of early Christian
days had been provided with its long lines of porticos, under

which the pilgrims, for instance, could walk without a break
the miles between the basilicas of S. Peter and S. Paul.
We must imagine that many of the arcades and porticos
were destroyed at the time of the fire of Robert Guiscard, especially where the level of the city was raised, and that those

Gothic Window of House in Piazza Capranica.

that were rebuilt were of less monumental character. Doubtless
they were extremely irregular, and were composed largely of
ancient materials, unmatched shafts and capitals, bits of architraves and cornices. In less artistic fashion they reminded of
the church porticos, and were seldom arched, almost always
with the pseudo-classic architrave.

With the return of the Papacy and the Renaissance, all these porticos were destroyed or closed up as occupying valuable room. Not a single one remains open.

To the same style of the thirteenth century belongs a house in the Piazza S. Cecilia. To the more advanced Middle Ages

Court of Vitelleschi Palace at Corneto.

and the Gothic invasion belong such typical palaces as that which has been turned into a theatre in the Piazza Capranica, with rather charming windows and on a large scale — probably a rich cardinal's house, quite similar to the better-preserved Anguillara palace which will be described under Military Architecture. But the fourteenth century was more concerned with tearing down than building up civil structures, which were then almost inextricably interwoven with that feudal military architecture, which the popular uprisings of this age sought to destroy.

It is not easy to dissociate the civil buildings in Rome itself with those in the province, where so many of the Roman nobility and clergy had palaces and castles, but the limits of this volume forbid more than an allusion to this rich field. Perhaps the two main distinctions are of material and style; for stone was substituted for brick nearly always in the provincial cities, and the classic influence was largely wanting, so that the porticoed

Late Gothic Windows in Vitelleschi Palace at Corneto.

streets either did not exist, or were in the Romanesque and Gothic styles. The towns both north and south of Rome are particularly rich in material of this period. Alatri, Ferentino, Anagni and Veroli, to the south; Civita-Castellana, Corneto, Viterbo, Orvieto, to the north, are still largely mediæval in their street architecture, and among the most picturesque cities of Italy. The palace of Cardinal Vitelleschi at Corneto, with its grandiose court and rich gothic fenestration, probably had counterparts in Rome.

MILITARY ARCHITECTURE

In a history of the military architecture of the Middle Ages, or even in a general history of the subject, neither of which has yet been written, the monuments of Rome and her province would take an unexpectedly important place, not so much for their fine preservation or intrinsic interest, as because they form in their early examples the connecting link with antiquity.

Specialists are aware of the fact that Roman military science in the sphere of fortifications was quite rudimentary in comparison with that of the Oriental nations. The Oriental tradition of curved lines, and of concentric parallel defences on different levels, handed down from Hittites and Syrians to Assyrians and Persians and transmitted by the Byzantines to the Mohammedans, seems to have been a closed book to purely Roman strategists, and was brought to the West only by the crusading leaders, who had learned of the excellence of these Eastern methods in the hard field of bitter experience.

But before this transformation was thoroughly completed in Europe, at the opening of the thirteenth century, a unique place was held by the mediæval fortresses of the Roman province. Elsewhere, in France, England and Germany, there is a slow and painful evolution from the earthworks of the Merovingian age, through the square keep within a circuit at first of earth and palisades and finally of stone, of which the best type is the Norman — a type which does not entirely replace the outer earthworks by stone until the beginning of the twelfth century.

In the Roman province, on the contrary, there is no such long lacuna and violent difference during the early Middle Ages. In this as in so many other branches antiquity and the Middle Ages clasp hands. But, curiously enough, nothing,

216

absolutely nothing, has been done to illustrate the numerous examples of mediæval Roman military architecture and engineering. Here they can be but lightly touched upon, as they do not belong, by strict construction, to the field of pure art.

Two conditions gave birth to the great development of military structures in this region, and these conditions arose almost simultaneously, in the ninth century : the establishment of the

Castle of Celano.
(Thirteenth century.)

feudal system ; and the great Saracenic raid. Both of these conditions were largely local. In the history of feudalism it is not generally understood that the feudal nobility of Rome was the earliest to acquire importance in mediæval society. A curious blow at the theory of its strictly Germanic and northern character ! The chaotic social and political condition resulting from the enfeeblement and extinction of the Carlovingian dynasty and the decay at the same time of the spiritual power of the Papacy, made it necessary for every strong man to fend for himself and opened the way to private ambition in a manner previously impossible when there was a strong central power. The great secular officers, such as the chiefs of the Roman army, the head officials of the Papal court, carved out for themselves important fiefs. Large estates and their towns, the property of the Church, were for a financial consideration turned over for life by the Popes to some prominent family, and what was intended as merely a life tenure became a hereditary possession. Such families as that of Alberic and Crescentius had at an early time both their palaces in the city and their fortresses in the country. The Frangipani, Orsini, Colonna, Anguillara and others soon followed, for the terrible condition of the Papacy in the tenth century, at the mercy of ambitious and dissolute women and nobles, gave free scope to the partition of the province among the ambitious magnates.

But an even more precise and far-reaching cause for the spread of military engineering was the Saracen invasion. It turned the Popes into generals and admirals, led again to the creation of a Roman fleet and to Roman naval victories. The permanent establishment of the Saracens in many military centres throughout the Roman and Neapolitan provinces, with their centre in a city on the river Garigliano, laid the whole country at their mercy for thirty years. Even now the eyrie-town of Saracinesca is peopled by their descendants. All country life ceased; all monasteries, even when fortified, were destroyed; no open town was safe. Far more than even the previous invasions of Vandals, Goths or Lombards, this raid, so little noticed in history amid the other more spectacular events of the Arab conquests, radically changed the aspect of the land in this part of Italy.

Cities were provided with strong battlemented walls and towers and defended by trained militia. The monasteries were turned into fortresses and the abbots into feudal military lords with a swarm of vassal soldiery. Every peak was fortified. At every point of vantage, at every proper interval between towns, were built watch-towers to guard the roads, and to give warning of raids. The chronicle of the great Benedictine monastery of Subiaco, which held sway over so many towns and built so many fortresses, is typical of the whole class.

This defensive military engineering as a feudal institution seems to have been developed in the province for some time before it was introduced into Rome itself; and when this

Castle and Fortifications of Nepi.

happened it was largely because of rivalry between the great feudal families. But there was one field — that of general public defence — in which we must picture Rome and the Papacy as at once taking the lead and showing the way. There was, for about a century, a tremendous activity and lavish expenditure in this field: the creation and fortification of the Leonine city around S. Peter; of the suburb of Johannipolis, around S. Paul; of the later fort of S. Lorenzo; of the fortified ports of Ostia, Portus and Civitavecchia, as well as the extensive repairing of the walls and gates of Rome itself. One stands amazed at the millions that must have come out of the Papal and imperial treasuries for this work of defence.

One of the most conspicuous of the feudal castles of this primitive period seems to be that crowning a rise overlooking

Palace of the Anguillara, in Trastevere.

the Campagna on the edge of the Alban hills near Grottaferrata. It is called Borghetto or Castel Savelli, but was called in the tenth century *Civitella* and may have been the primitive seats of the counts of Tusculum.

It is an oblong rectangle about 134 by 55 metres, with six squarish towers on each long side. Inside the walls, besides the main keep, a church and several other buildings, there were two inner bastions on either side of the main gate, facing Rome. The plan remained that of the ninth-tenth century, and the lower part of the walls is of the large blocks of Alban stone or tufa then commonly used. But the fortress was changed at two periods. In the thirteenth century, when it passed to the Savelli, they built the parts in small blocks of peperino, as well in the castle proper as in the bastion in front of it. Then in the fifteenth century it was changed, but not fundamentally, by Cardinal della Rovere. It is now totally abandoned, and worthy of careful study.

In the city itself the fortresses of the Frangipani and Pierleone and other great nobles were so strong in the twelfth century as to defy assault even when the city itself was captured. So in the Trastevere were the towers of the Tebaldi and near S. Martino those of the Capocci. The most prominent present ruins of such city fortresses belong to the following century and are the great towers of the Conti and the Milizie which still stand in only part of their original enormous bulk as part of great enclosures; that of the Conti included all the Forum of Nerva. Both could hold large garrisons and outdid the older fortresses of the Frangipani and Pierleone. Latest and best preserved is the fortress-palace of the Anguillara family in the Trastevere, where the Middle Ages join hands with the early Renaissance. It has fortunately been preserved from the fate of most civil structures in Rome by a careful restoration and use as a civic museum. Its halls are built around two sides of a court, while the third is occupied by vestibules and the keep, and the fourth side is protected by a high battlemented wall. This was a common plan.

SCULPTURE

THE decadence in technical ability that afflicted Italian art during the fourth century was offset by no redeeming traits

Statue of Hippolytus, Bishop of Porto.

in the sphere of Sculpture. In the new Christian dispensation it was the only art for which no mission was found; so that for it there was no rebirth on the plane of the new idealism such as transformed painting and architecture. More and more sculpture fell into the hands of mere practitioners and survived as an unoriginal product until the extinction of the art guilds in the fifth and sixth centuries.

In one way it has a peculiar interest, because, unlike sectarian painting, it was a common meeting ground. Pagan, non-sectarian (civil), and distinctly Christian forms all existed side by side. Triumphal arches, imperial statues and busts, consular, and other secular figures, continued the traditions of pagan public monuments with practically no change except from the

222

natural evolution of style. Even in the Christian field it was only in the reliefs that sculpture showed a dogmatic tendency.

It was inherent in the nature of statuary that it should be the least affected by a change of faith, as its very simplicity makes it a form of art but ill adapted to the expression of religious dogma. The most precious and early example

Bronze Statue of S. Peter.

Statue of Constantine, Lateran.

of Christian statuary, the more than life-size seated figure of Bishop Hippolytus of Porto, author of the reform in the ecclesiastical calendar for Easter, is almost an absolute counterpart of contemporary seated statues of philosophers and poets. While partly restored, it is true, it is a work of the age of Septimius Severus that challenges comparison with the classic works of the period; nothing about it suggests a religious creed of any sort. It was found at Porto itself and is now in the Lateran Museum.

Even more famous is the life-size seated bronze figure of
S. Peter, still existing in his basilica and an object of great
veneration. Tradition has attributed it to the middle of the
fifth century and the time of Pope Leo the Great. Some
recent critics have denied that so good a work could have been
produced at that time and have assigned it to one of the masters of the early revival of sculpture in the thirteenth century
(Arnolfo). I am still inclined to feel that it belongs to the
flourishing age of Theodoric and Symmachus. There is every
reason to believe that ability to produce good works of bronze
casting lasted much longer than that of carving in marble.
It is possible that while the corporation of marble cutters
was dispersed in 410, that of the metal workers remained to a
large extent in Rome, probably because it was far more generally patronized by the Church, while the marble cutters depended more on the favor of the defunct imperial court. The
numerous and varied forms in which gold, silver and bronze
were used for the decoration of the basilicas from Constantine
to Theodoric is proved by the extracts from the papal inventories given in the *Liber Pontificalis.* Among these there are
many figures in relief and in the round, including statues of
Christ and of the Apostles. Such an art was more traditional
and conservative than that of marble carving, depended less on
the actual handling of the practitioner, which had so sadly
deteriorated, and more on a skilful use and adaptation of ancient moulds, which had been handed down from previous
generations of good artists.

We may consider, therefore, this sacred statue of S. Peter as
the solitary survivor of a large class of works whose material always made them a prey to the spoiler. Here also there
is but little to distinguish the work of Christian art: only the
symbolism of the keys, analogous to the emblems held by so
many pagan divinities, and the gesture of blessing that suits
the air of alertness and authority.

Constantinian Works. — It is comparatively easy, even with
the few remaining examples found in Rome, to illustrate the
decadence in marble statuary under Constantine and his successors. Perhaps the two most famous statues of Constantine

were those in the square of the Forum, the Basilica and Thermæ, none of which have been preserved. But there is one, also colossal, which now stands in the atrium of the Lateran basilica and another in the Capitoline museum.

It seems quite impossible to attribute to the same age the very high reliefs on the porphyry sarcophagus of the Empress Helena, mother of Constantine, found in her mausoleum. The high finish and good action of the figures indicate unusual artistic ability and a far earlier date. One of his most striking busts, with summary treatment in broad planes and a return to archaic frontal pose, is in the Conservatori museum, probably from the colossal statue in the apse of the New Basilica. Less numerous and even more inartistic are the statues and busts of his sons and successors, of whom Julian the Apostate is the latest to be represented in busts whose authenticity is more than doubtful. There is still some ability at reproducing individual traits, but the technique is so faulty as to make detailed examination disappointing. The colossal statue on the balustrade of the Capitol Square is thought to represent Constantine II and to be from the Thermæ of Constantine. These works probably all antedate the time of the removal of the imperial school of sculpture from Rome to Constantinople, shortly before 330. They are superior to contemporary reliefs.

The far greater strength and character shown in the colossal bronze statue of Barletta, thought to represent Theodosius, is another proof of the superiority of metal over marble sculpture in the last days of antique art. This statue with the Emperor holding the historic Christian standard, the labarum, is probably typical of such colossal imperial statues in the fourth and early fifth centuries.

This secular imperial art was exemplified in a number of later spectacular monuments. The memorial arch of Valentinian and Theodosius at the entrance to their bridge was surmounted by bronze statuary which was precipitated into the river when the arch fell in the Middle Ages, and the fragments that have been recovered are now in the *Museo delle Terme.* A solitary base with sacrifice and soldiers belonging to a trium-

Q

phal monument of Diocletiam in the Forum, is similar, except for greater barbarism, to the corresponding bases of the arch of Constantine a few years later.

Of works in relief the best known are those on the arch of Constantine. In theme they reproduce the same subjects commonly given on the arches for over two centuries : the imperial gifts to the people (*congiarium*); the imperial victories; the emblems of the four seasons; the groups of captives; the river gods; the victories. Even the scenes taken from earlier monuments and set into the new arch are sometimes crudely con-

Sculptures on Arch of Constantine, by Constantine's Sculptors, with Victory of Mulvian Bridge over Maxentius.

nected with Constantine by substituting his head for that of the various original emperors!

One of the narrow reliefs of the time of Constantine himself is of special interest, as it gives us the architecture of the Forum at that time in its background.

The recently discovered small statues of consuls, which stood on pedestals in the Roman Forum, have at least furnished the material for an interesting study on the development of the ecclesiastical costume from the civil official costumes of the day. They are on about the same low level as the reliefs on the arch of Constantine.

Still, life-size or colossal marble statues were carved and

set up until the close of the fifth century. None are more interesting for the annals of the last days of paganism than those placed in 364 and 380 in the atrium of the House of the Vestals and representing the head vestal, recently deceased. This shows that until the very end the institution continued to function.

Before complete extinction some stray works seem to have been produced between the times of Leo the Great and Justinian; for instance, the head of the statue of an empress or lady of the imperial family, found in Rome a few years ago. The precision of the rich coiffure, the ivory-like finish of the technique, place it rather among the early products of Byzantine art than among those of the last Roman sculptors. There is also a male head in the Capitoline, of an unknown personage of the fifth century, with characteristics that faintly remind of archaic Greek or Etruscan treatment, perhaps a development of the characteristics noticed in the bust of Constantine.

Sarcophagi. — The main bulk, however, of the surviving sculpture of the fourth, fifth and sixth centuries is in the form of sarcophagi. Until recently it had been taken for granted that hardly a half-dozen of these sarcophagi antedated the reign of Constantine. The numerous instances of the use of pagan sarcophagi for Christian burial and of early Christian sarcophagi during the dark ages, as at S. Maria Antiqua, make it highly probable that a large number of the finest of the sarcophagi should be assigned to the third century instead of to a later date. Otherwise we should be forced to recognize the absurd anomaly that the sarcophagi produced by mere artisans were far superior artistically to the contemporary works executed by the best artists for imperial monuments, such as the Arch of Constantine!

This use of earlier sarcophagi was made doubly possible by the conditions which we found to exist after the beginning of the third century in the guilds, by which hereditary occupation and family workshops were made obligatory. The traditional teaching not only transmitted methods and mannerisms from father to son, but helped to establish a permanent stock in trade — a collection of "old masters."

The great majority of the sarcophagus reliefs consist of scenes from the Old Testament and from the life and miracles of Christ, with a predominance of the latter. In the Old Testament themes the symbolism is the prominent characteristic. The correspondences between the two series are not informed by the same historic sense that governs the later series in the basilicas. It is only toward the close of the period of the sarcophagi, after the middle of the fourth century, that we see the infusion of some themes inspired by the official art of triumphant Christianity, not by the symbolic and simple spirit of the era of persecution.

It is when the sarcophagus carver begins to represent Christ as the king and lawgiver, as triumphing in a supersensual

Sarcophagus in Lateran Museum.
(Fourth century.)

sphere, that he enters the field we are concerned with. But the perfection of this late development must not be sought in Rome itself; it is to be found in Ravenna and in the south of France, especially at Arles, a favorite metropolis of Constantine. Here sculpture flourished long after the guilds had fled from Rome in the days of Alaric (410) and Genseric (455).

There are two sarcophagi in the crypt of S. Peter which illustrate this tendency of the school just before and after 400. One was utilized as the tomb of Pope Pius II and has the bearded Christ on the rock with the four rivers in the scene of the Mission of the Apostles. The same scene is repeated in another sarcophagus of a slightly later date, used in 979 as the

Carved Wooden Doors, S. Sabina.

tomb of Gregory V. In both cases there are scenes from the life of Christ to supplement the central subject of Christ flanked by Peter and Paul.

Doors at S. Sabina. — In a place by itself stands the double door of carved cedarwood at S. Sabina, now generally ascribed to

Panel of Doors, S. Sabina.
"Adoration of Christ."

the time of Sixtus III (432–440), when the church was founded. A number of its panels have disappeared, but the majority remain in good preservation, though not in their original order. The panels are of two very different sizes as well as by at least two hands. The more perfect artist is characterized by slender figures full of action and life, and he also shows greater poetry and idealism in the choice and treatment of his themes. Characteristic of his style is the Adoration of Christ and the Ascent of Elijah. To the other artist should be credited scenes such as the Ascension and the greater part of the life and miracles of Christ, with heavier figures and a historic and material conception of the themes.

Originally the doors presented a parallel of Old and New Testament scenes far more elaborate than any on the sarcophagi and comparable to those that were being created at about this time in the frescos and mosaics of the basilicas. The Crucifixion scene is famous as the earliest known. It is symbolic; the three figures simply stand with arms outstretched, but unfastened, for there are no crosses behind them. One peculiarity is the grouping of two, three, or even four scenes above each other on the same panel, or the treatment of a single scene in superposed stories in the panel. There is the greatest similarity in this work to certain ivory carvings of the same century and to one sarcophagus in the Lateran. Certainly this art is not purely Roman.

Metal Sculpture. — If it is possible to point almost with certainty to a time when marble figure-carving ceased in Rome, we have found it impossible to be as positive about the sister branch of metal sculpture. The records used in the *Liber Pontificalis* describe a multitude of statues and reliefs of bronze, silver and gold executed for the churches during the more than five centuries between Constantine and the successors of Charlemagne, but we cannot judge of their artistic quality because none of them have survived; the metal was too tempting a spoils and was all turned into minted money.

These works were concentrated ordinarily around the high altar and were usually combined with metal ciboria, parapets, etc., to form a brilliant metallic combination. There were statues of Christ, angels, apostles and saints erected on railings or bases; cast or beaten reliefs on rails or altar fronts or gables. Occasionally there was a secondary group in connection with the baptistery. Combined with them to give effectiveness to the interior decoration of the churches were the richly colored hangings and the heavy metal hanging lamps.

The following is a contemporary description of the ciborium and its accessories given by Constantine to the Lateran basilica which will serve as a clue to the series: —

" A *fastidium* (*i.e.* ciborium) of hammered silver, having on its main front the enthroned figure of the Saviour, 5 feet high, weighing 120 pounds, and the twelve apostles, 5 feet high, weighing 90 pounds, holding crowns of pure silver. Also on the side facing the apse, the Saviour enthroned, 5 feet high, of pure silver, weighing 140 pounds, and four archangels of silver, 5 feet high, each weighing 105 pounds, with lapis lazuli gems set in their eyes and holding staffs. The fastidium itself weighed 2025 pounds, of ductile silver. Its ceiling is of pure gold and the lamp of pure gold which hangs from it with 50 dolphin lights, weighs 50 pounds and is held by chains weighing 25. (Under the centre of the architraves) hang four circular lamps of pure gold, each with twenty dolphin lights, each weighing 15 pounds."

To the same group around the altar belonged seven silver gilt candelabra, 10 feet high, each weighing 300 pounds and decorated with reliefs of the prophets. To the Lateran baptistery the Emperor gave for the decoration of the font a figure of the Saviour, of pure silver, 5 feet high and weighing 170 pounds, next to which stood a figure in silver, also 5 feet high, of John the Baptist, weighing 125 pounds, while between them was a Lamb, of pure gold, weighing 30 pounds, from which the baptismal waters flowed, and all around was a line of seven stags of silver, each weighing 80 pounds, from which the water also flowed.

There were never any but temporary interruptions in the flow of such gifts as these; the annals of Popes Sixtus (432–440), Hilary (461–468) and Symmachus (498–514) are particularly rich. When the above Lateran ciborium and all its accessories had been carried off by the soldiers of Alaric (410), the Emperor Valentinian replaced it by another of almost equal splendor, also of silver, and weighing 2000 pounds. That it must have been decorated with reliefs and statues is shown by the description of the ciborium which Valentinian gave at the same time to the Vatican basilica, which had the figures of the Saviour and the twelve apostles in gold, framed in precious stones, under arcades.

This tradition was continued by Pope Symmachus, who erected over the high altar at S. Paul's a relief in silver, weighing 120 pounds, with figures of the Saviour and the twelve apostles. Apparently reliefs were then taking the place of statuary.

The Gothic Wars. — Even the Gothic wars did not put an end to metal sculpture — though it may be considered now as inferior in splendor and workmanship. Pelagius I (556–561) replenished as best he could the church furniture. Pelagius II (579–590) decorated with silver reliefs the confessions of S. Peter and S. Lawrence. Gregory the Great (590–604) placed a silver ciborium in S. Peter. Honorius I (625–638) made silver reliefs for the confession of S. Peter and silvered doors; a silvered bronze ciborium of great size and silver confession reliefs for S. Agnes.

The life of Sergius I (687–700) not only credits to him the making of a gold statue of S. Peter, for his basilica, but mentions *three* gold statues of the apostle as existing there. It is under this Pope that we see the first traces of a substitution of marble for metal in ciboria as well as ambones, a substitution that militated against figured sculpture, because marble carving was purely decorative, and marked, perhaps, the downfall of the old school of metal workers on a large scale.

Carlovingian Works. — With the eighth century the text of the *Liber Pontificalis* begins once more to give greater details of art works, and we can see that if the Carlovingian popes, especially Hadrian I and Leo III, were thus able to give to the churches such a quantity of works in precious metals, there must still have existed a school of metal workers with some proficiency in figured reliefs; perhaps even there was a revival in this as in other branches. Still, it probably applied mainly to works of small size, such as may still be studied in the unique papal treasury of the Sancta Sanctorum chapel at the Lateran, recently made known after centuries of concealment. An example of these Carlovingian works is a gift of Leo IV to the Vatican basilica, where he placed a silver image of Christ enthroned, flanked by two angels and with the figures of the twelve apostles and the twenty-four elders on either side of the throne.

Between works of metal sculpture that have been destroyed, and marble sculptures that are merely decorative, there is therefore a hiatus in our knowledge of figured sculpture at Rome between the sixth and the eleventh centuries, except in the case of a few works of small size.

Revival in Twelfth Century. — The revival in sculpture that swept Europe during the latter part of the eleventh and the beginning of the twelfth centuries did not affect Rome perceptibly. While the Lombard and Tuscan schools were multiplying sculptures, barbarous, it is true, but showing constant effort at improvement, and adding materially to decorative effect in connection with architecture, Roman artists did not allow it to enter into their new scheme. It is a fact that the farther one goes southward in Italy during the Middle Ages the less does sculpture play its part and the more is its place taken by color.[1] The large strain of Byzantinism in Rome also helped to delay the plastic development. And yet there were some curious and original sporadic efforts, leading up to a half century of successful and artistic work just before the end of the school's career, — a half-century when the Roman sculptors were rivals and collaborators of the Pisans in certain branches of the art.

One general fact is characteristic : the school never once attempted to coördinate figured sculpture with the structure of its churches. There were no carved lintels or archivolts ; no galleries or arcades filled with statuary, no porches with columnar figures, no façade reliefs. These features, so common in Lombardy, Tuscany and Apulia, were *taboo* in Rome. There were not even any figured capitals.

In church furniture the prevailing fashion of mosaic inlay shut the door against sculptured decoration in more than one direction. For instance, it was in the form of pulpits that Niccola Pisano gave his main masterpieces ; that of the Pisan baptistery (1260) and that of Siena cathedral (1268), which his son Giovanni followed in those of Pisa cathedral and Pistoia (S. Andrea), not to mention many others by the Pisan school. The Roman love for color and for complete unity of design in interior decoration prevented their adoption of sculpture in a single pulpit.

[1] The exceptional use of decorative sculpture in the province of Apulia is probably due to Northern emigration.

Architectural figured sculpture and the decoration of church furniture being excluded, let us see what use the Roman school did make of figured sculpture.

The earliest piece is a baptismal font in the abbey church at Grottaferrata, near Rome. Its circular surface is covered with a scene symbolic of the sacrament of baptism and its effects. Upon a high rock on which is carved a gateway are seated two nude figures, catching fish that swim in the encircling seas and drawing them upward. On the left side a column rises high above the waters, and from it a nude figure is casting himself headlong into the water. The sea is the world, into which Christ descended to lose His life, so that He might become the great Fisher of men and keep them from drifting through the gates of hell. The extreme symbolism and the use of the nude, clumsy as it is, are both characteristics, not of Lombard or other Northern artists, but of some Byzantine school. This is historically confirmed by the fact that the monastery of Grottaferrata was built and inhabited by Greek monks, and that its mosaics and early decoration are purely Byzantine.

Well of Relics at S. Bartolommeo all' Isola.
(Twelfth century.)

To this Byzantine font of the eleventh century, which served as first model to the Roman school, we can compare a curious somewhat later work of purely Roman art, the sacred well-head of S. Bartolommeo all' Isola, which probably dates after the time of Paschal II (1113). Its circular surface is covered with the large figures of Christ and of the martyrs whose relics were placed below, Bishops Adalbert and Paulinus and S. Bartholomew. They stand under arcades and gables. The composition is in every way an evident copy of Roman sarcophagi, especially of those early Christian examples with single figures standing under such arcades separated by columns.

Equally a copy from antique models is a somewhat later, though cruder work, the paschal candlestick in the basilica

of S. Paul. It is signed by two Roman artists who worked after the middle of the twelfth century: *Ego Niconaus de Angelo cum Petro Bassaletto hoc opus complevi.* The entire surface of the column is covered with small figures in relief, in superposed rows, reproducing incidents of the life of Christ, including the Passion and Christ in glory. It seems a far-away miniature echo of Roman memorial columns, like other larger works, of substantially the same age, beginning with the bronze column of Bernward at Hildesheim (c. 1000) and ending with the marble column in the cathedral square at Gaeta (c. 1330). In style the figures are no better and no worse than contemporary work everywhere else in Italy, if we except certain charming and delicate Byzantine reliefs, such as those at the Pisan baptistery. The finish is crude and the proportions heavy, with enormous heads, though the general design is felicitous.

Paschal Candlestick
at S. Paolo.
By Niccolo di Angelo
and Pietro Vassaletto.

Statuary. — But where the Roman sculptor began to show unusual originality as the thirteenth century advanced is in the revival of sculpture in the round. The Roman artist had at this time acquired a great facility and firmness in handling marble, and after he had successfully reproduced the antique methods and styles in decorative work, in capitals, mouldings and cornices, it seemed a natural transition for him to imitate also the numerous draped statues that might easily serve as models for apostles and saints. Natural, perhaps, and yet a leap into the unknown, for had not some seven centuries elapsed since the chisel had fallen from the impotent hands of the last carver of an image in the round in Rome and the entire West?

The great leader in the revival of Italian sculpture, Niccola Pisano himself, cannot be said to have produced such a work unless we attribute to him the seated statue of the Emperor Frederic II on the triumphal arch at Capua; and the success in this style of work of his colleague Arnolfo was due to his residence in Rome. That the Roman artists of this age were alive to the influence of Roman statuary is shown by the statue of Aesculapius, with the signature of one of the Vassalletti, found in the school's workshop, and evidently used as a model.

There are two statues of SS. Peter and Paul, about life-size, which originally stood in front of the façade of S. John Lateran. They present the traditional types, such as we find in mosaics and frescos of the twelfth century. Though heavy and clumsy in proportions, they yet have all the interest of pioneer work, and are frankly classic in their aspirations. The treatment of details in the Lateran statues is excellent; the hair and beard have as much finish as in Cavallini's frescos. The simple tunic and toga have broad and natural folds. While the effect is that of pure statuary, these figures were set against a marble ground decorated with mosaic bands and circles; and this makes it logical to connect with them, as forming a single group, the kneeling statue (or very high relief) of a Pope, with exactly similar background, which has been commonly called a figure of Pope Nicholas IV (1288–1292), simply because of its single tiara, which points to a predecessor of Boniface VIII, who was the first to adopt the triple tiara. The difference in treatment between apostles and Pope is due to the contrast between the free use of types and classic costume in one case, and the attempt at portraiture and ecclesiastical costume on the other. While it is difficult to be positive in face of such unusual works, I am inclined to regard this group as earlier than Arnolfo and earlier even than the middle of the thirteenth century.   It was perhaps the most important work of sculpture in Rome, holding the place of honor in the atrium of the Lateran basilica.

Similar statues existed at S. Peter, where they can be seen in the crypt, and S. Croce in Gerusalemme.   The latter are much smaller and much later, showing a refinement of form and a polish of surface treatment that savor of foreign influence, but far from being an improvement on the burly but

Statue of S. Peter at S. John Lateran.

Statue of S. Peter at S. Croce in Gerusalemme.

impressive Lateran figures.   In fact, they may be part of a ciborium attributable to the time of Urban V (c. 1370).

There is some work nearly or wholly in the round at the Lateran cloister which helps to assign a date to the Lateran statues.   The cloister was erected between 1220 and 1230 by one of the greatest masters of the Roman school, Vassallettus or Vassalletto.   His feeling for the round is shown not only in the sphinxes that flank the entrances, and are clear reproductions of the antique, but in some heads that project from the

outer cornice of the court. They are so full of vigorous character and spiritual life that they can stand in the same class as
similar contemporary works of the sort in some French cathe-

Detail of frieze of Lateran Cloister by Vassaletto.

drals (*e.g.* Reims) and others by Niccola Pisano and in the pulpit at Ravello. They are mostly youthful heads, types of
pages and young aristocrats, with an occasional monk and old
woman. Delicately silhouetted in firm and well-marked planes, .

they produce an effect more sparkling than anything of this class in Italian art. One suspects an infusion of Gallic salt. A recent writer, finding some spirited heads on the tomb of Hadrian V and comparing them with others by Arnolfo and Niccola Pisano, has used them as an argument for the attribution of this tomb to Arnolfo, and has ascribed to Niccola, whose

early work does not antedate 1250, the merit of conceiving this class of delicate creations — a merit which these Lateran heads prove to belong to the Roman Vassalletto, in about 1225. The quality of vitality, so absolutely lacking hitherto in Italian sculpture, appears therefore for the first time in Vassalletto. Either the Lateran statues precede him, or are by a master of less power. The son of this Vassalletto inherited his father's talent; witness the spirited little kneeling figure on his paschal candlestick at Anagni.

Top of Paschal Candlestick at Cathedral, Anagni, by Vassalletto.

While the works I have just mentioned are almost unnoticed by historians of art, there is one statue which has not been overlooked, partly because of its historic interest. It is the seated statue of King Charles of Anjou, which the Roman Senate ordered set up in the Capitol in his honor when the king became civic ruler of the city in 1268, and was inaugurated as senator. As a portrait, the head is characteristic and interesting; as a work of art, the statue is stiff and awkward, decidedly inferior to its more classic immediate predecessor, the statue of the Emperor Frederic at Capua. The king wears a crown and holds a sceptre, but this mediævalism is tempered by a Roman costume and the curule chair. The stern face, with its prominent features, and the large head form a carefully studied portrait. The extreme shortness of the upper limbs indicates that the statue originally stood on a high pedestal. It is a grim record of this tamer of Popes and destroyer of the imperial power in Italy.

This statue, the second of its class in Italy, has been attributed to Arnolfo, the Florentine architect and sculptor, and has been used as an argument for assigning to the same artist the bronze statue of S. Peter, for which I have adhered to the traditional date of the fifth century. I can trace as little resemblance in style as in material.

Tombs. — During this same decade (1260–1270) the Roman school, after having thus attempted to revive statuary, perfected a type of sepulchral monu-
ment by combining the three arts of architecture, sculpture and painting in a form that was to affect Italian art even as late as the Renaissance. Until recently there had been no fixed type of funeral monument, no purely mediæval creation. In the majority of cases the body was placed in some pagan or early Christian sarcophagus, of which so many were always coming to light. In the twelfth century we find for the first time a homogeneous type of which there are examples in the atria of S. Maria in Cosmedin (tomb of Alfanus) and S.

Tomb of Cardinal Fieschi at S. Lorenzo.

Lorenzo. Here a plain sarcophagus is surmounted by a gable resting on columns and the recess is filled with a fresco; or else four columns support a plain low canopy over the sarcophagus : but there was no sculpture, either figured or decorative.

This type was developed and culminated in the middle of the thirteenth century in the tomb of Cardinal Fieschi at S. Lorenzo (1256), where a finely carved classic sarcophagus is surrounded by a large architraved and gabled canopy which

R

encloses a fresco of the Virgin and Child accompanied by saints and adored by the defunct.

Soon after this, a leader of the Roman school, Peter, son of Oderisius, made the first attempt to introduce both sculpture and mosaic decoration in sepulchral art, in his tomb of Pope Clement IV at Viterbo in 1268. At least, if there were any

Tomb of the Savelli at S. Maria in Aracœli.
(With use of ancient sarcophagus.)

earlier examples of this type, they have perished: the monument of Cardinal Bernardo Caraccioli († 1261) at the Lateran, of which only the statue remains, may have been such an example. In doing this he also for the first time substituted for the antique architrave and classic orders, the Gothic trefoil arch and foliated capitals. It was quite a revolution. The accompanying illustration of the tomb of Hadrian V, made only a few years later, also at Viterbo, is of a similar type, but by an artist of greater plastic skill, who gave more charming lines and more delicate ornamentation to his design, and showed himself a masterly sculptor in the reclining figure and the carved details, — probably Arnolfo.

The tomb of Clement IV is unusual in having as its annex that of his nephew, Pierre le Gros. The Pope's effigy is tilted forward to meet the eye; that of Pierre, being below, lies perfectly flat. They are not by the same hand. The Pope's is a painstaking portrait, even to the heavily marked lines of chin and neck, and the heavy folds of drapery are both effective and artistic. The two defunct were French; the man charged by the cardinals with ordering the monument was a Frenchman, Peter, archbishop of Narbonne. Why is it not natural to suppose that the Roman artist's adoption of both sculpture and Gothic design were due to French influence, since reclining figures were then a commonplace of French sculpture, whereas they were yet unknown in Italy? The monument as it stands gives but little idea of the original, and is due to a reconstruction from existing fragments. Originally the canopy was far loftier and enclosed a group of statuary, the Virgin and Child and probably some saints and the Pope, as in the later monument of Cardinal de Braye. Most of the mosaic decoration, also, has disappeared.

Even more drastic has been the damage suffered by the tomb of the famous prefect of Rome, Peter de Vico, executed in the same year (1268), in the same design, for the same church at Viterbo (S. Maria ai Gradi), evidently by the same artist. Even its statue has disappeared.

Arnolfo. — The master who dominated the school for the last quarter of the century now appears on the scene, Arnolfo di Lapo. He is the famous Florentine architect and sculptor, a contemporary and early coadjutor of

Tomb of Pope Hadrian V,
S. Francesco, Viterbo.

Niccola Pisano, whose artistic activity centred in Rome during the best part of his career. He assimilated so much of the spirit of the Roman school, especially from the Vassalletti, that it is difficult not to regard him as part of it. At the same time he added to its patrimony a distinct element through his greater plastic sense, which led to the increased use of sculpture in church furniture, especially in ciboria and sepulchral monuments.

Arnolfo's career cannot yet be clearly traced. He had a share in the pulpit at Siena, assisting Niccola Pisano in 1268. When, in 1277, Charles of Anjou released him to complete this sculptor's beautiful fountain at Perugia, Arnolfo had probably been working in or near Rome, though at what we cannot tell unless it was on the destroyed monument of Innocent V. The

Ciborium at S. Cecilia, by Arnolfo.

monument to Cardinal Riccardo Annibaldi, done at this time (1276–1277), of which many fragments remain at the Lateran, has been recently attributed to him on account of its plastic beauty. The frieze in high relief which originally stood under the canopy, over the reclining figure, and is now in the Cloister, strikes a very individual note. It is a procession of figures of clerics in high relief, bearing an incense-burner, book, candles and mitre for the celebration of the funeral service. The ease of movement, variety and naturalness of action, perfection of workmanship, make of this little-known work one of the most charming pieces of the early Renaissance of Italian sculpture. Or he may have been engaged on the monument of Hadrian V at Viterbo (S. Francesco), a superb masterpiece which Venturi attributes to him — instead of to Vassallettus II, as I had suggested. The face of Hadrian certainly has the softness of texture and the smooth gradations that we shall later find in authentic works of Arnolfo, though the slender proportions are quite different from his usual massive norm.

After 1282 we find him erecting the monument of Cardinal de Braye in S. Domenico at Perugia. His signature is at the bottom of the memorial metrical inscription: *Hoc opus fecit Arnolfus*. It is distinctly an amplification of the type inaugurated fourteen years before by Pietro Oderisi in the tomb of Clement IV, and more of its sculptures have been preserved, though its effect is destroyed by the loss of the trefoil tabernacle that formed its original framework. When still perfect, it was the most sumptuous combination of mosaic work and sculpture saved from the ravages of the Renaissance, surpassing even all known monuments of the Popes. The lower basement supported the two shafts of the canopy, now destroyed. The second section is a cenotaph on which rests the body of the deceased on a draped bier. Above it projects a pitch roof from which curtains hang, drawn away from the front by two angels. Over the canopy on a flaring base is a symmetrical composition. In the centre the dedicatory inscription; above, in a pointed niche, the enthroned Virgin and Child; on one side the kneeling cardinal, presented by S. Paul, and on the other S. Dominick — all gazing toward the divine Child.

There are qualities here that do not reappear in the other known works by Arnolfo: a slenderness of proportion, a projection in the draperies, a delicacy of type, an almost over-refinement and asceticism. The feeling of life culminates in overaction in the angels, perhaps a relic of the influence of Giovanni's *furia*, which will wear off after more protracted contact with the calm classic masterpieces of Rome, whose influence is also to give greater solidity to Arnolfo's figures.

Arnolfo's next signed and dated work is the ciborium of S. Paul in Rome, in which he was assisted by an artist named Pietro, who has been without proof identified with the painter Pietro Cavallini. There are but too many Roman artists named Pietro in the thirteenth century! This work is both signed and dated, 1285. *Hoc opus fecit Arnolfus cum suo socio Petro.* The Gothic design is here first applied to the altar canopy transforming it as the tomb had been transformed twenty years before.   Its four superb columns of *rosso antico* have capitals of almost purely French Gothic design.   The pointed structure they support, with its pinnacles and gables, is a harmonious combination of mosaic and sculpture.

The sculpture on this ciborium is unusually interesting because it is probably the earliest of its class and therefore an epoch-making creation, which was to set the fashion for the

Monument of Cardinal Ancher at S. Prassede, by Arnolfo.

next generation.   At each corner is a statuette; those on the front are S. Peter and S. Paul.   In the pendentives is a scene in relief, divided into two parts by the arch; *e.g.* the abbot Bartholomew offering the model of the ciborium to S. Paul. The gable is filled with a wheel-window supported by two flying angels, — one of the peculiarities in which Arnolfo betrays the growing influence of the antique, for they are neither more nor less than Roman Victories.

To the following year (1286) I am disposed to attribute the superb statue of an otherwise destroyed monument: that of

Cardinal Ancher in S. Prassede. Here we see the soft *pastoso* treatment of the face so characteristic of Arnolfo, used in so masterly a manner as to be by none but the master. It is, in fact, superior to the authenticated statue of Boniface VIII. The handling of the drapery is equally masterly in its feeling for textures. This tomb should be restored with basement and canopy and probably with votive sculptures. This work had not been as yet attributed to Arnolfo.

Shortly after ·(1287) Arnolfo executed the monument of Honorius IV in S. Peter's, a work that suffered the fate of

Detail of Opening to Chapel of the Presepe, S. Maria Maggiore.
A Prophet, by Arnolfo.

nearly all the works of art in the old basilica when it was torn down. Only the recumbent statue was saved and transferred to decorate the tomb of the Savelli family (to which the Pope belonged) in the church of Aracœli.

To Arnolfo is to be credited another conspicuous novelty, in another of the great basilicas, S. Maria Maggiore. This basilica was called *ad præsepe*, from containing the relic of the Manger of Bethlehem. To provide a fitting shrine for it, Pope Nicholas IV (1288–1292) erected a chapel which is the prototype of the sacred *tableaux* in the round, of marble, terracotta or wood carving, so numerous in Northern Italian, such as those of Modena and Varallo. This little chapel, now moved underground and transformed, is occupied by a life-size group of the Magi adoring the Infant Christ in the arms of the Virgin. At its entrance, over the door, two small figures of prophets in high relief occupy the pendentives. They are full of alert awkwardness and sharpness of line, and their counterparts by Niccola Pisano and Giovanni may be seen in their pulpits. The group of statues within the shrine is less successful. In

Angle of Ciborium at S. Cecilia, by Arnolfo.

it there is an attempt to transpose into statuary the pictorial scheme of composition. In the centre are the Virgin and Child on a throne, restored. On their right is the bearded figure of Joseph, leaning forward on his staff. From their left the Magi are approaching, in order of age. The oldest, with flowing beard, is kneeling, while the other two are conversing. The composition is easy, but the figures are clumsy, though the drapery is flowing and classic. The heaviness of the figure is unexpected when one remembers the slenderness of those on the De Braye monument. But it has been rightly ascribed to Arnolfo for several centuries.

The design of the ciborium of S. Cecilia in 1292 is an improvement on that of S. Paul's in harmony. There was no dedicatory tablet to break up the architectural lines, and the simpler arrangement of the corner statuettes does away with the awkward juxtaposition of overhanging niche and column. The sculpture is entirely by the hand of Arnolfo. The statuettes are connected with the legend of S. Cecilia and represent the contemporary Pope Urban, her brother, Tiburtius, her husband, Valerian and herself. In the pendentives are the Evangelists and their symbols, the apostles Peter and Paul and two female saints. Angels of classic type hold the wheel-windows in the gables. All the figures stand out from a mosaic ground and are richly colored. The effect is even more pictorial than at S. Paolo, and there is far greater suppleness and skill in the handling. Of course Arnolfo was assisted by a mosaicist and painter.

Probably Arnolfo's last work in Rome was the chapel and monument of Boniface VIII (1294–1303). Some critics have been sceptical as to his authorship of it because the artist died about two years *before* the pope, but their scruples were unnecessary for it is well ascertained that the Pope had Arnolfo make in S. Peter the chapel dedicated to his namesake Boniface IV during his own lifetime and had his own monument prepared at the same time. If further proof were needed, there was the signature of Arnolfo, reported before its destruction by several writers of the Renaissance : *Hoc opus fecit Arnolphus architectus*, alone sufficient, also, to prove the identity of Arnolfo the sculptor with Arnolfo the architect. The statue was originally surmounted by a mosaic of the Virgin and Child in a medallion, to whom the kneeling Pope is being presented by S. Peter, while S. Paul stands on the other side. The mosaic was by Giovanni Cosmati. The whole was framed by a very rich ciborium in which Arnolfo combined the old architraved style with an elaborate grouping of Gothic pinnacles and niches. The statue itself is full of repose, and is in Arnolfo's later *pastoso* manner, even softer than that of Ancher and more easy in pose than that of Honorius IV. A bust of Boniface VIII, also in the crypt, probably belonged to the same chapel.

There exist at S. Peter's and in its crypt a number of statues that are torn from their original monuments, from tombs and ciboria. We can only conjecture that two beautiful angels in the crypt, still holding back folds of drapery, may have belonged to Arnolfo's tomb of Boniface VIII. Another angel, now flanking the seated marble statue of S. Peter, is also in his later style (see p. 143).

The marble statue of S. Peter, now in the crypt, which has just been alluded to, was once in great veneration in the old basilica. It is an extremely rare example of mediæval adaptation of antique work. The statue itself is certainly Roman; the head and hands are the work of some good sculptor of the age of Arnolfo, for such soft treatment of flesh and hair cannot be earlier.

Meanwhile other sculptors of less developed art were producing works in Rome of considerable interest. In the Lateran basilica is a fragment from the chapel of S. Mary Magdalen, where the figures of Christ and of the Cardinal of Milan presented by John the Baptist, and offering the model of the chapel, are careful studies in portraiture and type, but rather labored and not rising to beauty of line and form. They are set against the same mosaic ground that has appeared in Arnolfo's work. It seems characteristic of the Roman school. Polychromy played a greater part in sculpture than was the case with any other school. First of all, the marble figures were placed usually in a colored setting and often against a mosaic background. This was brilliantly successful in Arnolfo's ciboria at S. Paolo and S. Cecilia, and in the procession of clerics at the Lateran. The color scheme is continued in the inlaid surfaces of colonnettes and slabs and in the compositions in mosaic and fresco that surmount the sarcophagi in the sepulchral monuments. But, more than this, the carving itself was strongly colored both in drapery and flesh; witness the same ciboria, the statues of Clement IV, Boniface VIII and Honorius IV. The angels' wings are solidly gilt; the details of garment-patterns, of architectural and other accessories, are minutely picked out in color. Of course a great deal of this is restoration, but probably on the original lines.

The family of Cosmatus furnished two sculptors whose work is contemporary with the last years of Arnolfo. Their names are Deodato and Giovanni, two of the four known sons of Cosmatus. Of the two, Deodato was the more subtle and able artist and fertile designer. He was the true successor of

Arnolfo. We see his hand in the reclining statue of Cardinal Pietro da Piperno († 1302) in the Lateran basilica, where the artist has mastered Arnolfo's later soft *pastoso* manner.

Deodato was also a decorator. Part of a ciborium, with his signature attached, is in the Lateran Cloister, and the superb but fragmentary papal throne from the old apse is also probably his. He did not, however, follow Arnolfo's lead in applying sculpture to ciboria, as we see by his work in S. Maria in Cosmedin.

Giovanni Cosmati. — His brother, Giovanni, was productive but not a genius. His known works are sepulchral monuments executed during the decade just before and after 1300, at the same time as Deodato's work. He signed the tombs of Cardinal Consalvo († 1299) in S. Maria Maggiore, of Cardinal dè Surdis († 1302) at S. Balbina and of Bishop Durand († 1304) at S. Maria in Aracœli. Evidently by him, though without signature, is the tomb of Cardinal Acquasparta († 1302) also in the Aracœli. The De Surdis tomb is mutilated.

Tomb of Cardinal d'Acquasparta,
S. Maria in Aracœli.
By Giovanni Cosmati.

All the others show the same type of a double base surmounted by the reclining figure, with an angel at head and foot handling the hangings that encircle the figure at back and sides. The whole is surrounded by a tabernacle, formed by a trefoil gable resting on columns or pilasters.

In these works the design is meagre and both less artistic and less monumental than that of the tombs of the previous generation. The sculpture is rather stiff and lifeless, and the transitions between planes are rather sharp and awkward both in drapery and flesh. In the monument of Cardinal de Surdis at S. Balbina (1302), Giovanni is at his best: the face is perfectly expressive of sleep and the body is really resting, not uncomfortably perched sideways. If the statue of Bishop Durand at S. Maria sopra Minerva were restored to its proper position by the removal of the stone blocks under its head, it would probably have a similar restful effect. Both give the impression of good portraits, though the handling is lacking

Figure from De Surdis Tomb at S. Balbina.
By Giovanni Cosmati.

in suppleness. The angels holding up the ends of the drapery that surrounds the cenotaph are graceful and quite a contrast to the restless angels of the De Braye tomb.

Of almost precisely the same design is the unsigned monument of Cardinal Acquasparta, and yet the figure, tipped forward according to the older type of the Hadrian V statue, and the greater realism of the face, would suggest another hand than Giovanni's — that of an older artist, were it not for the tomb of Cardinal Consalvo, the exact duplicate of Durand's, which Giovanni executed and signed in 1299, and which leaves no doubt that all these works are by the same hand. Evidently some influence was brought to bear upon Giovanni toward 1301 or 1302 which gave greater naturalness to his style.

A specialty of the Roman school were statuettes, either entirely in the round or in three-quarter relief. From the many destroyed ciboria and tombs of this period (c. 1250–1300) there were saved a number of such statuettes that are hidden away in churches, crowning doorways or perched on façades. They can be seen at S. Maria in Trastevere, S. Alessio, S. Saba, etc.

A smaller class of monument that was built on similar lines to the altar ciboria and gave some scope to the sculptor were the tabernacles or ciboria holding the Eucharist, placed ordinarily near the apse. The most graceful and well-preserved is that in S. Clemente, dated 1299, and given by Cardinal Giovanni Gaetani.

The unnatural ending of the school came with the Avignon exile. So thoroughly was it depleted that when, toward the middle of the fourteenth century and later, the Popes ordered an occasional monument or ciborium,

Tabernacle at S. Clemente.

it was found necessary to call sculptors to Rome, especially from Umbria and Tuscany. Such works as the ciborium of the Lateran, the tombs of Benedict XII († 1342) and Urban VI († 1389), and the monument of Cardinal d'Alençon at S. Maria in Trastevere, date from this period and illustrate the death of the school.

PAINTING

It is neither practical nor logical to separate, as many writers have done, the two main branches of Christian mural decoration — mosaics and wall paintings. Much as they differ in technique, they stand together in all matters important for the history of mediæval painting. Together they embody the mission of the Roman school of art as long as the Christian Church had something to teach the classes and the masses through the medium of the eye as well as the ear. Rome was the centre and source of the Western school of pictorial theology; as theological views changed, so did artistic themes vary and keep in touch with prevailing thought. That artists were not free to represent their personal fancies gave to their works the stamp of the leading minds of the Church whose ideas they embodied. Elsewhere than in Rome and its immediate circle there were innumerable variations, because the principles that governed were less clearly perceived. But in Rome and her school we may hope to surprise in their purity the pictorial forms of the mediæval West. The history of ideas and of themes must then be studied simultaneously with that of style and technique.

Use by the Church. — There is hardly a single man among the great writers and fathers of the Church who cannot be appealed to if necessary to prove the importance attributed to and the close supervision exercised on painting. S. John Chrysostom confessed the inferiority of language to art in urging the painters of Antioch to depict the acts of the martyrs. S. Jerome wrote of painting, that one can understand far better what is perceived by the eye than by the ear. The appeal to the emotions and the understanding to which these men allude is along the broadest lines, though it applies more particularly to persons of the highest education and sensibilities.

But there were other forms of appeal to other classes. The first was the combined effect of the picture and of the explanatory inscription usually placed under it, thus making the literary and pictorial arts unite in presenting a single idea. When S. Augustine delivered his famous sermon on S. Stephen in the new chapel then consecrated, he ended: "Why should I further enlarge? Read the four lines inscribed on these walls. They are here in this public place so that all may

Interior of S. Angelo in Formis.
(Showing arrangement of frescos in basilica of eleventh century.)

read; they are few so that they may be memorized by all. There is no need of a book on the matter: this apse is your book."

The explanatory lines that accompanied paintings as a rule made it therefore possible for the great middle class of moderately educated persons who could read and write to understand the scenes without help and to explain them to others.

Descending farther in the social and educational scale to the masses who could neither read nor write, a proportion of the population which increased tremendously after the sixth century, we find that the Church considered painting as making an unparalleled appeal to them. Even as early as about

400 Bishop Paulinus of Nola, in explaining why he depicted in his churches the scenes of the Old and New Testaments, the sufferings of the martyrs and the triumphant reign of Christ, says that it was for the instruction of the crowds of ignorant peasants and other poor and illiterate people who congregated in crowds to the churches on all great feasts and holidays and whose minds would thus be instructed and their religious feelings stimulated. S. Gregory, with his usual happy terseness, says, "What writing is for those who can read, painting is for the uneducated who can only look." At the other end of the Middle Ages the continuity of the Catholic tradition is confirmed by the French prelate Durand, in the thirteenth century, who says, "In churches we pay less reverence to books than to images and pictures; pictures and ornaments in churches are the teachings and scriptures of the laity." In this way painting was made to enforce its appeal on each and every class in the community from the most highly educated to the poor and illiterate.

Even the Councils of the Church took a hand in guiding the development of painting. In 692, when the old symbolic thought, so well exemplified in the art of the Catacombs, had become thoroughly obsolete and out of harmony with the more psychological trend of current theology, the Quinisext Council ordered that the old types and figures and shadows under which the truth had been presented should be superseded and that Christ should henceforth be given by artists in his human form and not in the shape of the Lamb. The second Council of Nice was held in 787 largely to decide as to the use of religious compositions and whether to stop the iconoclastic crusade against them. Painters were not held responsible for what they produced, for it says, "The composition is not an invention of the painter but a product of the legislation and tradition of the Catholic Church; . . . the art alone is the painter's; the choice and arrangement are of the fathers who build the churches."

It was the zealous defence of religious art by the Roman pontiffs that at this time turned the tide and put an end to the war against images which had almost destroyed religious art in the East, after the Emperor Leo the Isaurian had inaugurated his anti-artistic crusade in 726, decreeing the destruction of images and death or mutilation for artists who disobeyed. Characteristic documents at this time were Pope Hadrian's message to the Council through his legates, and his letter to Charlemagne at the time of the Council of Frankfort (794) in defence of the acts of the Council. He here reviews the history of painting in Rome from the time of Constantine, enumerating the principal extant works and implying that the Popes made themselves personally responsible for the paintings in the churches of Rome.

"From their time until the present," he writes, "the large churches built by Popes Sylvester, Marc and Julius have remained decorated with sacred subjects in mosaic and wall painting. The same thing was done, at the time of the second council, by S. Damasus for his own Church . . . which is still full of religious paintings. . . . Then, at the time of the third council, Pope Celestin decorated his cemeterial basilica with paintings. But especially did his successor, Pope Sixtus, when he built the basilica of S. Maria Maggiore, called *ad præsepe*, decorate it with religious compositions both in mosaic and in wall painting. . . . At the time of the fourth council . . . Pope Leo built several churches which he decorated with both mosaics and frescos. Especially did he make, in the basilica of S. Paul, and attach to it his name in verse, the great arch with its mosaic representing our Saviour Jesus Christ and the twenty-four elders." Hadrian continues, enumerating the paintings by Pope Vigilius at the Lateran, the very extensive series by Pelagius in the Church of the Apostles, etc.

The case was really stated in a nutshell, centuries before, by Pope Sixtus, when he dedicated his mosaics at S. Maria Maggiore to the Christian people in the simple inscription, *Sixtus episcopus plebi Dei*.

But painting served these purposes not merely in the old established communities, in which the great majority had long since become Christians : it was also called upon to do missionary work in new lands, to assist in converting the nations

s

that were successively brought into the fold, — Lombards, Anglo-Saxons, Germans, Bulgarians, Russians. Rome furnished the pictorial scheme, as well as the artists themselves, in the majority of the historic constructive labors out of which the Christian civilization of the North was to grow. The balance came from Byzantium.

When Gregory the Great sent S. Augustine to evangelize England he gave him model pictures — one group of which still exists. When the second and even greater evangelizing effort was made, over half a century later, under Theodore of Tarsus and Benedict Biscop, several more series of pictures were sent over, systematically grouped, for the decoration of the new churches.

We will now study the monuments historically : not without hesitation, because there has hardly yet been time to digest the mass of interesting but fragmentary wall paintings which recent discoveries force us to assign to their place in a field yet wrapped in obscurity and not yet treated adequately by any writer on the history of art.

Catacomb Frescos. — The Catacombs contain quite a number of paintings with which the principal crypts were decorated for centuries after they ceased to be used for burial. The Popes, especially Damasus, took great care to identify the tombs of the principal martyrs in the Catacombs, to mark them with monumental inscriptions and decorate the crypt in which they were with appropriate pictures. Until the ninth century the majority of the Catacombs were kept open for occasional worship and the visits of pilgrims; the basilicas built above ground, over the graves of the principal martyrs, were the centre of the cult. The graves in the Catacomb crypts were kept in good condition, guarded and continually redecorated with new wall-paintings. The main stairways were kept open for pilgrims. Thousands of names scratched on the walls and tombs attest the popularity of these shrines that encircled Rome with an added odor of sanctity. The written itineraries or reports of several of these pilgrims have been preserved and help to identify many of the monuments. Not until the Lombard and Saracen invasions of the ninth

century made it necessary to abandon all the monuments outside the walls, did the Popes cease to beautify these subterranean crypts with paintings, to be, therefore, studied side
by side with the frescos and mosaics of the basilicas and
oratories. But the bulk of the catacomb frescos of the
second, third and early fourth centuries will not be discussed, as they represent the pre-Constantinian stage that is
excluded from the scope of this handbook.

Mosaics. — In one field, at least, early Christian art can lay
a claim to distinct originality and progress beyond the attain-
ments of classic art: the field of mosaic painting. It would
seem as if classic art had not gauged its possibilities, for the
decorative vertical mosaics of fountains and lararia, such as we
see at Pompeii, are quite inferior both in technique and purely
ornamental value to the decorative wall mosaics of the early
Christian Church. What Christian art did at once, both in the
East and West, was to sublimate the art of mosaic work by
consecrating its almost imperishable technique, its wealth
of deep and brilliant color, to the service of the most sacred
themes on church walls. In doing this it took a step that
influenced the development of religious art most radically for
over a thousand years; and one of the greatest centres where
this can be studied during the whole period is Rome. These
scenes are found in every part of the principal churches; on
the exterior walls of façade and even of apse, on the interior
surface of the walls of apse, transept, triumphal arch, nave and
façade.

Some modern critics relegate mosaic painting to the domain
of the mechanical industrial arts; but they make the mistake
of applying to an earlier period a judgment which is correct
only for mosaic painting since the Renaissance. It is true
that for the last four hundred years mosaicists have contented
themselves with being mere copyists of the great masters of
oil-painting, tempera and wall-painting, and that their work has
been mechanical. But in the early Christian period and the
better part of the Middle Ages the actual execution of the
mosaics was the work, not of artisans, but of the most noted
master painters. The same men who made the preliminary

sketches and cartoons, squared off the wall surfaces, transferred the cartoons in outline to the wet plaster, and then, with the help of assistants, set in the cubes.

Constantine and the Fourth Century. — The assets of Christian painting in Rome in the fourth century, beginning with Constantine's time, are very numerous in the field of wall-painting, while the mosaics are quite scarce. But such mosaics as there are far exceed the paintings in importance because they were executed by a higher class of artists, those of the imperial school, whereas we may consider the Catacomb painters to belong more to the class of artisans, and not usually to represent the standards of the new official basilical art, but to be belated echoes of the art of preceding generations of simpler thought. The mosaics are those of the mausoleum of S. Costanza, the nave of S. Maria Maggiore, the apses of S. Rufina and of S. Pudentiana. Some of the contemporary Catacomb wall-paintings that may be compared with them are those attributable to Pope Damasus in the Catacombs of Domitilla, S. Sebastian and S. Callixtus, and the somewhat later works at SS. Marcellinus and Peter, S. Domitilla and S. Agnes.

S. Costanza. — The mosaics which originally filled S. Costanza (or S. Constantia) are typical of two phases: of the passage from decorative to didactic art, of the indefinite phase of art and culture that was non-sectarian, so that it was possible to discuss whether the art were pagan or Christian. It was typical of the border-land between the poetic imagery of the Catacombs, the historic narrative of Bible scenes, and the didactic tendencies beginning to take shape in theological forms.

The principal part of the ornamentation was that of the central dome. It was divided into twelve compartments corresponding to the number of arcades and columns below. The main scheme for dividing and framing them was by twelve picturesque caryatid figures in mosaic with raised arms, whose feet rested on rocks rising from the sea of the world that flowed uninterruptedly around the base, peopled with playful genii in boats and on shore, fishing and playing with swans and other aquatic birds. Above and between the caryatids were framed scenes of both Old and New Testament and also of Allegory, the selection being based not on historic sequence, as was later the case in the basilical series, but on symbolism and analogy, after the fashion of the Catacomb frescos and sarcophagi, with even greater resources of fancy. All this, the most significant part of the decoration of this building, was destroyed centuries ago, leaving only the more purely decorative mosaics of the annular vault.

To any one familiar with Roman imperial pavements, with the stuccoed vaults of the tombs on the Via Latina, with their

Drawing of Sixteenth Century of Lost Mosaics in Dome of S. Constantia.

architectural compartments, with the frescos in the houses and tombs of Rome and Pompeii, with the scenes on the Christian sarcophagi and in the Catacombs, it will be quite clear from what mixed sources the mosaicists of the mausoleum of Constantia derived their art. It is a matter of superficial decoration, with no attempt at pictorial illusion. There was more breadth and unity, of course, in the destroyed compositions of the central vault, but in the annular vault that forms a continuous aisle around this central section, there is, in perfect preservation, an uninterrupted line of the earliest Chris-

tian mosaics in existence, cut up into a series of eleven dis-
connected compositions, not only separately framed, but each
one sometimes subdivided into many sections.

The most interesting and the freest in design is the compartment almost entirely filled with wandering grape-vines that
spread from the four corners toward the centre where a charming youthful bust, almost a portrait, picturesquely impression-

Mosaic of Annular Vault at S. Constantia.

istic, looks down from an aureole of the grape — a spiritualized
god of the vine. For the scene is the only one to which a
meaning can be attached, a scene with unity. Among the
vines, where birds are pecking, the naked genii, such as we see
on the contemporary sarcophagus of Junius Bassus and many
others, are picking the grapes and letting down the filled
baskets. Along the edges of the scene are four-wheeled carts
drawn by two oxen, guided by a genius, carrying their load of
grapes from the vineyard. And then, under a gabled roof, sup-

ported by four piers, is the great vat in which three genii, with much gesticulation and glee, are dancing as they tread the must.

The charming freedom of the rambling vine carries one back to the fresco of the Catacomb of Domitilla, which is attributed to the second century, far more than it reminds of other works of the fourth century. This is quite paralleled by the resem-

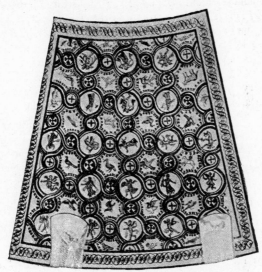

Mosaic of Annular Vault at S. Constantia.

blance of another compartment to the stuccoes of the Augustan and Flavian periods. Evidently the artist of S. Costanza was a thorough eclectic and took his motifs from any period as well as from any art. He was a good imitator.

Even more exactly a replica of the classic stucco-work is another compartment, in which the ornamental motifs are enclosed not in rows of medallions of equal size, but in a series of interlaced large medallions connected by smaller circles and with concave hexagons between them. The larger medallions each contain a figure — flying cupid, psyche or genius of some sort — while the hexagons enclose an animal or a bird and the connecting circlet has a floral pattern. There is a great deal of animation and irregularity of design to relieve the geometric patterns. A little farther in the series this design is almost duplicated, though no single detail is the same, and the greatest ingenuity is used in securing variations. In fact, there are several *quasi* repetitions of this sort, and only seven out of the eleven compartments are of perfectly distinct types.

There is no solid background in these mosaics. The patterns and figures are in color against white, so that the outlines are clear, and everything seems detached, separate, unreal, without atmosphere. The mosaicist here is not a painter: he is not even a great decorator, though technically his art is excellent, and every now and then in his side-scenes of country life and his fantastic vegetable and floral scrollwork, he shows that he can unbend and cast aside the trammels of set figures.

S. Maria Maggiore: Nave. — Of quite another caliber are the mosaics of S. Maria Maggiore. Here is something of a mystery. Both walls of the nave above the architrave have a series of oblong compositions from the Old Testament. Around the Triumphal Arch is a corresponding series from the New Testament. In the apse, beneath mediæval accretions, are remains of a further scene. Now, this series is certainly one of the brightest stars in the constellation of early Christian monuments, for its beauty, its early date and its comprehensiveness. It gives for the first time some general scheme of subjects selected by the leaders of the Church and her artists for the teaching of the masses when the somewhat desultory symbolism of the Catacombs had been abandoned for the more systematic methods of an official Church in charge of the world's spiritual welfare.

The question is complicated by curious differences of opinion among critics. According to Richter, all the mosaics belong to the second century, a revolutionary theory which will hardly find a following; the majority of critics assign them all to the time of Sixtus I in the fifth century (432–440), to whom the dedicatory inscription on the arch belongs; some of the best judges are inclined to see two periods and styles, attributing the mosaics of the triumphal arch to Sixtus I, and those of the nave to the earlier date of Pope Liberius (352–366). I feel inclined to agree with the latter critics, for reasons that affect fundamentally both the spirit and technique of these mosaics, though the fact that the inscription cuts into the feet of Peter and Paul would connect it with a restoration and give equality but not priority of date to these arch mosaics. Those of the nave are material in conception; they are far more originally impressionistic and Roman in their technique, as compared to the more clearly articulated, more orientally poetic and idealized compositions above the arch. The main difficulty in a study of these mosaics has been their distance from the ground, their small size and the confusion of their composition, so that, however we may disagree with Dr. Richter, his careful tracings and colored drawings have for the first time given us a true idea of the wonderful, in fact, unique, technique of the nave mosaics.[1] They are the only instances of true *impressionism* in mosaic painting. The cubes are of large size and of varied shapes; they are not set close together, but widely spaced in their bed, so that the artist could turn and twist them to his taste. It is extraordinary how the brilliantly gleaming eye, so characteristic of many of the figures, is produced by the juxtaposition of just two sharply contrasting mosaic cubes. Closely examined, the design seems coarse, rough, ineffective, aimless; as one draws off to a distance, everything takes shape and springs startlingly into life. For mosaics such as these the conventional long, squared sticks, chopped off into regular rectangular cubes, were quite insufficient. For the features, extremities and even draperies, there were required irregular cubes of all shapes and sizes, that had to be made for their particular places. Such work as this was as far removed as brush work from anything mechanical, and required even more artistic imagination to secure the right effect.

The compartments number twenty-eight. Those on the left are episodes taken from the stories of Abraham, Isaac, Jacob

---

[1] We may hope to know them still better when Dr. Wilpert's photographs and drawings, now being made, shall have been published.

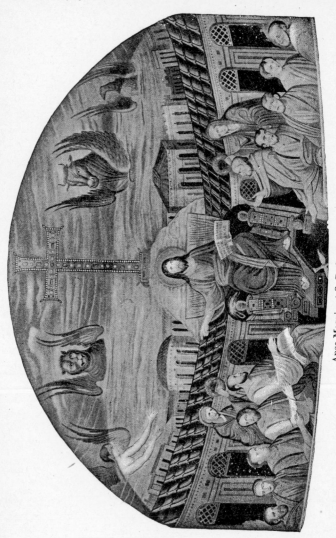

Apse Mosaic at S. Pudentiana (c. 395).

and Esau; those on the right from those of Moses and Joshua. Undoubtedly there were more in the original series, perhaps a second row. The scenes are natural and full of life and animation. It has seemed to many critics that there was a striking analogy between the battle scenes from the story of Joshua and the Roman battle scenes in the reliefs of the Columns of Trajan and Marcus Aurelius. The art is still antique in its naturalness.

S. Pudentiana. — Equally removed from the mechanical precision of S. Costanza and the impressionism and poetry of S. Maria Maggiore is the apsidal mosaic of S. Pudentiana, an example of solid sincere brush-work effect in mosaic, and of plain unimaginative Roman realism. It is the earliest and most beautiful apsidal mosaic in existence, made in the last decade of the fourth century by the priest Leopardus by order of Pope Siricius (384–399).

Mutilated as it is both above and below by Barocco vandals, the scene represents the Spiritual Church, in all its main elements, in the Heavenly Jerusalem. Christ, enthroned, surrounded by the figures of the twelve apostles, seated in a hemicycle like Roman senators, forms the exact spiritual counterpart of the scene daily enacted in the lower part of the apse of the churches, where the bishop's throne and the seats for the presbyters around the hemicycle were occupied in the same fashion by the officers of the earthly Church. The rest of the composition, in more abstract form, completes the idea. The Universal Church, in early symbolism, was formed of two main sections: the Jewish, or Church of the Circumcision, and the Gentile, or Church of the Nations. They were represented in the form of allegorical female figures in varied types that were popular in art even as late as the Gothic period. Here we see them, standing behind the row of seated apostles, placing a wreath on the head of the two who represented these two elements: S. Paul, apostle of the Gentiles, and S. Peter, the apostle of the Church of the Circumcision. Above, in the clouds, are the symbols of the four great witnesses, the evangelists, the earliest remaining examples of these emblems: the Angel, the Lion, the Ox and the Eagle. They flank the great central jewelled cross, standing on the sacred mount from which the four rivers of paradise flow. Between the upper and lower elements of this scene is an elaborate series of buildings behind a continuous arched portico, which forms the

Figure of Christ in Apsidal Mosaic of S. Pudentiana.

background and gives the artist's idea of the structures of the Heavenly Jerusalem in which the scene is laid. In the sixteenth century the two end apostles were destroyed, as well as the lower part of all the figures with whatever was below them.

To supplement this mosaic, there must have been two other scenes: a narrow band immediately below, in the hemicycle of the apse, and a composition covering the face of the apse above the hemicycle. Of the first of these, enough remains, in the Lamb of God standing on a rock, to show that here was the theme so frequent in later apses, of the twelve sheep on either side of the Lamb.

To reconstruct the destroyed scene on the face of the apse,

Apse Mosaic of S. Pudentiana (Apostles on left).

we can turn to an even earlier replica of the same scene (c. 330–360) in a church at Naples, described by its early church chronicler, where, beside the twelve seated apostles were the four greater prophets: Isaiah, with an olive crown, Jeremiah, Daniel and Ezekiel. At S. Pudentiana the prophets doubtless occupied the spandrels of the arch.

To restore the aspect of even the main scene of the seated convention of apostles we must turn to a Catacomb fresco, to the mosaic of S. Aquilino in Milan, and to some sarcophagi of about the same age, for later art and most contemporary monuments give the apostles as standing. Even so, one must beware of the enormous percentage of restoration, particularly on the right side, where the heads of all the apostles, except of Peter, seem to be largely Barocco restorations, especially those in the extreme right and left. Above, the angel of S. Matthew, on the left, is a Barocco creation, and the right lower side of the head of Christ is badly deformed.

Yet, for all these mutilations, there breathes from this mosaic a unique air of power and beauty. The realism of the heavy Roman types is redeemed by the spirituality of the Christ, and is lighted up by the glint of the sunlit gold on his throne and his garments, in those of the two Allegories of the Church, and in the buildings of the Heavenly Jerusalem, whose roofs and window traceries gleam brilliantly, while above them the clouds with their golden lining almost hide the blue sky.

The technical characteristics of this mosaic that make it preëminent in its class, are particularly the realistic solidity of the figures, with their deeply lined drapery, their varied and lifelike attitudes, their portrait-like heads. The eye sinks into the picture; it has perspective, has different planes. The artist makes of his figures more than abstract types for purposes of religious instruction: he gives them the real life that was characteristic of the simple art of the Catacombs and which was to disappear very soon from art under the influence of more abstract theoretical thought.

Something of the breadth and strength in the heads also can be understood from the almost contemporary heads of apostles in the baptistery of the cathedral at Ravenna.

Lateran Baptistery. — At about the same time the apsidal ends of the porch of the Lateran baptistery received their mosaic decoration. That on the right, dedicated to SS. Rufina e Seconda, has preserved the mosaic, and while it may at first sight appear merely decorative, it is a straight piece of symbolism suited to the place where the chrism of confirmation was administered after baptism — the promise of the new life of the Vine. The entire field is occupied by rich volutes springing from a common centre. The fan-shaped crown contains the Lamb (Christ) and four doves (the evangelists) under arches and between flowers. Beneath the vine is the world of sea and shore, as at S. Costanza, with its sportive scenes. Further symbolism in the border includes twelve crosses (Apostles) and doves at vases (water of life).

Here, as at S. Costanza, is the Catacomb art spiritualized. Technically, the work is superb, though it is badly restored. The destroyed companion scene in the opposite hemicycle represented the shepherding of the sheep of the Church.

S. Maria Maggiore: Arch and Apse. — The next work is the triumphal arch at S. Maria Maggiore, as well as the original apsidal mosaic. From a description of c. 1100 A.D. the composition in the apse must have been almost the counterpart of S. Rufina with more details: a vine with a sea scene below, with birds and animals and fishes. But on the triumphal arch we see the advent of a new art and thought derived from the Hellenic Orient.

How explain the effect, as of soft and mellow Persian carpets, in the decorative framework under the triumphal arch? Only a colorist from the East could have done it for Pope Sixtus. How explain the poetic use of oriental apocryphal legends in these same mosaics by any artist schooled in the simple symbolism and historic parallels of the Roman school?

Critics disagree as to whether any part of the present apsidal mosaic can be dated in its actual workmanship to the time of Liberius or Sixtus. I believe that all the volutes of the vine, except where they are twisted, in the lower part, away from their original lines to admit of the inserted mediæval figures, are actually part of the original mosaic. The plastic beauty and depth of color, the skilful interweaving of the birds, are indications of early date. Of the water scene below, part seems original, part mediæval reproduction in which the playful, graceful air of the scene has not been lost.

The mosaic on the face of the triumphal arch has preserved its original character far better than those of apse or nave. Its scenes are of the New Testament, partly symbolic, partly historic. In the centre, in a band above the summit of the arch, is an apocalyptic scene, the Adoration of the Throne. The throne is cushioned and jewelled, surmounted by a cross and surrounded by a double glory. Under it is the dedicatory inscription of Pope Sixtus — *Xystus Episcopus Plebi Dei.* On either side, hovering in the air, are the four Beasts or symbols of the Evangelists; and between and below them two figures holding books, two prophets or "witnesses," usually called erroneously SS. Peter and Paul. Connected theoretically with this composition, though separated materially by all the evangelical subjects, are the scenes at the very bottom of the arch on each side, representing the sacred cities of Jerusalem and Bethlehem, and below them the twelve sheep or apostles in two picturesque groups.

There are three tiers of scenes between these groups just described, interrupted by the curve of the arch. They relate to the Birth of Christ, and are more closely related to early apocryphal legends of the Infancy of Christ than any other known works of art. I. (*a*) Annunciation; (*b*) Message to Joseph; (*c*) Presentation in the Temple; (*d*) Flight into Egypt (?). II. (*a*) Adoration of the Magi; (*b*) Triumphal Reception in Egypt. III. (*a*) Murder of the Innocents; (*b*) The Magi before Herod. In these scenes the presence of many angels as attendants is a Hellenic trait. In this unique way of treating the Annunciation, the Virgin is enthroned between angels, while Gabriel hovers above. The scene of the angel bringing the message to Joseph is also unusual. The Adoration of the Magi is lifted above the commonplace by the fact that the Child is not held, but sits alone on an immense throne behind which four angels stand, while on either side are seated the attendant symbolic figures of the two Churches, — of the Circumcision and the Gentiles. The next scene is supposed to be from one of the apocryphal narratives of the Infancy of Christ (pseudo-Matthew) and to represent one of the kinglets of Egypt issuing forth to do homage to the Child. The art of these mosaics seems to vary from those of the nave in the richer tonality of the coloring, in a lesser amount of impressionistic handling, and a greater precision in the composition; though these differences must not be unduly emphasized.

S. Sabina. — Not many years after, the church of S. Sabina received a superb mosaic decoration, of which the little that remains is quite closely connected with part of the scene at S. Pudentiana, as it consists of the two allegorical figures we

The Church of the Circumcision, Mosaic at S. Sabina.
(Early fifth century.)

have already seen there and at S. Maria Maggiore, which are clearly identified at S. Sabina by inscriptions as *Ecclesia ex Circumcisione* and *Ecclesia ex Gentibus*. As at S. Pudentiana, these figures are each associated with a prince of the apostles,

T

S. Peter being placed above the one, S. Paul above the other. If we compare the same figures in the two mosaics, it would appear as if a quarter of a century had led to some decrease of realistic ability. The female figures at S. Sabina still have the grave and stately matronly type; but their coloring is not only deeper, but more monotonous, unrelieved by high lights, and the effect is flatter and less rounded. This scene was placed on the inside wall of the façade of the church and was completed above by the Christ and the symbols of the four evangelists. Originally it was a small part of a general mosaic ornamentation that covered the apse, the triumphal arch, and perhaps the walls of the nave, as at S. Maria Maggiore.

S. Paul. — The original mosaic of the triumphal arch at S. Paul followed closely after S. Sabina. It was famous in Church annals, being praised by Pope Hadrian in his letter to Charlemagne. In the centre is the half-figure of Christ in a luminous circle, like a rainbow, and with a nimbus radiating long rays of light, according to the description in Revelation. Above, on either side, are the four symbols of the Evangelists, the Beasts of Revelation. Near the lower part of Christ's aureole are two angels. Farther off, on both sides, are the twenty-four Elders. In the lower part of the pendentives are the figures of the princes of the apostles: Paul on the right, Peter on the left. This mosaic is entirely modern and is valuable merely as preserving the design of the original, badly damaged in the fire of 1823. The mistake of regarding it as genuine is common in handbooks of art history. The hard, flat, severe head of Christ on the arch at S. Paul is often used as giving the type of the fifth-century Christ — which is distinctly a libel on the century and as far as possible from the truth. The Christ of the fifth and sixth centuries is far from ascetic: works that retain the actual handiwork of the time show softness, *morbidezza* of handling, mildness of expression; the type, in fact, of the so-called Veronica head.

Lateran Baptistery. — The continuation of the symbolic semi-decorative style even after the middle of the fifth century is illustrated by the little mosaic in the chapel of S. John the Evangelist added to the Lateran Baptistery by Pope Hilary.

This groin vault has a very schematic decoration on a gold ground. The centre is occupied by the Lamb within a rich wreath of flowers, which is itself enclosed in an ornamental square frame. From the corners and centres of this radiate

Figure of Christ in Apsidal Mosaic of SS. Cosma e Damiano.

frame-like ornamental bands and triple candelabra forming eight compartments and intersected by four large garlands of flowers festooned from the central frame; the flowers represent the four seasons.

In each of the eight compartments is a similar group of a

central vase full of fruit and on either side a bird pointed toward it. Each of the four sections of the vault has a particular kind of bird — of which there are four. They are: ducks, partridges, doves, parrots. These birds are supposed to symbolize the four elements: water, earth, air and fire. Some decoration remains in two lunettes.

Had the two apsidal mosaics of S. Andrea in Catabarbara (c. 471) and S. Agata in Suburra (c. 461) been preserved we should

Painted Decoration of House of John and Paul (SS. Giovanni e Paolo).

undoubtedly have found in them the connecting links between S. Pudentiana and SS. Cosma e Damiano — strong-featured, heavily modelled, realistic apostles, richly shadowed in flesh and drapery. The names were attached to each apostle at S. Agata and with their loss we have missed the chance of seeing what the earlier Western tradition held to be the type of each one.

SS. Cosma e Damiano. — It was under Felix IV (526–530) that the apse of SS. Cosma e Damiano received its mosaic (ill. on p. 73). The theme is that of the typical apsidal mosaic of the

Roman school: on the face of the apse the apocalyptic scene of the Lamb, the Angels and the twenty-four Elders and, in the semi-dome, Christ, Peter, and Paul, Cosmas and Damian, Theodore and Pope Felix; while below are the Lamb and the twelve sheep. Compared with earlier treatments of the same scene, such as S. Pudentiana, there is here an elimination of all accessories, such as the buildings of the Heavenly Jerusalem. This step had already been taken in the fifth century. But, further, the figure of Christ does not stand on the solid level on which the saints are placed, but in the midst of clouds on a higher plane. Here and in the angels above we trace the Orient, but in the heavy types of the heads rather

Orante, Fresco in House of John and Paul.

a modification of antique Roman by the Gothic art of Ravenna. The substitution here of the statuesque for the early pictorial type has been noticed by keen critics as an important innovation, and this mosaic has also the glory of being the prototype of subsequent Roman compositions for over five centuries.

Frescos: House of John and Paul. — The frescos that belong to the same century and a half as all these mosaics throw an interesting side-light.

The series may be opened with the most remarkable frescos outside of the Catacombs, those in the house of John and Paul on the Cœlian, turned into a church by Pammachius in c. 400. Several rooms, preserved below the present church, have a decoration sometimes religious in character, sometimes purely decorative. The most beautiful is a series of wreath-carrying figures encircling one room, so beautiful as to make an earlier date probable. In another room the orante is more highly finished and lifelike than any in the Catacombs. But most remarkable if not as beautiful is the scene of martyrdom in the chapel improvised in the very room of the house where the saints were killed — John, Paul and their friend Gorgonius. We see one of them on his knees, his eyes bandaged, while the executioner stands back to swing the sword to his neck. The other martyrs stand waiting in the background. It is a unique scene, painted shortly after the event.

S. Felicitas, etc. — To the fifth century belongs the apsidal fresco of the chapel of S. Felicitas, with this martyr in large size surrounded by her sons. It is illustrated on p. 56. It helps to bridge the distance between the easy familiar art of the catacombs and that of the basilicas. The composition of Christ surrounded by saints and the two apostles is repeated in the catacombs: twice, for instance, in the cemetery of S. Maria della Stella at Albano, in the pure Roman style of the fifth century. The three broadly treated saints (Policamus, Sebastian, Quirinus) in the cubiculum of S. Cecilia at S. Callixtus, in graceful tunic and pallium, are about contemporary with Sixtus III (432–440).

Perhaps even earlier and decidedly more interesting is a composition in the main crypt of the cemetery of SS. Peter and Marcellinus. It is a fresco with large figures in two tiers. In the upper and larger tier is Christ enthroned; on his right S. Paul and on his left S. Peter, neither with any emblem or nimbus. In the lower tier the Lamb is in the centre with cruciform nimbus, the Constantinian monogram and A–Ω, on the mount from which flow the four rivers. Two saints on either side are acclaiming the Lamb with raised arm as they approach. They are inscribed; on the right Petrus and Gorgonius and on the left Marcellinus and Tiburtius. These saints were buried in the crypt.

Papal Portraits. — A decided novelty, however, is the series of portraits of the popes in medallions, which were originally placed in a row above the arcades of the nave at S. Paul. These portraits were added to at different periods. The first series seems to have been painted either in the time of Pope Leo the Great (440–465) or in the time of the Antipope Laurentius (501–505). Those that were saved from the fire of 1823 were detached and can be studied in the gallery. About fifteen years ago I had a series of photographs made. The earlier heads, while in no sense exact portraits, are excellent examples of the treatment of artists of the fifth century, with broad effects of light and shade, easy transitions in planes, and without the heaviness that soon appears at SS. Cosma e Damiano. The latter have the ascetic type and linear technique of the eighth century.

Commodilla. — The principal painting among those recently discovered at the Catacombs of Commodilla confirms, by its style, the attribution to John I (523–526) which may be inferred from the text of the *Liber Pontificalis*, for it stands midway between the mosaics of the time of Theodoric and those of Justinian at Ravenna. Christ, youthful and beardless, is seated on a globe, the exact counterpart in type and position of the Christ in the apse of S. Vitale at Ravenna (c. 530–540). On the right is S. Peter, on the left S. Paul, and beyond, on either side, the martyrs to whom the chapel is dedicated, SS. Felix and Adauctus. These four figures do not stand facing the audience, but are looking toward Christ and moving toward him with that bending rush so characteristic of the Magi approaching the Infant Christ in S. Apollinare Nuovo at Ravenna (c. 540). Framing the scene at either end, but not strictly part of it, are two other saints, Emerita, who was also buried here and shared the local honors with Felix and Adauctus, and Stephen. These two figures are immobile and face the spectator ; yet they are not lifeless, ascetic and attenuated as such figures became in the following seventh century, but stand in graceful dignity, like youthful oranti, or like Theodoric's prophets between the win-

Mosaic on Triumphal Arch, S. Lorenzo.

dows at S. Apollinare, or some of the figures in the galleries at S. Vitale. In every fibre they breathe the air of Ravenna in its most Hellenic proto-Byzantinism.

Other paintings in the same crypt are in the same style, but may be later, especially the single figure of S. Luke, which seems to be dated in the seventh century by the inscription *sub tempora Constantini Augusti nostri*, probably Constantine Pogonatus.

Another large painting in this crypt is a votive picture over the tomb of a lady named "Turtura." Here the Virgin and Child are enthroned in the centre, with the young Felix on the right and the old bearded Adauctus on the left, who is presenting the woman in rich dark robes whose tomb was below. In all these works the technique is quite distinct from the thin sketchy work of the catacomb frescos heretofore. The rich solidity of the coloring shows the reaction of mosaics on fresco painting. It is not a development, however, of the Roman school. Technique, style, composition — all are an importation from Ravenna.

The Gothic wars now come to interrupt the course of artistic events, and the rest of the sixth century is comparatively barren, unless we place here the earliest frescos at S. Maria Antiqua and S. Saba. But while Rome suffered almost complete artistic eclipse, Ravenna continued to flourish artistically, so that it is not surprising to find that the next products of the art in Rome are somewhat ineffective echoes of Ravenna; ineffective, because the school of Ravenna was itself declining.

Mosaics: S. Lorenzo and S. Teodoro. — Pope Pelagius (578–590) placed a mosaic on the face of the triumphal arch of the older basilica of S. Lorenzo (*ad corpus*) when he enlarged the Church. Christ is seated on the globe of the world, blessing with his right and holding the long cross in his left. On either side are three figures, each with his name inscribed above his head. On the right of Christ, S. Peter with cross and keys and S. Lawrence with cross and open book, presenting Pope Pelagius (who carries a model of the basilica *ad corpus*). On the left of Christ, S. Paul with two scrolls, S. Stephen with open book and S. Hippolytus carrying his martyr's crown. Under two highly decorated windows, which frame the composition at either end, are the two sacred cities, Jerusalem and Bethlehem, in the pendentives. SS. Stephen and Hippolytus were introduced because their bodies were buried in this church, as well as that of the titular saint, Lawrence. Nearly the whole of the body of Pelagius is modern, also unimportant parts of SS. Lawrence and Hippolytus.

Earmarks of the Byzantine traditions of Ravenna are the seating of Christ on the globe and the placing of S. Peter on the right instead of the left side of Christ. In the interesting and necessarily theological discussion as to the meaning of the position of the apostles, in which Catholic critics show a somewhat natural susceptibility, it appears not to have been noticed that the constant and invariable Roman tradition from the fourth to the thirteenth century places S. Peter on Christ's left side, while the Byzantine tradition, with equal persistency, places him on Christ's right side. In several cases the position on the right is sufficient to prove Byzantine influence.

Perhaps a little later is the semi-dome of the little circular church of S. Teodoro, where the presence of S. Paul on the right of Christ shows that Roman tradition was beginning to reassert itself, though the seating of Christ on the globe is a sign of the imitation of Ravenna models. The restoration of it in the fifteenth century under Nicholas V was so fundamental as almost to obliterate the original style.

Increased Influence of Ravenna and Constantinople. — When Pope Pelagius and his successors set about their work of artistic restoration of the city, their problem was extremely difficult, almost insoluble. We have seen how pitifully they failed in architecture. The situation was perhaps not so desperate in the field of painting. But certainly Rome herself had not preserved any painters or mosaicists. Once more we must believe that she turned to Ravenna, where art had continued its uninterrupted course, though beginning a decline that was to become a landslide in the second part of the seventh century. But now, before the close of the sixth century, mosaic and wall painting were still cultivated with at least sufficient vigor to account for the source of the works produced in Rome. In fact, no other origin seems possible, as we must exclude a direct influence from Constantinople, and no other city in Italy then possessed an important school of art. There is one possible exception. The great church of the Apostles, built with the aid of the Byzantine general Narses himself, was decorated with a series of mosaics mentioned by Pope Hadrian. In a work that was a sort of consecration of the Byzantine triumph it is possible that Constantinople furnished the artists; we cannot say. But certainly the mosaics at S. Lorenzo and S. Teodoro cannot be attributed to artists from the capital. They combine the traditions of Ravenna and Rome. To Ravenna belongs the type of Christ seated on the globe of the world instead of enthroned or standing in the

clouds.   Foreign to Roman tradition is the placing of S. Paul
on the left instead of the right of Christ, and the placing of a
cross in the hands of Christ and S. Peter.   While the technique
of these works is still excellent, the figures have no life or
substance; they are flat and expressionless manikins.

It seems to have been quite different in the field of wall-
painting.   We are forced to attribute to the period shortly
before or after 600 a number of the recently discovered
frescos at S. Maria Antiqua and S. Saba, and to find in them
the charm and beauty of a masterly art.   In fact with the
opening of the seventh century the invasion of the field of
fresco painting by Byzantine art becomes most pronounced.
So much so that it is not easy to say whether the thread of
Roman tradition was not altogether broken.   There has been
until now an entire misconception of the character of painting
during this century because the judgment of critics was based
on mosaics, which were then undeniably stiff and lifeless.
But, thanks to recent discoveries, it appears that the contemporary painters possessed far greater suppleness and life.

S. Agnese and S. Venanzio. — But, to begin with the better
known mosaics.   These are : the semi-domes of S. Agnese and
of S. Stefano Rotondo; the apse of S. Venanzio; the altar-piece
at S. Pietro in Vincoli.

At S. Agnese only the hemicycle of the apse is preserved,
dating from Honorius I (625–638).   It contains but three
figures, standing stiffly against a gold ground.   In the centre
S. Agnes, in rich court costume, diadem and jewelled pectoral,
is flanked by the figures of two Popes, one holding the model
of the basilica (Honorius I ?), the other, with modern head
and holding a book (Sylvester or Symmachus).   Though there
is not much relief to the figures, the stiff costume of S. Agnes
has led to a somewhat unfair estimate of the painting of this
period, and of Byzantine art in general.

Any rich and heavy costume that conceals the figure is apt
to be called Byzantine and as proving the influence of Byzantine art, commencing with this S. Agnes in her apse, and
continuing until the revival of the thirteenth century.
Nothing could be more fallacious.   The courtly and ecclesias-

tical costumes since the time of Constantine had taken on that richness, whether in East or West, and, later, the use even of specifically Eastern styles does not prove that Byzantine art was the cause, but rather that, as we know it to have been a fact in the Rome of the seventh and eighth centuries and in the Venice of the tenth and eleventh centuries, Byzantine costume

Mosaics of Chapel S. Venanzio (left side), Lateran.

prevailed among the wealthy and upper classes, and this style was, therefore, not foreign but national and naturally reproduced by native artists from life.

In the same fashion that all such heavy and bejewelled costumes have been foisted upon Byzantine art, it has been supposed that this art had lost the ability to use simple classic draperies. So that when such draperies are found in the Roman frescos or elsewhere, they are adduced as a return to early Christian models, as a proof of the absence of Byzantine influence. A study of Byzantine illuminations — where larger works fail us — show on the contrary that the mastery of classic Greek and Roman drapery remained an undying heritage in the Orient, even when eclipsed in the West. For figures of ideal character, except in the case of warrior saints and the like, for apostles and prophets and even for the common multitudes in many biblical scenes, the costume was thoroughly antique. This is of incalculable influence over the form of artistic expression.

In another mosaic of this time, that of S. Venanzio, the prevalence of figures of saints in ecclesiastical costume gives a general effect of stiffness that is contradicted by the Christ and angels in the upper part of the composition. Pope John IV (640–642) began and Pope Theodore (642–649) completed this decoration of S. Venanzio.

In the upper part of the semi-dome a half-figure of Christ emerges from clouds and blesses in Greek fashion. On either side, also half-hidden in clouds, is an adoring angel. Below, representing the Church on earth, is the Virgin in the centre as *orans*, with arms raised. On her right, S. Paul, John the Evangelist, S. Venantius and Pope John IV, founder of the oratory. He carries the model; all the rest books. On the left are S. Peter and John the Baptist with the crosses, S. Domnio of Salona in Dalmatia whence came the relics of the saints for which the oratory was built, and finally Pope Theodore, who completed the decoration of the chapel. At the base is the dedicatory inscription in two lines.

The decoration of the face of the arch is in two tiers. .The upper tier is broken by three windows which interfered, undoubtedly, with the completeness of the theme. On either side of the central window (where the Lamb, the Cross or the bust of Christ should have been) are the symbols of the evangelists. Beyond the two other windows are the two sacred cities. The lower tier consists of eight figures — four in each spandrel representing the principal martyrs and saints of Istria and Dalmatia whose relics were brought here by Pope John IV. They are, beginning on our left, SS. Paulinianus, Telius, Asterius, Anastasius, Maurus, Septimius, Antiochianus, Gaianus. The principal and titular saint, Venantius, had already been represented in the apse itself. Each figure is inscribed above its head. This is a work not without character and life. The court costume of some of the saints gives some relief from the stiffer ecclesiastical robes of the bishops and deacons; and there is some attempt at relief and shading, especially in the whites. It is the best mosaic of the century.

To the same Pope Theodore is due a much weaker and badly restored apsidal mosaic at S. Stefano Rotondo. In the centre a jewelled cross stands in the garden of Paradise. On its summit rests a medallion enclosing the bust of Christ, above which, within a starry firmament, is the hand of the Father, holding the wreath. A saint stands on either side, identified by his inscribed name; S. Primus on the right and S. Felicianus on the left of Christ. The restorations are very considerable, but not sufficient to undermine the general character and soft coloring, which is not nearly as abounding in contrasts of light and shade as S. Venanzio.

At S. Pietro in Vincoli the single figure of S. Sebastian formed an ancient altar-piece, probably erected in 680 by Pope Agatho at the time of the plague. The saint is a middle-aged, bearded man in the military costume of short tunic and chlamys, that prevailed in Constantinople at this time. The type is the absolute opposite of the effeminate youth popularized by the Renaissance.

With this work the series of seventh-century mosaics closes.

Pope John VII. — At the opening of the eighth century only a few fragments show the style of a precious series of mosaics at the Vatican basilica in the chapel of the Virgin erected by Pope John VII. They strike a new note; new in technique, in composition, in ideas. There is nothing like them before or after. They are a stray visitor from the Orient.

Though merely the decoration of a chapel these mosaics formed an elaborate series. On the outside façade were eight scenes from the life of S. Peter, mostly from apocryphal sources, beginning with his preaching in Jerusalem and ending with his martyrdom. Inside the chapel was a series from the life of Christ. Though there are but seven framed compartments, the subjects are sixteen. Two, three and even four scenes are picturesquely thrown together in a manner that we are apt to associate only with such Renaissance artists as Ghiberti in his bronze gates or Botticelli in his Sistine frescos. The themes begin with the Annunciation and Visitation and end with the Crucifixion and Descent into Limbo. On a larger scale, framed by these scenes on both sides, is the Virgin as *orans*, to whom the Pope is offering the chapel.

Of the apse mosaic, where the Virgin and Child were flanked by Peter and Paul, nothing remains; but the colossal Virgin as *orans* is in S. Marco at Florence, the Adoration of the Magi (part) at S. Maria in Cosmedin, and smaller fragments in the Vatican crypts, the Lateran Museum and at Orte.

The color scheme is very light and unusual, with a predominance of whites, yellows and greens. The effect is flat, coarse when examined closely, but unconventional and at a distance picturesque and effective. The white draperies are lined with thin blue shadows, the flesh has red shadows. It is a return, in another way, to an impressionism corresponding to that of S. Maria Maggiore's nave. There is a movement and variety of pose quite different from the statuesque front-view method of the rest of Roman mosaics; profiles and three-quarter views are not avoided. The most interesting of the themes is the Crucifixion, which here appears for the first time in an official and dated Roman monument, though that painted in the catacomb of S. Valentinus is probably earlier (642–649).

Frescos of the Seventh Century and of John VII. — But before proceeding further we must review the works of fresco-painting for the century and a half between the mosaic of Pelagius II at S. Lorenzo (578–590) and that of John VII (705–707) at S. Peter.

Aside from the frescos in the Catacomb of Commodilla, already described, there is a fresco in that of Pontianus, which is of about the time of the mosaics of S. Venanzio (c. 625–650), and illustrates the greater suppleness of fresco technique. In a composition with five figures, Christ, as a half-figure, appears above on the clouds, with cruciform nimbus. He is crowning, with far-extended arms, S. Abdon on his right and S. Sennen on his left. These noble Persian martyrs wear their national costume — a hooded (pileus) short mantle fastened in front over a short fringed tunic and anaxarydes which leave the legs entirely exposed. Further on the right is S. Milix in short tunic and chlamys fastened on the right shoulder. The corresponding figure on the left is S. Vincent in ecclesiastical costume. Both these saints have their arms extended in the attitude of *oranti*, while the Persian martyrs are pointing toward Christ. The site is marked as Paradise by the flowers.

Head from Apse of Lower Church, S. Saba.
(Sixth to seventh centuries.)

Of the same period is a scene in the baptistery. It is the Baptism of Christ, who stands in the Jordan up to his waist. His head has the nimbus, and to it, through clouds, descends the dove of the Holy Ghost; over the right bank a ministering angel hovers, holding Christ's garments, and in front a stag is drinking. On the left bank stands John the Baptist in a scanty skin garment, carrying a crook and leaning forward to lay his hand on Christ's head. There are here also two famous portrait-busts of Christ. The first, at the foot of the main stairway, with simple cruciform nimbus, broad and oval face with short beard and low-growing hair; the second, with jewelled cruciform nimbus, heavy long hair and chin-beard. The former is earlier and better; the latter is debased and crude.

In the cemetery of Callixtus a figure of S. Cecilia, as an orans, with arms extended, painted in the crypt sacred to her, is interesting to compare with the figure of S. Agnes in that saint's basilica, of about the same time. S. Cecilia is in rich jewelled costume, embroidered with lines of pearls and with heavy bracelets, her head decorated with a nimbus and a pearl frontlet.

The finest fresco of the time in a Catacomb, and a good Byzantine work of the early seventh century, is one in the cubiculum of the four saints in the cemetery of Generosa, where Christ is surrounded by four martyrs carrying their crowns and in typical Byzantine costume, SS. Simplicius and Viatrix on his right and SS. Faustinianus and Rufinianus on his left.

There was certainly a continuous interaction between the two arts during this period.

Saint from Apse of Lower Church, S. Saba.
(Sixth to seventh centuries.)

The mosaicists of John VII borrowed from wall-painting their light tones and sketchiness. In turn the heavy outlines which they were obliged to use in consequence in order to accentuate their rather substanceless figures, were afterward adopted by the painters themselves when they became, in the following century, unable to handle softly graded body colors. The later works at S. Saba show this, especially the group of heads of

U

Oriental eremites. At the same time the advantage is entirely with the fresco-painter.

For a real understanding of the possibilities of fresco-painting at this time we must study those at S. Saba and S. Maria Antiqua.

Frescos of S. Saba. — The primitive small single-naved church attached to the Greek monastery of S. Saba on the Aventine has been recently unearthed in its lower part, under the

Greek Eremites in Fresco of Lower Church, S. Saba.
(Seventh to eighth centuries.)

larger basilica of the twelfth century. Injured, probably, by the fire of Robert Guiscard, it was demolished to within less than two metres of its pavement, this space filled with dirt and the new church built on the higher level. Its walls were entirely covered with frescos. There appear not to be as many successive strata as we shall find at S. Maria Antiqua, though all the scenes were not painted at the same time — those in and near the apse being the earlier and a second stratum being evident in parts. The eighteen large figures of saints occupying the lower part of the circuit of the apse, after the fashion of S. Venanzio, with their purity and sureness of outline, and the early classic Byzantinism of their physiognomy, seem by the same early hand as the exquisite head of Christ with its softly graded flesh tints and its round contours. The eyes are open and mild, the mouth is sweet and rather small, with full lips. These are traits impossible much after c. 600 in Italy, so that we must suppose an early colony of Greek monks to have decorated the church just before or after that date. Perhaps the group of heads of Eastern monks, with their ungraded flat surfaces and broad brushwork, belongs to some cruder, more sketchy compositions of the seventh or early eighth century. There are also some small-sized scenes which correspond perfectly with the frescos of John VII at S. Maria Antiqua and were, with these, the prototypes of later similar scenes of the eighth century in the older S. Clemente, by the hand of inferior native Roman imitators. This miniature series is from the life of Christ.

Head of Christ, S. Saba.
(Sixth to seventh centuries.)

There can be no doubt in the mind of an unprejudiced student that these frescos are all by Byzantine artists, probably by Greek monks of the monastery itself, such as the *Martinus Monachus mag(ister)*, who is represented on the left wall.

Frescos of S. Maria Antiqua. — Although the church of S. Maria Antiqua in the Forum was a far more important building than S. Saba, none of its frescos are quite equal to the earliest there, except a few fragments of the two earliest strata, especially the head of an angel, among those that are in adoration of the enthroned Virgin and Child. This three-quarter head is of the same beautiful early Byzantine type as the famous archangel of the British Museum diptych (c. 500), and gives a high idea of what these first frescos at S. Maria Antiqua may have been.

When the Library of the temple of Augustus, between the Palatine and the Forum, was transformed, toward the close of

Miracles of Christ: Frescos in Lower Church of S. Saba.
(Seventh century.)

the sixth century, into a Christian church under the name of S. Maria Antiqua, it received a wall decoration in fresco which was supplemented and renewed at short intervals during the following two centuries, especially under Popes Martin I (649–653), John VII (705–708), Paul I (757–767) and Hadrian I (772–793). As the church was abandoned under Leo IV (845–850) none of its frescos can be later.

There is a general scheme of decoration. The left-hand wall was covered with scenes from the Old, the right wall with those of the New Testament. Both series overflow into the presbytery and choir-screen. This is supplemented by others in the two rooms on either side of the apse, by those in the apse and adjacent presbytery walls, and finally the others near the entrance to the church in the Chapel of the Forty Martyrs. The history of fresco-painting in Rome during the two centuries, between the age of Justinian and that of Charlemagne, is epitomized in this one building. It represents official Roman art because the church was the Papal chapel and John VII established his residence in a palace next to it, and the frescos bear evidence of being official attempts to glorify the Papacy and its policy.

The apse best illustrates the history of this pictorial decoration. When the building was first turned into a chapel, it was not provided with an apse. At this time it received the first stratum of frescos. To this belongs a bejewelled Madonna, with adoring angels, of the Odegetria type. When the apse was cut, this stratum was overlaid by another and the same scene was repeated; the head of one of the adoring angels is the masterpiece already referred to. As this second stratum is connected with Pope Martin I (649–653), it may be supposed that the earlier stratum is not later than the time of Gregory the Great, just before or after 600, and may well be even earlier. After another half-century the church was again enlarged, and Pope John VII (705–708) superposed a third series in which the former theme was concealed by a row of single figures of saints with their names, among which are Gregory Nazianzen and Basil. Christ flanked by tetramorphs filled the semi-dome. Other fragments of the second stratum represent Church fathers with names and inscribed scrolls. The apostles are also placed as busts in medallions. The entire presbytery was devoted to the Life of Christ culminating in the Crucifixion.

With each renovation the frescos appear to have spread further from the apse and presbytery, and, under John VII, to have covered the walls of the nave. With few exceptions all the inscriptions of these three earlier strata are in Greek, and this confirms the stylistic evidence of the paintings themselves.

The scheme of the decoration was to place the scenes from the Old Testament on the left, as one faces the apse; the New Testament scene on the right, not only on the walls of the nave, but on the piers at the entrance to the presbytery. The New Testament scenes are less thoroughly destroyed. The Annunciation, in its repetition of the scene on two strata, shows the two periods (John VII and Paul I ?). Other subjects are Judith with the head of Holophernes and the Mother of the Maccabees with her seven sons, which are extremely effective.

The original arrangement appears almost perfectly in the left side-aisle. Below is a tasteful dado painted to imitate a rich hanging. Then, a line of large figures, three-quarter size. Here the scene is Christ enthroned with nine Greek saints and Church fathers on his left and eleven Latin saints and fathers on his right. All the names are in Greek, so this picture is not later than John VII. Above this are two rows of oblong compositions with Old Testament scenes. The upper row began with the Creation, and ended with the Flood. The lower row are from the stories of Jacob and Joseph. The different style and the Latin inscriptions show that these rows are a little later than John VII, probably as late as Zachariah and Paul I. The heavier outlines and lack of moulded shadows betray an artist inferior to the author of the other Old Testament scenes at the entrance to the presbytery, such as the scene of King Hezechiah and Isaiah.

The best preserved scenes of the New Testament are inside the presbytery. The Adoration of the Magi recalls the scene at Ravenna in the mosaic at S. Apollinare and the tomb of the Exarch Isaac. An unusual scene is the Carrying of the Cross by Simon of Cyrene, — a scene which leads up to the great Crucifixion in the centre. Another one is S. Anne enthroned, holding the Virgin as a child.

In studying these series of Bible history on so small a scale, framed in their decorative patterns, one is reminded of the theory that such series originated in the early illuminated Bibles.

S. Valentinus. — To confirm the date of these frescos of S. Maria Antiqua and S. Saba, and their Greek origin, come the frescos of a crypt in the cemetery of S. Valentinus, which have been proved to belong to the time of Pope Theodore (642–648). The style is crude in comparison. The artist is not an originator, but a native copyist. The series is in four parts. Its condition is almost too bad to allow of criticism. Its importance, however, is increased by the fact that its Crucifixion scene is probably the earliest known.

In the Crucifixion Christ is robed in the long sleeveless colobium; his feet rest, side by side, on the *suppedaneum.* His eyes are wide open. Above his nimbed head is the title *Jesus. Rex. Iudeorum.* On either side are the sun and moon. Below, on the right, the Virgin; on the left, S. John, holding a book. There also are single figures of S. Lawrence, and of another martyr, per-

The Crucifixion, Fresco at S. Maria Antiqua.

haps S. Valentinus, and a scene of the Virgin holding the Child straight in front in the centre, in the position of the sacred pictures of Constantinople such as the Odegetria. Finally there are three episodes in the life of the Virgin. (*a*) The Visitation; (*b*) the washing of the Child; (*c*) the miraculous cure of the incredulous midwife (apocryphal legends). These frescos at S. Valentino presuppose the earliest at S. Saba and S. Maria.

I will add here another example of the Crucifixion, in the

house of SS. John and Paul under their church, of similar type
to both the Crucifixions just described.

Mosaics and Frescos of the Eighth Century. — To return,
now, to mosaic-painting, there is a gap in the continuity of
existing mosaics in Rome between those of the first decade
of the eighth century and those of c. 800, when the face
of the apse of SS. Nereo ed Achilleo was done by the

Apsidal Mosaic of SS. Nereo ed Achilleo (c. 800).

hand of Greek artists under Leo III (795–816). The semi-
dome of the apse was decorated, of course, at the same time,
but has not survived. The composition consists of three
scenes, not at all germane to the Roman tradition, but belonging to Byzantine art. In the centre is the Transfiguration.
Christ in an oval aureole is robed in pallium and white tunic
trimmed with purple and gold. Outside the aureole, on the
mountain, stand Moses and Elias, while below them kneel,
on the right Peter and on the left John and James, who veil
themselves from the glory. All are in white. At the right
end is the Annunciation, in which the Angel approaches the

seated Virgin, who has laid aside her spinning. At the left end are the Virgin and Child adored by an angel, in the attitude of the famous miraculous "Theotocos" (Mother of God), — pictures so popular after the Council of Ephesus.

The principal part of the mosaic, that on the semidome of the apse, was destroyed during the Renaissance, but it is known to have included, in the centre, a large cross in front of a large pavilion, while sheep are approaching on both sides. This is merely a symbolic representation of the same theme — the Transfiguration. Compare the Transfiguration in the apse of S. Apollinare in Classe at Ravenna.

The mosaic of the Mission of the Apostles and the scene with Leo III and Charlemagne from the Lateran triclinium hardly requires mention, as it is merely a Renaissance reproduction.

Before describing the mosaics of Pope Paschal I and his successors later in the ninth century, the frescos painted between c. 710 and 816 must be studied.

The eighth century saw no abating in the activity of Roman painters. Gregory III (731–741) in particular, the opponent of the Iconoclasts, patronized them, and his letter on the subjects painted in Roman churches shows his intelligent interest. Under Zacharias the frescos of S. Maria Antiqua were supplemented by new ones in the chapel of Quiricus and Julitta, which are in especially good condition. They have recently been ascribed in part to an earlier date, and to have been merely supplemented and restored by Zacharias. The apsidal niche has the best-preserved early Crucifixion scene in existence. The figure of Christ occupies nearly the entire width; beneath the arms of the cross are the Virgin and S. John; between them and Christ are Longinus, piercing His side, and a second soldier with sponge and vinegar. Above are the sun and moon. In the background is a rocky landscape on the right. A peculiarity is the classification of individual figures by their size, which corresponds to their relative importance. Here there are three very distinct categories. Christ is of the usual early type with wide-open eyes, without any trace of suffering or weakness, as He seems to rest against the Cross, not to hang from it. The long blue *colobium* covers Him entirely in soft fine folds. In the figures of the Virgin and S. John we see no longer the Hellenic beauty so clear in the works of the previous century; and the type of the two soldiers, lank and awkward, is one that will continue in Rome until the eleventh century and be repeated at S. Urbano alla Caffarella and S. Paul (Martirologio Chapel).

Underneath is a line of figures centred around the enthroned Virgin and Child. SS. Peter and Paul stand on either side. Beyond them are the persons to whom the chapel is dedicated, SS. Quiricus and Julitta, and at the ends Pope Zacharias and the donor Theodotus, uncle of Pope Hadrian. They have the square nimbus, showing them to have been living. These two heads were added over those of the original donors. Each figure is inscribed. A long inscription identifies Theodotus: *Theodotus primicerio defensorum et dispensatore sanctæ Dei genetricis semperque Virginis Mariæ quæ appellatur Antiqua.* It is this inscription which made the identification of this church certain.

The history of the two titular martyrs is developed on the side-walls in eight compositions, which are described in Latin inscriptions and are among the most precious and earliest of preserved lives of the saints. The scenes relate to the trial and martyrdom of mother and son in Tarsus of Cilicia. Of peculiar interest is another scene, near the door, which is unique as giving the portrait-figures of the founder of the chapel, Theodotus and his two children. It is true that there are different opinions as to whether these portraits were not later substitutions for earlier originals.

It is not certain that these frescos may not be by Greek hands, but the balance of probability is that they are by local artists trained by Greeks in their solid color-system.

In the apse and presbytery of the church the confusing super-position of frescos and their scaling off in certain parts more than others make it difficult to distinguish always what belongs to the latest series — probably that of Pope Paul I (757–767). This Pope appears in the apse worshipping an enthroned Christ, who is attended by six-winged cherubim.

I am inclined to attribute to this series some scenes of the Old and New Testaments in and near the presbytery to which Latin inscriptions are attached. One suspects, from the delicacy and miniature-like quality of such scenes as the sickness of King Hezechiah, that there had been a new influx of Greek artists under Paul I, if we do not ascribe them to John VII.

There was a second and probably earlier Crucifixion scene on the wall above the main apse, so badly injured that only the upper part of the Christ, parts of adoring angels and of S. John can be distinguished. It was probably originally the grandest scene of its kind in Rome, and more an ideal interpretation than the others. This we gather from the very long Greek inscriptions underneath it composed of quotations from the Song of Solomon (iii, 2), Zachariah (ix, 11; xiv, 6–7), Amos (viii, 9–10), Jeremiah (Baruch iii, 36) and John (xix, 37). It is a glorification of the Crucifixion, placed on this most prominent position; and suggests a connection with the Quinisext Council of 696, which ordered Christ to be represented crucified in human shape, not as the Lamb. This and the Greek inscription relates this painting to the series of John VII, not to the later ones.

Perhaps here should be mentioned two damaged scenes in the subterranean church of S. Martino ai Monti (VII cent. ?), of similar effect to others of the type of S. Venanzio. In the first Christ stands in the centre blessing in the Greek manner and holding a scroll. S. Paul on right and S. Peter on left hold books. SS. Processus and Martinianus, one on either side, hold martyrs' crowns and small crosses. Each figure had his name inscribed above his head. In the second scene the Virgin stands holding the Child. Four female martyrs accompany her, two on each side, each carrying a ring and a martyr's crown. They are in embroidered and jewelled robes, similar to the S. Agnes type and only one saint, "Agnes," has preserved her name.

It is curious that the great artistic activity of Pope Hadrian I, Charlemagne's contemporary, should have left so few certain traces in Rome. His care for the Catacombs and their decoration resulted in an abundance of frescos, and some scattered fragments may remain. Such are the four single figures in the crypt of S. Cornelius at S. Callixtus (Cornelius, Cyprian, Sixtus II and Optatus), also attributed to his successor Leo III.

There still seem to have remained some Greek painters in Rome in connection with the Schola Græca of S. Maria in Cosmedin, for the frescos in the church restored by Hadrian which were recently uncovered appear to belong to this time rather than to the twelfth century. Those on the face of the apse represent a scene thoroughly Byzantine, the Trisagion. The colossal Christ is surrounded by choirs of worshipping, singing angels.

The Ninth Century : S. Prassede, etc. — As an instance of the manner of the Roman school of this time, still following the Byzantine scheme but in quite a different style, is a group of four small scenes in the lower church of S. Clemente. The first, a Crucifixion, is a derivative of the type of John VII, but the earmarks of the Western, or rather Northern Carlovingian energy, is shown in the gesticulating attitude of the Virgin and S. John. The other scenes are: the Maries at the tomb; the Descent into Hades; and the Marriage at Cana. The rather vulgar and crude style and the coarse outlines show how the school had lost ground since even the days of Paul I.

The decadence in fresco is reflected in mosaic. The fall from SS. Nereo ed Achilleo, where Greek refinement was joined to some solidity and depth of color, to the lifelessness of the mosaics of Paschal I is rapid. It is not so extreme at S. Prassede as in other and slightly later works. In sheer bulk and mass of color the S. Prassede mosaics are very impressive, for it is the largest series in Rome except that of S. Maria Maggiore and was entirely the work of Pope Paschal I. There are two groups: those of the semi-dome and face of the apse and of the triumphal arch ; those of the exterior and interior of the chapel of S. Zeno.

On the face of the apse, within a circle in the centre, is a Lamb on a cushioned throne with the cross rising behind and the seven-sealed book (scroll) on a stand below. On either side are the seven candlesticks, the four archangels and the four symbols of the Evangelists, in the midst of clouds. Below, in the pendentives, the twenty-four elders are offering up their crowns.

Within the apse is Christ, standing in clouds, right hand raised in teaching, scroll in left. Slightly in front of him, and standing on the ground of Paradise, are six figures. On the right S. Paul with his right arm over the shoulder of S. Praxedis, whom he is presenting; beyond, the much-restored figure of the builder, Pope Paschal I. On the left S. Peter similarly presenting S. Pudentiana (sister of Praxedis), while beyond her is S. Zeno. At each end is the usual palm-tree, with the nimbed phœnix of the resurrection in that on the right. Beneath the feet of the figures runs the sacred river Jordan, signifying that the scene is beyond the present world. In the predella below is the usual procession of the twelve sheep issuing from Jerusalem and Bethlehem, toward the central Lamb from whose sacred mount issue the four rivers of Paradise.

On the triumphal arch is a unique presentation of the Heavenly Jerusalem, not at all according to the specification in Revelation xxi., except that the walls seem decorated with precious stones and the gates guarded by angels. In the hosts of the saved that fill the two pendentives, robed in white and with palms in their hands, we can also see the echo of Revelation viii. 9, "a great multitude . . . of all nations and kindreds and people and tongues . . . clothed with white robes and with palms in their hands." The heavenly city does not contain as yet the hosts of the saved. In the centre is Christ flanked by two archangels. On a lower level the two female figures nearest Christ are the Church of the Circumcision and the Church of the Gentiles followed by John the Baptist and the twelve apostles, all carrying crowns, extending in a line on each side as far as the gates. Above them are three figures that are pointing toward Christ: the beardless Moses, with the book of the law (*lege*), and the bearded Elias, the two prophets of the Transfiguration, probably thought to be the two witnesses of Revelation (xi. 3). The angel is the Angel of the Proclamation of the Gospel (xiv. 6). Outside the gates of the Heavenly Jerusalem, a group of the elect approach on either side.

Mosaics of Triumphal Arch and Apse, S. Prassede (Ninth Century)

Taking restorations into account, — which are more destructive at these ends than anywhere else, — it would seem as if the approaching cohorts on the right consisted originally of women and those on the left of men. The former are being received only by two angels, the latter by S. Paul and S. Peter, to whom an angel is pointing as to the doorkeeper.

The chapel of S. Zeno projects from the body of the church with which it is connected by a sort of façade centring around

Mosaic Vault in Chapel of S. Zeno, at S. Prassede.

a doorway, whose window is encircled by a double row of medallion busts: Christ and the apostles in the outer, the Virgin and Child and saints in the inner row. The entire interior is covered with mosaics. The chapel is in the form of a Greek cross with a central cross-vault. There are mosaics on (1) central vault; (2) four drums of vault; (3) arcades forming cross; (4) end walls of arcades.

The central vault is occupied by the half-figure of Christ in a medallion supported by four angels with arms raised and feet resting on globes. The drums are filled by the Virgin and S. John the Baptist; by SS. Peter and Paul; by SS. John, Andrew and James; by SS. Agnes, Pudentiana and Praxedis. The curves of the arcades forming the short tunnel vaults of the cross have simply decorative patterns of geometric design. The end walls had two compositions except on the entrance side — one in the lunette, the other below. One of these represents the Mother of Paschal, Theodora, who is called "Episcopa!" and has a square nimbus. She accompanies the Virgin

Apsidal Mosaic of S. Maria in Domnica (Ninth Century).

and SS. Praxedis and Pudentiana. Above is the Lamb on a rock accompanied by four stags. On the right Christ is between S. Zeno and S. Valentinus. An unusual scene is Christ descending into Hades.

Even more Byzantine in their general scheme are the face and semi-dome of S. Maria in Domnica. These rigidly ordered, heavily framed mosaics contain the unusual multitude of figures characteristic of the mosaics of Pope Paschal. But the compositions are not stereotyped. On the face of the arch Christ is seated on the curved arch of heaven inside the oval aureole, with an archangel on each side. Then come the twelve apostles, six on each side, headed by Paul and Peter. They all carry in veiled hands either books or scrolls, except S. Peter, who has the keys. All are robed in white and stand on the flowery ground of Paradise. In each pendentive is a prophet, with his scroll pointing upward, — one bearded and long-haired, (Elias ?) of the more usual prophetic type ; the other younger and beardless, like the type of Moses at SS. Nereo ed Achilleo and S. Prassede.

In the semi-dome of the apse the scene is the veneration by the heavenly hosts of Mary as the Mother of God. The Virgin, holding the Child, sits on a splendid throne. On either side are innumerable angels in white who bend forward in adoration, their heads encircled with a nimbus. It is impossible to decide whether any distinct number of angelic classes is intended — such as the nine of pseudo-Dionysius or the six or seven of earlier writers. They are probably represented as singing the Trisagion. Pope Paschal is kneeling before the Virgin, one of whose feet he holds.

At S. Cecilia we find the third and least successful of the mosaics of Pope Paschal I. On the face is the Adoration of the Virgin and Child (or of Mary, as Theotokos). The rich arched-back throne is guarded by two archangels. From either side approaches an adoring procession of female martyrs, both crowned and bearing on veiled hands their martyr's crown. That the scene is laid in heaven is shown by the buildings of the two heavenly cities at either end and by the figures of the twenty-four elders offering up their crowns, in the pendentives below. The ten female saints — five on each side — are certainly those whose bodies (including those of SS. Cecilia and Agatha) were transferred to this church from the Catacombs by Pope Paschal.

In the semi-dome is the usual stereotyped scene, almost identical with those of S. Prassede and S. Marco: Christ, surrounded by clouds and surmounted by the hand of God holding the wreath ; on His right S. Paul and S. Cecilia, who presents Pope Paschal holding the model of the church. On the other side S. Peter, a young beardless martyr and a

x

female martyr, probably S. Agatha, who was venerated here immediately after S. Cecilia. The usual palm-tree at each end (a phœnix on the right-hand tree), and the flowers that carpet the ground, are intended to give the local color of Paradise. Below this is the dedicatory inscription of Paschal in three lines. The scene is completed below by the usual predella of the Lamb, the twelve sheep, the two cities and the rivers of Paradise.

Paschal's successor, Gregory IV, was the author of the mosaic of S. Marco, which is both the last and the worst of the Roman mosaics of the early Middle Ages. As usual, they occupy the semi-dome and the face of the apse. The coloring is defective, the tints blurred, the types quite effete and lifeless, without even the illusion of humanity.

There are seven figures in each composition. Those on the face are framed in a heavy double band of jewels and scroll-work. Busts of Christ and the four symbols of the Evangelists enclosed within medallions form an upper row below which S. Paul on the right and S. Peter on the left occupy the pendentives, in vigorous attitudes pointing toward Christ.

The figures of the semi-dome stand upon separate inscribed bases, like inanimate statues. Christ has on His right S. Felicissimus and S. Mark the Evangelist who presents Pope Gregory IV (828–844), holding a model of the church; on his left Pope S. Mark, S. Agapitus and S. Agnes. Beneath Christ is the symbolic phœnix, while the usual predella band occurs below, the garden of Paradise with the twelve sheep issuing from the two sacred cities toward the central Lamb standing on the mount with the four rivers.

Carlovingian Frescos. — In painting, however, we find before 850 an attempt to relieve the lifelessness that had settled upon art, by the introduction of the element of vivacity of gesture and attitude so characteristic of the Carlovingian art of the North. It was not found, to be sure, in the purely hieratic sacred scenes where the figures retained the immobility that was regarded as their essential superhuman quality, but in the more human element of the compositions.

It is worth citing a fresco in the old S. Clemente as illustrating these two rather disregarded facts. It is an Ascension, in which Christ rises in an aureole carried by four angels, while below are the Virgin and the Apostles. Included in the composition, though foreign to the scene, are two figures that frame it on either side: one is S. Vitus, the other Pope Leo IV, whose square nimbus shows him to be the donor of the fresco. The

Ascension of Christ. Fresco at S. Clemente.

contrast between the extreme vivacity and varied attitudes of all the participants in the Ascension scene and the absolute immobility and frontality of the two end figures is typical of a general fact: that for several centuries (VII–XII) there were two canons, one of immobility and frontality for the divine sphere and for juxtaposed or single saints, and one of relative action and variety of pose in historic and other narrative scenes. Ordinarily the two styles are not mixed, so that critics are apt to think that a period that produces the one is incapable of the other. It needs a scene such as this, where by exception the two manners are combined, to prove that even a single artist was a master of both manners. A similarly treated scene had been painted as early as the sixth century in the Catacomb of Commodilla.

Even during the two centuries of decadence from the close of the ninth to that of the eleventh century, painting was not only practised in Rome, but was called upon to produce some of the most extensive works in the history of the school. It is true that mosaic painting was no longer in use. The knowledge of it seems to have been lost. Neither can it be denied that the fresco-paintings show less of artistic quality than at any other time. Still, even now the Roman school seems to have been preëminent in Europe.

Handbook of Painting. — Curiously enough there appeared at this time a handbook or practical guide for painters with all necessary receipts and directions for mixing and using colors and for making mosaics. It was written by a painter named Heraclius, who called it *" De Coloribus et artibus Romanorum."* Internal evidence points to the post-Carlovingian age, certainly before the revival. That Heraclius belongs to the Roman school seems clear from the preface, where a passage reminds one of the well-known lament on the decay of Rome which I have already cited. He says, of the city : —

> " *Jam decus ingenii quod plebs Romana probatur*
> *Decidit, ut periit sapientum cura Senatum*
> *Quis nunc has artes investigare valebit*
> *Quas isti artifices, immensa mente potentes*
> *Invenire sibi, potens est ostendere nobis.*"

Heraclius expressly says that he is himself a painter : " I am not writing of anything that I have not previously tested." A study of the text of this practical manual would show exactly how painters then worked.

Great Cycles of Frescos. — Until the destruction of the old S. Peter in the sixteenth and seventeenth centuries there remained on the two walls of its nave the partly obliterated frescos of the Old and New Testament, painted by order of Pope Formosus in 897. The bulging walls, slanting outward on one side, accumulated so much dust as practically to conceal most of the scenes from the New Testament, and while those of the Old Testament on the opposite wall were clearer, the drawings and descriptions of them give no idea of their style. We must merely admit that in sheer extent these works surpassed all their known predecessors.

About ten years later the school, perhaps the same artists, were obliged to repeat the same feat by covering with similar subjects the walls of the nave of the newly reconstructed Lateran basilica. These were destroyed in 1310.

There are, however, five works of this school still wholly or partly extant, produced within the same half century or more, which will give a fair clew to the style of these greater works : in a chapel on the Cœlian; in S. Maria in Pallara on the Palatine; in S. Silvestro at Tivoli; in S. Abbondio at Rignano; and, especially, in S. Elia near Nepi.

The defaced scene in the chapel of S. Lorenzo near SS. Giovanni e Paolo on the Cœlian, is interesting mainly as a record of the successful attempt of Methodius and Pope Formosus to convert the Bulgarians whose king is here represented as doing homage to Christ under the patronage of the Pope.

The apsidal fresco in S. Silvestro at Tivoli is more important and shows that painters were reverting, after the Byzantine epoch had closed, to the models of the early Christian period, for the composition here is clearly modelled on the apse of SS. Cosma e Damiano, though it contains fewer figures. Christ is standing on clouds, above the Jordan, with S. Paul on His right and S. Peter on His left, to whom He is handing a scroll.

S. Elia, Nepi, and Other Monasteries. — Almost the same can be said of part of the extensive series in the ruined monastic church of S. Maria in Pallara on the Palatine, which was one of the foremost monuments of the tenth and eleventh centuries, the residence and fortress of several popes. The frescos were ordered, in about the middle of the tenth century, by a wealthy physician named Peter, who also endowed the monastery.

In the centre of the apse is the figure of Christ standing on the clouds with hand raised and open book: on either side are two saints; S. Sebastian and S. Zoticus, S. Stephen and S. Lawrence. Underneath is the narrow zone of the Lamb on the rock and the twelve sheep. Farther below is a line of figures adopted from the Byzantine school: the Virgin between two archangels and four female saints, two of whom are S. Agnes and S. Lucia. It is only in this lower zone that we find the painters of this century innovating on the early Christian composition. This part of the frescos has been preserved, though in very poor condition; but originally the series was much more extensive: on either side of the nave were scenes from the Old and New Testaments, and in or near the porch the lives of the martyrs buried in the church and represented in the apse. Even the donor, Peter, and his wife were depicted on either side of the apse.

If none of the works in Rome itself are sufficiently well preserved to allow of a clear opinion as to their style, it is not so with the frescos in a monastic church not far to the north, S. Elia near Nepi. This large series fill the apse and transept, are fairly well preserved and are important not only in themselves, but because they are signed by their authors, three painters from Rome — two brothers Johannes and Stephanus, and their nephew Nicholas. It has been assumed that their date is the eleventh century, but the church was rebuilt after 939 and there is no reason to doubt that the frescos are between c. 950 and 975. The main scene in the hemicycle of the apse is a frank imitation of that of SS. Cosma e Damiano.

Christ stands in the centre on the mystic mount with the four rivers, with S. Peter on His left and S. Paul on His right, beyond whom, on either side, is a saint, one of them probably S. Elias, in Byzantine costume. At each end is a palm-tree, in one of which is a phœnix. Below is the traditional frieze of the twelve sheep on either side of the Lamb, whose blood is pouring into a chalice. Still lower is a line of figures, as at S. Maria in Pallara, of Christ enthroned, flanked by two archangels, beyond whom on either side are four Virgins with crowns, recalling those of S. Apollinare Nuovo at Ravenna of the sixth century, and those of S. Maria in Pallara.

On the face of the apse are the long ascetic figures of the twenty-four elders in two rows, as at Rignano; only here twelve of them raise crowns and twelve chalices, — a transition between the early mediæval type where all have crowns, and the later where they are entirely replaced by chalices.

Below the elders and beyond them on the transept walls

Female Saints and Archangel, Fresco in Apse of S. Elia, near Nepi.
(Tenth century.)

was a series of oblong compositions in three tiers; those on the right, which alone are preserved, are mostly scenes of great originality and rarity taken from the Apocalypse. The series appears to have illustrated this book in the greatest detail. Doubtless the nave was filled with scenes from the Old and New Testaments. The entire series may be attributed to the three artists of the apse.

The dependence of these works on earlier mosaics is indicated by the yellow ground for the row of sheep, to imitate the gold cubes; by the strong contrasts of color and sharp outlines. The extreme flatness reminds one of the last mosaics in Rome, at S. Marco. There is a single yellowish flesh tone, rouged, and a single verdigris body color, heightened by white streaks and broken by black lines with which the slight reddish and gray shadings fail absolutely to unite. As a result the bodies are almost flat outlined transparencies. There is absolutely nothing Byzantine in the technique, which is far removed from the works of the seventh and eight centuries at S. Saba and S. Maria Antiqua.

The apocalyptic scenes that have been identified are on the right: (1) John having the vision of the enthroned Lord; (2) the four angels having dominion over the four seas; (3) the angel chaining the dragon; (4) the four riders; (5) a dragon episode. On the left side: (6) conflict of angels with the dragon; (7) the dragon pursuing the woman. These are the earliest known examples of such scenes on church walls.

The deserted monastic church of S. Abbondio near Rignano, close to the Tiber and to Mt. Soracte, is of the same school and period as the frescos at S. Elia, though less careful in drawing. The connection with mosaic compositions and with earlier traditions is evident, but there are interesting variations. The remaining frescos cover only the face of the apse, those in the hemicycle having been destroyed. The upper row has the Lamb in the centre of the symbols of the four evangelists; below, in a second row and on a larger scale, is a half-figure of Christ in a circular medallion flanked by two seven-branched candlesticks, two seraphim with six wings and two groups of angels. Below, on either side of the hemicycle, are the twenty-four elders in two rows. The type of both the seraphim and the half-figure of Christ may be traced to the Byzantine school, for they do not belong to Western and Roman tradition. Such medallion busts of Christ are very common in the centre of Byzantine domes of every age. The rest of the scene belongs to the native stock.

It was especially in the large monasteries throughout the province of Rome that art found a haven from the religious indifference, penury and ignorance of the Papal Rome of the tenth and eleventh centuries. Farfa, Subiaco, Soracte, Monte Amiata helped to stay the ebb tide in painting, though not endeavoring to revive the art of mosaic, a task reserved to the other great monastery of Monte Cassino, which, in order to do so, was obliged to import artists from Constantinople, for the Byzantine mosaicists had not yet gone to Venice to decorate S. Marco. The works I have just described in the minor monasteries of S. Elia and S. Abbondio are merely fragments saved out of the ruined multitude.

In an indirect way a German Emperor was also the means of encouraging Roman painting. The monument of the Emperor Otho III contained the only work of mosaic painting extant in Rome for a stretch of over two centuries, so that it is as historically interesting as it is little known. The burial of this Italo-phile in Rome, where he died, near the east door in the vestibule of S. Peter, gave him a congruous resting-place. Here, as Thietmar's chronicle relates, the figure of Christ stood, blessing all who approach. This figure in mosaic, flanked by the princes of the apostles, still remains in the Vatican crypt, in fair preservation, though the mosaic picture is severed from the immense sarcophagus over which it stood.

Otho III himself gives a proof of the high esteem in which the Roman school of painting was held, for his chief court painter was the Italian artist John, almost certainly a Roman, whom he took back with him in c. 990 to fresco the imperial palace at Aix-la-Chapelle. His works there were so much admired that the Emperor appointed him to an Italian bishopric. John, after a brief visit to his native land, returned to Germany and then settled at Liège, where he painted for the bishops a series of frescos. It is impossible to say what influence he had on the German school.

Not much later comes a series of frescos in Rome itself, in one of the pagan temples turned into a hall-church and dubbed S. Urbano alla Caffarella. Its deserted, isolated position outside the city saved these frescos from destruction, but not from much repainting. The date of 1011 under the Crucifixion scene may be accurate. In the apse is Christ enthroned between two angels and SS. Peter and Paul. At the opposite end, on the inside of the façade, is the Crucifixion. On the side walls are lines of oblong compositions taken both from the New Testament and from the lives of S. Urban, S. Cecilia, S. Lawrence and other saints whose relics were here.

The Crucifixion is rather notable from the presence of the two crucified thieves, the angels above, and the two donors

Crucifixion, Fresco in S. Urbano alla Caffarella (Eleventh Century).

below reverently approaching with cloths the *suppedaneum* on which Christ's feet rest, to catch some of the sacred blood. The Virgin and S. John, Longinus and the soldier with the spear complete the scene. The two donors seem especially interesting because they herald in their types the style of S. Clemente. Through the repainting it seems possible to detect a change from the style of S. Elia: greater solidity and naturalness as well as more action.

Revival at S. Clemente. — Shortly after the middle of the eleventh century some unknown painters decorated a large part of what is now the subterranean basilica of S. Clemente, together with its porch, with a series of fresco compositions larger in size and fuller of figures than any we have previously encountered.

The art of these frescos at S. Clemente is on a higher level than that of anything produced in Rome for many centuries. It distinctly raises the banner of an epoch-making revival in painting. There were other works of the same age and style, but this series is the only important remaining example. It illustrates still further what we have recognized as a new fact for the seventh, eighth and ninth centuries, that for these centuries, at least, the highest achievement is to be sought here and not in the stiffer field of mosaic painting.

It would seem as if once more the artist kindled to the feeling of pure beauty and looked beyond his task of purveyor of mere ecclesiastical information. And this feeling for beauty was not restricted. It shows itself in rhythm of composition, in simplicity and directness of narrative, in variety of attitude, in beauty of pose, as well as in purity of outline, symmetry of drapery, softness of shading and lightness of coloring. These qualities are to a certain extent offset by the lack of life and dramatic force that were to come in the more psychologic age of Giotto. Yet, even here, several of the faces are expressive of varied emotions, — such as the pall-bearers in the funeral procession of the unknown saint, the father of Alexius and his bride in the death-scene. The action of the mother as she gathers up and carries the child, in the scene of his rescue from the Black Sea, are full of naturalness, even if awkward.

Of the four scenes belonging to this series two relate to the life and legend of S. Clement and one each to that of S. Alexius and an unknown saint. Two were given by Beno de Rapiza and his wife; one by Mary, the wife of a butcher! The first couple are themselves given in small size approaching the saint in the scene of the miracle by which Clement restores the sight of the blind Sisinnius. The scene is laid in a church interior and Clement stands in attitude of adoration beside the altar. Theodora, the Christian wife of the pagan Sisinnius, has come to divine service and has been followed by her wrathful husband, who, as he enters, is struck by blindness, to be led forward and healed by Clement. The figure of Theodora is soft and graceful in its antique costume and filleted head, standing foremost in the group of worshippers.

The two donors are repeated, by themselves with two children and nurse, below their other painting, — the rescue of the child Clement, — and these are far removed from the previously prevalent stiffness of such single figures. The gracefully poised head of the wife, with its turban-like headdress, is more modern in its appeal even than anything Giottesque.

There is no uniformity in the method of composition. In the scene where Clement is celebrating mass, the frame encloses but the one theme, except for the intruding donors. The same unity appears in the funeral procession with its reception at S. Clemente. In the Rescue of the Child there are two successive stages: one where the mother is taking the child from the water; the other where she is bringing him to the local clergy assembled to honor the miracle.

Then, in the life of Alexius there are three successive scenes in the same picture. The saint presents himself in the garb of a pilgrim before his father, who fails to recognize him, and he serves in his father's house without being recognized. In the centre, he reappears, mortally sick and visited by the Pope, who gives him absolution and receives from him the written story of his life. On the right, the truth has been published; the father and mother of Alexius are lamenting his death and his bride is embracing him.

There is a curious small composition under the Sisinnius picture, which has a more homely and everyday aspect. It is the explanation of the blindness of Sisinnius and portrays the episode when Sisinnius, then Roman prefect, having sought out Clement in the Catacombs and brought his slaves to seize him, is directing and cursing them, because they are so slow in roping and hauling a column which in their common miraculous blindness they have all taken to be S. Clement! The objurgatory remarks of Sisinnius are among the earliest and choicest specimens of the early Italian dialect of the people.

How are we to account for the artist or artists of S. Clemente?

Frescos in Lower Church, S. Clemente.

Miracle of S. Clement (above).   Donors of Frescos (below).

What were their antecedents ?   It has been suggested that they
are to be found largely in the frescos of the Catacombs and
other works of early Christian art.   I do not believe so.   At
the same time they cannot be linked to the decadent art that
immediately preceded.   For the careful student of the newly
discovered frescos at S. Maria Antiqua and S. Saba, the problem is solved by the recognition in them, or such as they, of the
inspiration for the artist of S. Clemente.   So, after all, it is,
though Roman, another tribute to Byzantium — not to the ascetic and unæsthetic Byzantinism of the time in which the Roman
painter lived, but to the Hellenic school that still interpreted
the beautiful.   Light coloring, pure outline, clear story-telling
— these qualities are especially evident in the earlier frescos
at S. Saba.   These works were visible in good preservation
before the fire of Guiscard which involved S. Clemente and
S. Saba in a common ruin.

The restoration of the basilica and monastery of S. Paul
undertaken by Hildebrand perhaps even before he became
Pope Gregory VII, gives, I believe, the date of some frescos
in the *Cappella del Martirologio*, between the basilica and the
cloister, which escaped the fire of 1823.   Here, as at S. Urbano,
the Crucifixion occupies the end wall, treated in almost identical fashion, and in direct descent from that of S. Maria Antiqua.   It is flanked by figures of Peter and Paul.   The rest of
the apostles, supplemented by saints, form a continuous frieze
of large-sized immobile figures along the side-walls, separated
by palm-trees and carrying inscribed scrolls and emblems.
Though much repainted, they show enough of their original
character to prove their distinctly local and non-Byzantine
style ; they act as a connecting link between the S. Urbano
and S. Clemente frescos.

There are still in Rome other traces of the school just before
the fire of 1084.   In one case — the chapel of S. Gabriel — the
donor is the same Beno de Rapiza of S. Clemente.

Byzantine Artists. — It was not from ignorance that the contemporary Byzantine style had so little influence on Roman
artists, for works of pure Byzantine art were being executed
now at the very gates of Rome by artists themselves evidently

Greeks, whether brought over by Desiderius of Monte Cassino or mosaicists of the Greek Basilian order. The main doorway and the triumphal arch of the church of the Greek monastery at Grottaferrata each have a mosaic in excellent preservation by Greek hands; that over the door has in the centre Christ enthroned, and on one side John the Baptist, on the other S. Basil, propedeutical to the true faith. The workmanship is excellent and the style free from excessive asceticism. There is depth and reality to the figures.

The mosaic of the arch represents the adoration of the Throne, in a form common in the East, but unknown to West-

Pentecost (Etimasia), Apsidal Mosaic in Monastic Church, Grottaferrata.
(Twelfth century.)

ern art. On either side of the vacant throne of the apocalyptic vision are seated the twelve apostles, upon whom are descending the Pentecostal rays.

It was at this time that the Monte Cassino school frescoed the basilica of S. Angelo in Formis, of which I give a view (p. 255), both because it is a good example of a basilica built with materials from Rome and because it is the best-preserved example of an interior completely frescoed, even though the work was not done by the Roman school. It gives, in a modest way, the same effect that must have been given by so many interiors in Rome before the Renaissance devastation.

New Roman School. — When Paschal II called artists about him to rebuild and decorate the churches, it was not, therefore, necessary for him to re-create a monumental school of painting, as it was found necessary to do in architecture and church furniture and ornament. At the same time there was a difference in the two branches — fresco and mosaic.   The Roman school had certainly omitted mosaic work from its *répertoire* for over two centuries; at first for lack of funds, later from ignorance also.   Where did Paschal II find the mosaicists whom he employed?   One can only guess.   He could draw from Venice, as his successors did, for S. Marco's decoration was then begun; or from Sicily, where Cefalù had already been decorated; or, perhaps, from Monte Cassino, of which school we know but little.   At all events from somewhere mosaicists came to Rome

Apse Mosaic of S. Clemente.

and decorated the façade of S. Bartolommeo all' Isola with a work of which only the central half-figure of Christ remains; and the apse of S. Maria in Monticelli.   The former Christ has a flatness of effect and an inexperience of handling that argue native talent.

And yet, in a few years, still under Paschal II, the apse of S. Clemente was produced, a work which in its essentials is based on old Roman traditions, and in its technique is almost perfect.   In its general design it figures the vine, representing the redeemed Church, whose spirals cover the apse, and Christ the Redeemer on the Cross in the centre; the main difference between this and the early Christian interpretation of the scene being the substitution of the human figure for the lamb on the cross. The earthly Paradise and the river Jordan at the base, with their abundance of animal and symbolic life, are purely classic in idea and even in technique, whereas the little figures of mediæval creation that are interwoven in the spirals are of heavy Romanesque type. Only on the face of the apse, where the large figures of SS. Peter and Paul, SS. Lawrence

Apse Mosaic of S. Maria Nuova (S. Francesca Romana).

and Clement, loom up in distinct contrast, do we see a touch of Byzantine influence in their being seated instead of standing.

On the other hand the group of foreign artists produced one apsidal mosaic in Rome in the years immediately after Paschal II, in the newly rebuilt S. Maria Nuova (S. Francesca Romana) in the Forum. It is unique in design and style and far from a success; its authors were not at home in their medium. As the Rhenish and other sculptors of the North (even the Tuscans) reproduced at this time the motif of early Christian sarcophagi, where arcades frame single or coupled figures, so

Y

here each figure is placed under an arcade, with archivolts and shafts imitated from illuminated manuscripts, which also inspired the patterns of the fan-shaped top. The tormented lines of the drapery show the descent from the Carlovingian type, a style common among Northern artists of this time.

There are but five figures. In the centre the enthroned, richly robed and bejewelled Virgin, holding the Child not in the Byzantine fashion, straight before her in her lap, but

Apsidal Mosaics of S. Maria in Trastevere.

standing and turning toward her almost in profile. On her right are S. James and S. John; on her left S. Peter and S. Andrew in costumes that ape the classic. There is a curious attempt to imitate solid masonry above the arcades that encircle the figures.

S. Maria in Trastevere. — As the twelfth century advances Byzantine influences penetrate beyond mere superficialities, in mosaics if not in frescos, probably because Roman artists were learning again to handle the cubes, after long disuse, under the instruction of Byzantine masters. The apse and façade of S. Maria in Trastevere are both attributed to about 1140, and bear no connection with the contemporary work at S. Maria Nuova. The façade mosaic is badly restored. In the centre are the Virgin and Child enthroned; at their feet two small kneeling figures, probably the Popes who built and restored the church. A line of ten female figures stands, five on either side of the centre. They are richly robed and carry lamps. Their nimbus proclaims them saints. They probably represent the female saints whose relics were placed here. They have been mistakenly interpreted as the wise and foolish virgins, and two of the figures have been erroneously restored with lamps reversed, on this supposition. The rest preserve their lighted lamps.

The mosaic of the apse is in far better preservation. In the centre is Christ enthroned, with book in left hand, while with His right arm He embraces the shoulder of the Virgin seated on His right. He is saying, in the words inscribed on the book, *Veni electa mea et ponam in te thronum meum.* Further to the right are S. Callixtus, S. Lawrence and Pope Innocent II, holding the model of the church. On the left are S. Peter, Popes Cornelius and Julius and S. Calepodius. In most cases these figures were selected because their relics are in the church. They are identified by inscriptions between their feet. Below is the usual predella band of the central lamb and the twelve sheep issuing from the two sacred cities.

On the face of the apse, in the centre, is the cross in a luminous circle; on either side the seven candlesticks, and beyond the four Beasts with the inscribed names of the evangelists. Below are the two prophets Isaiah and Jeremiah with inscribed scrolls. Under them an exquisite decorative panel of classic taste. It is particularly in the prophets that we see some analogy to the earlier mosaic at S. Clemente. The figures in the apse remind one of those in the *Cappella del Martirologio* at S. Paul.

Toscanella, S. Pietro. — There is at S. Pietro at Toscanella a fresco that seems one of the finest products of the Byzantine section of the Roman school and to date not after the middle of the twelfth century. It is the last great product of the old ideas of apocalyptic character that were soon to be superseded, and in that respect is the lineal descendant of S. Elia and Rignano. At S. Pietro the frescos cover the semi-dome and face of the apse.   In the semi-dome is a colossal standing figure of Christ in the centre, robed in white, holding a globe in His right and an open book in His left hand.   On either side of Him a long-robed angel withdraws from Him with gestures of amazement.   Below are two flying angels and four half-figures of angels with inscriptions.   Further below a line of the twelve apostles, separated by palm-trees, not in hieratic stiff attitudes, but conversing animatedly or gazing upward in truly Carlovingian style.   Under this is a line of busts of saints in medallions.

On the face of the apse the encircling band has the Lamb in the centre and three half-figures of angels on each side. On the centre of the wall-face is a half-figure of Christ in a medallion.   He blesses in the Greek manner.   On either side are the seven candlesticks, two seraphs and the symbols of the four evangelists.   Below, on either side of the arch, the twenty-four elders are offering up their crowns.

Several series in the Roman province seem to show the presence here of other artists than those trained in the Roman school itself, though it may be an error to exclude them from it when we understand how catholic in its tastes the school was.   In the cathedral of Anagni, for example, where the pavements and all the sacred furniture, such as canopies, altars, paschal candlesticks, tombs, were the work of Roman decorators, the crypt is covered on walls and vaults with frescos, the majority of which belong to the twelfth century.   Ignored by critics until very recently, they now appear as among the best preserved and most interesting examples of this period, full of force and originality.   Some of the themes, especially those from the Apocalypse, are unique.   The scene of the Elders offering up their chalices and the doctors, Galen, etc., are by a lineal descendant of the artists of S. Elia.

Subiaco. — At Subiaco, in the churches of the famous Benedictine monastery, there is even closer connection with Rome. These much-neglected frescos of the vaults and walls of the subterranean church of the Sacro Speco are now being carefully studied.   Those on the vaults seem to me slightly earlier than the rest.   Instead of dating them from Abbot John VI, after 1217, which is the correct date for most of the decoration of the walls, they might be attributed to the years succeeding 1165, when some Greek Basilian monks, fleeing from their own monastery of Grottaferrata, sought refuge at the Sacro Speco, bringing precious objects with them. We have seen that Grottaferrata possessed a school of mosaic and fresco painting, and some Byzantine elements of these Subiaco frescos would be reasonably ex-plained by this hypothesis. The three vaults and the walls are covered with them. But, through the veil of restorations we seem to trace a date rather later than this for the conception of these scenes, one that would connect them with the Roman art that afterward produced the Cosmatus work at the Sancta Sanc-torum. The vaults have a central figure in a heavily bor-dered medallion sur-rounded by eight figures; those in the pendentives being

Painting of Vault in Lower Church of Sacro Speco at Subiaco.
(Early thirteenth century.)

entire, the intermediate being three-quarter figures. In the central vault the medallion has the three-quarter figure of Christ; in the pendentives are four archangels and between them four apostles, Peter, Paul, John and Andrew. In the second vault S. Benedict occupies the centre. The third vault contains, in the centre, the Lamb, and in four fields the four evangelists. The later similar compositions by Cosmatus in the Sancta Sanctorum at Rome make the connection quite plain. The scenes on the walls, by Conxolus, are better preserved.

The lower chapel of S. Gregory, beneath the subterranean church at Subiaco, has some unusual frescos dated by a contemporary inscription in 1228, painted perhaps by a monk named Oddo. The principal scene is that of the consecration of the chapel by Pope Gregory IX, in the preceding year, 1227, the Pope bending over at the altar, assisted by two clerics. Another scene is a S. Gregory the Great in company with the ulcerous Job. The artist is of the purely native Roman school without a trace of Byzantinism. On the contrary the vault of the chapel shows a different and earlier hand, as Byzantine as that of the subterranean church, who has placed the four signs of the evangelists in as many medallions separated by six-winged seraphims. Besides a Crucifixion and a Christ between Peter and Paul the Roman artist's most remarkable product is a portrait of S. Francis, which is conjectured to be the most authentic in existence, a contemporary study made by Friar Oddo when S. Francis visited the Sacro Speco in 1223. This, however, is doubtful.

Varied Art of the Thirteenth Century. — Whatever comparative unity there may have been in Roman painting gave way in the thirteenth century to variety and individualism. The city became the main stamping-ground, the inspiring foster-mother of the painter, stimulating in its themes and opportunities. It is true that nothing is produced that breathes such pure classicism as the S. Clemente frescos, but the old Roman traditions are unbroken; they appear clearly in the series at S. Lorenzo-fuori-le-mura. At the same time there were produced in Rome, in the first decade of the century, some mosaics of pure Byzantine workmanship, the apses of S. Peter and S. Paul, by the mosaicists sent from Venice to Innocent III and Honorius III.

The apse of S. Peter has, of course, entirely disappeared, but can be studied in drawings. It stands alone in the use of a few colossal figures : Christ and SS. Peter and Paul.

At S. Paolo the apse mosaic still exists, but so thoroughly renovated after the fire that criticism can bear only on the composition. Christ has Paul and Luke on His right; Peter and Andrew on His left. In the frieze below, the rest of the apostles (ten) are adoring the throne flanked by angels. This scene we have seen at Grottaferrata. It is a purely Byzantine conception.

The native Roman artists, commonly called the Cosmati, at this time seem not to have gone beyond the creation of small mosaic pictures. Perhaps it was their inability to produce the more colossal works that led to the calling of the Greeks from Venice. In 1218 a small work of this sort was made by Jacobus Cosmati for the hospital of S. Tommaso in Formis. It is a circular mosaic in a medallion with gold ground. Christ is seated, and on either side of him is a released captive, one white, the other black. The white carries a cross and his feet are shackled; the negro is manacled. While unpretentious, it is a work in excellent taste and free style. A few years before the same artist had made a figure of Christ in mosaic over the side door of the façade of the Cathedral of Civita Castellana, also a pure product of Latin art.

S. Lorenzo. — The most considerable work now remaining in Rome itself by the painters of the first half of the thirteenth century, whose active productivity is incontestable, is the series painted in the porch and inner façade of S. Lorenzo in the time of Honorius III or shortly after. There are about forty small compositions in regular rows, telling the stories of saints whose relics are preserved in the church : Lawrence, Stephen, Hippolytus, Sixtus, as well as scenes connected with the foundation and history of the Church, ending with the coronation of Peter de Courtenay as king of Jerusalem by Honorius III. The wholesale repainting leaves it possible merely to see that while the peculiar charm and delicacy of S. Clemente are lacking, the same school has continued to exist in Rome. The compositions are simpler and with fewer figures; the attitudes more natural and easy, without the awkward grace and flowing lines of the older artists. A certain *bravura* of attitude and gesture reminds one of French miniatures.

In better preservation is the fresco over the tomb of Cardinal Fieschi in the same church, dated 1250. It is a votive picture with the scene that was to become so common: the Virgin and Child with a few saints and the donor and Pope; here it is SS. Lawrence and Stephen, Pope Innocent IV and Cardinal Fieschi.

Naturalism. — In the second half of the thirteenth century artists attempt in quite distinct ways to attain to the naturalness of style that was to be their goal. The two styles — Byzantine and Roman — continue to exist side by side. An almost farcical parody of the former is in the chapel of S. Silvestro annexed to the church of the SS. Quattro Coronati. The central composition is a peculiar interpretation of the Last Judgment, in abbreviated form. This is surrounded by eight scenes from the legend of Pope Sylvester and Constantine. Accessories and costume are unduly accentuated, and the figures are awkward and lifeless. Neither before nor after was so poor a work produced in Rome.

At the same time the native school was producing works at S. Agnese and S. Cecilia that show progress. In the former church the scenes from the life of S. Catherine and S. Agatha have the solid treatment of drapery and forms, the massing of shadows and the sculptural effects that reach their climax later in the masterly art of Cavallini. S. Agnese was, two centuries ago, a large picture-gallery for this period; the surviving fragments are now mainly in the Lateran museum. Compared with earlier work (S. Clemente) there is loss of delicacy and grace, but gain in life and reality.

At about this time there were painted in the churches of Toscanella, especially at S. Maria Maggiore, an extensive series, supplemented by some of earlier and some of later date. It is probable that the Byzantine section of the Roman school was responsible for most of this work.

Toscanella, S. Maria. — At S. Maria Maggiore in the apse is the colossal standing figure of Christ with an adoring angel on either side. Below, a line of the twelve apostles quietly dignified and not full of action, as at S. Pietro, considerably restored. It is a work of the twelfth century.

On the face of the apse is a grandiose composition of the Last Judgment, covering the entire wall to roof. At the summit, within an iridescent aureole, is the enthroned Christ surrounded by a multitude of angels. On either side are seated the apostles. Below, on the right, is the army of the elect, headed by the Virgin, who is presenting her mother, S. Anne. Adam and Eve are followed by the groups of patriarchs, kings, prophets, popes, bishops, priests and monks. Below Christ stands the cross surrounded by the instruments of the Passion, near which kneels the small figure of the donor, Secundianus. To the right, under the elect, is the scene of the resurrection from the dead, who are leaving their tombs to the sound of the angels' trumps.

From the throne of Christ proceeds toward the left a river of fire forming the boundary of the infernal regions, into which angels with long tridents are thrusting the damned, received and tormented by numerous demons who pass them along to a colossal Lucifer with snake-mouths above and exits below. He devours them with his snake mouths and spues them out into the enormous maw of hell. This seems to be later than the composition in the semi-dome and to date from the third quarter of the thirteenth century. It is a most important work.

In the right aisle, the Virgin and Child enthroned between two female saints, and the Flagellation of Christ, are of the same date and style as the apse. Another Virgin and Child enthroned with four flying angels and two saints, where the throne has a Roman mosaic decoration, is a work of the pre-Giottesque Roman school, in a free and humanistic style.

Sancta Sanctorum.— In order to find in Rome an echo of the epic compositions at Toscanella, we must turn to its greatest painter of the early revival, Pietro Cavallini. The work that immediately precedes him, besides the series at S. Agnese and S. Cecilia, already mentioned, is the decoration of the Sancta Sanctorum chapel in 1277 and 1278 by Cosmatus. Was Cosmatus the master of Cavallini? No answer deduced from the style seems possible on account of the serious restoration of the Sancta Sanctorum frescos and the difficulty of studying its mosaics. The chapel is closed to students, on account of its sanctity, and has been closed for about three centuries. It is reached through a vestibule whose vault is covered with a Virgin and Child in mosaic. Another mosaic in the apse represents S. Lawrence and S. Stephen with two angels, on either side of the enthroned Virgin and Child, before whom two Popes are kneeling. Below is a line of figures of Popes including Leo the Great, Gelasius and Paschal II. In the ellipsoidal vault of the apse is a mosaic of Christ in a medallion supported by angels with outspread wings. The vault and walls of the chapel itself are frescoed. In the vaulting compartments are the evangelists and their symbols on a blue ground, two of which are sufficiently well preserved to remind us distinctly of Cavallini's work and to connect Cosmatus with him. Below, on either side of the pointed windows, is a shell-crowned framework enclosing a composition. There are eight scenes, relating to the saints whose relics are in the chapel: (1) Decapitation of S. Paul; (2) Crucifixion of S. Peter; (3) (4) Miracles of S. Nicholas; (5) S. Lawrence on the gridiron; (6) Stoning of S. Stephen; (7) Christ enthroned; (8) S. Nicholas offering the Chapel to S. Peter. Beneath the windows in a series of twenty-eight trefoil arches are as many single figures: prophets, apostles, saints, bishops, monks, framed in twisted columns, — a design that Cavallini seems to have reproduced in the next decade at S. Cecilia.

The whole scheme of decoration is charmingly symmetrical and complete, and places Cosmatus in the front rank of his contemporaries. The restoration of the frescos by Nanni under Sixtus V has, however, deprived the frescos of their stylistic value. Still, one fact is certain: they are a product of direct Roman tradition with scarcely a trace of Byzantinism, and foreshadow the work of Cavallini.

Rome: S. Maria Maggiore. — A few years ago some fragments were found, between the present Renaissance coffered ceiling and the roof of the transept of S. Maria Maggiore at Rome, of a series of frescos which once must have entirely covered the walls above the mosaics of the nave. In the left transept there were eight large medallion-circles, enclosing busts of which four remain. Fragmentary as they are, their preservation is sufficiently good to show that they must belong to the time of Pope Nicholas IV, who built the palace next to the church (c. 1288), restored the apse-mosaic and added those on the façade. The heads of S. Peter and S. Paul, so familiar in many variations of the traditional features, may serve as touch-stones of comparison: they are not ascetic Byzantine; they do not have the hardness of Cimabue. The sense of life comes from a combination of portrait-study with adherence to type, and a method akin to impressionism in the use of color. The technique, with its hatched lines, is far from that of Giotto, as well as from that of the author of the decorative Roman Old Testament scenes at Assisi. There is a breadth, swing and vigor that bespeak a master then in the first fulness of his powers, who must be reckoned with as a "great unknown" preceding Giotto and greater than either Cimabue or Duccio. As this is not an example of the earlier manner of Cavallini, before his S. Cecilia work, then we must acknowledge the exist-ence of another almost equally great Roman master at this time, whose intense vigor and vitality show as plainly the new life as does the more sculpturesque calm and breadth of Caval-lini. From his hand, perhaps, are some of the Assisi scenes, such as the sacrifice of Isaac, and from his workshop proceeded, perhaps, a Virgin and Child with saints at S. Saba, and some of the Assisi compositions with heavy architectural frame-works. By a different master, more addicted to broad masses than to linear methods, is a unique Virgin and Child uncovered at S. Bartolommeo all' Isola.

Assisi. — Some time before this the work of decorating the double church of S. Francis at Assisi had begun. The theme of the succession of artists and schools who had a share in it is too complicated to be discussed here. Tuscans, Umbrians and Romans rubbed elbows there for over forty years. The relative shares of Cimabue and Giotto are still heatedly dis-puted. The hand of several Roman artists has been traced by recent writers, and names have been attributed to some of them: Cavallini, Gaddi, Rusutti, Torriti.

Cavallini. — The personality of Pietro Cavallini has been looming up very prominently during the last decade as a partner — even a predecessor — of Giotto in the revival of painting.   We were familiar with Vasari's fables which made of him Giotto's pupil and his assistant in the "Navicella" mosaic at S. Peter, and assigned to him frescos at S. Maria and S. Cecilia in Trastevere, S. Maria in Aracœli, in Rome, and others in Florentine churches and at S. Francis in Assisi.   The only two facts of which we were certain are: (1) that he completed in 1291 a series of six mosaic compositions in the apse of S.

Maria in Trastevere and (2) that in 1308 he was in the service of the court of Naples, having left Rome after the departure of the Popes for Avignon.   Ghiberti admired him as one of the greatest of masters and was Vasari's source for most of his list of works.   Ghiberti's judgment is now being confirmed.

At S. Maria in Trastevere it was a narrow frieze of six compositions that Cavallini added below the main mosaics in the curve and face of the apse, all illustrating the Life of the Virgin.   They are: the Nativity, Annunciation, Vision of the Shepherds, Adoration of the Magi, Presentation and Death of the Virgin.   Below this frieze is a single scene on a larger scale: the bust of the Virgin and Child in a medallion flanked by Peter and Paul and the kneeling donor, Bertoldo Stefaneschi.   Cavallini completed the work in 1291, according to an inscription now lost.

Mosaic by Cavallini in S. Maria, in Trastevere.
"Birth of the Virgin."

No artist can be as free in his handling when he uses the medium of mosaic cubes, and yet Cavallini almost approaches the untrammelled realism of the early Christian mosaicists in his handling of tones and masses in these frieze compositions. No sane critic can now call them "Byzantine." When we say that the composition is well balanced, the action often dramatic, the story well told, the accessories decorative but not overloaded, the figures graceful, natural and well draped, we will yet have missed the keynote, which is the sense of life and reality.

The art which Cavallini embodied in these Trastevere mosaics is that of a mature master, sure of his style and not an eclectic. At that time, in 1291, Giotto was only twenty-five years old; not old enough to have founded a school. As a matter of fact Giotto was then forming himself in Rome. So astonishing is the resemblance between these mosaics and the works assigned to Giotto's youth that one is forced to the alternative of either depriving Giotto of the honor of being the re-creator of painting, and conferring it on Cavallini; or of supposing that Giotto was the real author of these mosaics, Cavallini merely carrying out his cartoons. Now, it is certain that Cavallini signed and dated these mosaics; the words *Petrus fecit hoc opus* having existed in part until recently. Besides, the analogies are not identities. They are instinct with a calm and dignity that is less akin to Giotto than to the Roman tradition of S. Clemente, where Cavallini also found the Hellenic classicism of some of his female heads.

But where Cavallini shows himself in perfect freedom of technique and stylistic development is in the recently discovered frescos at S. Cecilia, which he executed in about 1290. What is left of them covers the inside wall of the apse and laps over the adjacent walls of the nave. Originally the entire nave was decorated with Old Testament scenes on one side and New Testament scenes on the other.

The composition of the Last Judgment occupied the whole interior of the façade. The figure of Christ in the centre, in an aureole surrounded by seraphs and angels, is flanked by the Virgin and John the Baptist, standing, and by the seated apostles, statuesque figures, with a strong play of light and shade to emphasize the antique drapery. They are as if consciously reproduced from Roman statues. The heads, especially that of Christ and the younger apostles, have a dignified sweetness that is new in art. In them the more physical strength and energy embodied by the artist of the frescos of S. Maria Maggiore has become transformed by a new spiritual grace. In the head and even the attitude of John the Baptist there is an expression of deepest reverence and faith. Below the throne of Christ is the altar with the emblems of the Passion. Further below is a part of the scene that has been nearly destroyed: the elect on the right being led by archangels into Paradise; the damned on the left being thrust into hell-fire. The angels, in the wonderful variety of the coloring of their wings, their foreshortening, the realism of their trumpeting, the ideality of their type, are an extraordinary creation. The entire composition has a new harmony, richness and boldness of coloring that is missed by all Cavallini's successors, including Giotto, and is reconquered only by the Renaissance. Nothing at Assisi can be classed with such works as these. The mosaic of the Virgin and Child at S. Crisogono is rather weak for him, and his frescos there have disappeared, as have also those with which he covered the nave of S. Paul.

From the activity of Cavallini's school we can infer that of the master during the last decade of the thirteenth century, but nothing has been saved or recovered that can be safely ascribed to him. The fresco in the apse of S. Giorgio in Velabro, painted at this time, may have been his, but it is repainted, and even in the composition there is little to mark it as Cavallini's, because the artist was probably obliged to follow the traditional composition of Roman apses that places here Christ flanked by the patrons and martyrs of the Church.

The only other incontestable work is one belonging to his old age: the frescos of S. Maria Donna Regina at Naples. When the school dispersed with the departure for Avignon, Cavallini went to Naples, and in 1308 and the subsequent years we find him receiving an annual pension of thirty ounces of gold from King Charles II of Anjou. In all probability he was not alone but at the head of a large workshop, if not as large as the one in Rome. Since the recovery of the S. Cecilia frescos, it has become clear that in the decoration of S. Maria Donna Regina we have three hands: Cavallini's for the great scene of the Last Judgment on the inner wall of the façade and the scenes from the Passion in the upper part of the nave; Cavallini's pupils in the choirs of angels on the triumphal arch; a Sienese master's in the scenes from the lives of the saints (*e.g.* S. Elizabeth of Hungary) in the lower part of the nave. It seems doubtful, as we study the almost monochromatic effect of the tones of terracotta with which the four superposed tiers of Cavallini's scenes are treated, whether this work was ever completed.

Giottesque Crucifixion at S. Saba.

These two epic pages of the Last Judgment scene in Rome and Naples make it unusually easy, from the unity of their theme, to trace the change in Cavallini's style in the course of about twenty-five years. The milder, more delicate types at Naples are due to broader expanses of unbroken tone, a greater use of whites and less brush and line work. It is a natural development and one that lessened the divergences between him and Giotto, whose work by this time at Rome, Assisi, Florence and Padua had given him the popular primacy in painting.

Giotto. — Giotto's work in Rome need only be referred to, because though he received his artistic education in Rome his style was so much his own as to place him outside the Roman school. He lived and worked there at intervals between c. 1285 and 1303, alternating with his work at Assisi and in Tuscany. The altar-piece at S. Peter's is thought by most critics to be one of his early Roman productions, though a critic has recently disputed his authorship. The "Navicella," a mosaic representing the Bark of the Church weathering the storms and Christ saving Peter from the waves, entirely made over during the Renaissance, is a tribute to the popularity of mosaic work in Rome in Giotto's younger days. He was probably engaged to refresco part of the ancient basilica of S. Peter, but made only a small beginning. His last work was also one of the very last works of art executed in Rome before the departure for Avignon. It was a colossal historic fresco representation of the proclamation of the Papal Jubilee of 1303 from the Lateran Loggia by Pope Boniface VIII, of which a small fragment remains.

Torriti. — Even while Cavallini was resuscitating the art of fresco-painting, there were other artists in Rome who were more mosaicists than frescoists, and who connected themselves rather with the Byzantine than with the antique element in the Roman school. It was this group of artists that influenced Cimabue. They were magnificent decorators and colorists, but poor story-tellers and not yet touched with the life, the sense of reality and dramatic power that seethe in Cavallini. The foremost of these artists was Torriti.

The mosaic in the apse of S. John Lateran is the earlier of the two Roman masterpieces of Jacopo Torriti, and was completed in 1291 with the assistance of Jacopo da Camerino, the year before Cavallini had completed his Life of the Virgin at S. Maria in Trastevere. The mosaic that we see is modern in its execution, as the present apse is a modern construction, when its position was moved back at the time of the recent restoration. But it is a faithful facsimile, and from it and from early photographs I feel certain that Torriti was by no means the creator but only the restorer of this mosaic, which

in some parts, notably the bust of Christ, retained the work of
the early Christian era (fourth to fifth century). Above is a
heavenly sphere, in which the bust of Christ, overhung by a
seraph and accompanied by eight angels, floats in the clouds.
Below is the church on earth. In the centre, on the sacred
mount, rises the Cross, on which the Holy Spirit is descending
from the Divine Christ. The four rivers flow from it, and
deer and lambs drink at their sources, while in and about their

Apse Mosaic of S. John Lateran (Reconstructed).
(Fourth to thirteenth centuries.)

united waters play a multitude of fishes, birds, animals and
genii. On the flowery background stand the saints; on the
right the Virgin, S. Peter and S. Paul; on the left John the
Baptist, John the Evangelist and S. Andrew. These figures
are regularly spaced, so that an awkward effect is produced by
the insertion, on one side of S. Francis of Assisi, between the
Virgin and S. Peter, and on the other of S. Antony of Padua
on a far smaller scale. In the same fashion the small figure
of Pope Nicholas IV is placed, kneeling, at the feet of the
Virgin. A peremptory proof that these three small figures
were added to a previously existing mosaic is given by the
figure of the Virgin. Her right hand was originally *raised,*

z

like that of the other figures, as is shown by the folds of
drapery, but Torriti when he placed the Pope at her feet,
brought her right arm down so as to rest her hand on his head,
though leaving the telltale drapery. Undoubtedly Torriti
restored the larger figures, but they belong to a far earlier
master, a Byzantine artist (Andrew is entirely modern). The
angels above are Torriti's. The charming scene of the
terrestrial paradise goes back, like the bust of Christ, to

Apse Mosaic of S. Maria Maggiore.
(Fourth to thirteenth centuries.)

the early Christian age. Below this large scene, between the
windows, are the figures of nine apostles, standing between
palm-trees. All this work at the Lateran has been so modernized that we must turn to Torriti's later activity at S.
Maria Maggiore for an appreciation of his style.

Planned by Nicholas IV and the two Colonna cardinals, the
mosaics of the façade and apse of S. Maria Maggiore were
carried out by several artists: Jacopo Torriti, Filippo Rusutti and Gaddo Gaddi, and are important works of unequal
merit and charm. The work commenced in the apse under
the direction of Torriti, by whom it was completed in 1295.
I agree with Müntz in regarding the main composition as by

no means entirely of the time of Torriti. This artist retained the old fourth (or fifth) century mosaic that still existed as a framework for his work. The decoration was then purely ornamental, without figures, an immense scroll-pattern of the Vine, unwinding its symbolic spirals over the entire semi-dome. Cutting out the centre and the lower section of these spirals, Torriti placed there: above, a large starry sphere almost filled by a cushioned throne on which are seated, side by side, Christ and the Virgin whom He is crowning. On either side and below, are choirs of adoring angels on a much smaller scale. Beneath, midway in size, is a line of figures stretching across the apse. On the right S. Peter, S. Paul and S. Francis, with the kneeling Pope, Nicholas IV; on the left, John the Baptist, John the Evangelist and S. Antony, with the kneeling figure of Cardinal Giacomo Colonna, who paid for the work. It is easy to see how unnaturally Torriti was obliged to twist and terminate the antique spirals in order to insert his figures.

Below, between the windows, are five small compositions from the Life of the Virgin, similar to those at S. Maria in Trastevere. They are: Annunciation, Nativity, Adoration of the Magi, Presentation in the Temple, Death of the Virgin (in the centre). A comparison between this and the similar frieze at S. Maria in Trastevere is interesting as demonstrating better than anything how Torriti represented the fine flower of Byzantine color-sense and skill in decorative design, transfused by the influence of the antique decorative elements in the Roman school, while Cavallini, disdaining the less fundamental elements of art, reached out for the expression of life, character and thought in the figures. Torriti charms our æsthetic sense; Cavallini grips our dramatic and religious sense. Torriti stands at the summit of the receding wave of art, delicate but lifeless; Cavallini leads the charge of the new-born breakers, instinct with life.

On the façade of S. Maria Maggiore the mosaics are both badly restored and by artists inferior to Torriti. The main central scene, on a large scale, has the figure of the enthroned Christ in an aureole accompanied by angels and evangelists;

below is a row of eight saints. This work is signed by a Roman artist named Filippo Rusutti. The scenes below refer to the legends of the founding of the basilica: the visions of Pope Liberius and of the Patricius, the miracle of the summer fall of snow that gave its mediæval name to the basilica of S. Maria *ad nives,* and the miraculous indication of the site for the new church. A number of small works have escaped the fate of the more extensive wall-paintings. This is especially the case with the frescos and mosaics protected by the canopies of the tombs. To Torriti and Giovanni Cosmati are assigned those of the tombs of Matteo d'Acquasparta, Gonzalvo, Durand, etc., dating c. 1300. Of similar style is a lunette over the side door of S. Maria in Aracœli, and a somewhat larger mosaic of the Colonna chapel. These are all school pieces.

Until the very close of its history Roman painting reflects, therefore, the two currents — classic and Byzantine. At the close the classic element, led by Cavallini, became paramount because of the newly awakened national spirit of Italy, which was showing itself in painting after having been embodied in every other form of culture. The painters who drifted from Rome to Naples, to Avignon and France, to Umbria and Tuscany, became more and more subjugated by the Giottesque version of the parent school. Rome itself has a number of such works that have been only slightly studied; some seem even to be unknown, like the superb scene in the monastery of S. Sisto. Thus, in the hour of the dispersal of the school, as its members moved north and south, they helped to spread the new Romano-Giottesque style.

I cannot close this chapter without referring again to the Assisi frescos, because they not only epitomize the activity of the Roman school during its last half-century, but also illustrate this passing on of the torch to the Tuscan artists of Florence and Siena. The Upper Church was undoubtedly not only the first to have its pictorial decoration planned, but the more important in regard to its subjects. The decoration commenced in the apse and transepts. This part is in such deplorable condition that no judgment can be given of its color scheme or technique; of anything, in fact, but the themes, composition and line effects. The Roman scheme was followed of giving here the dogmatic subjects and those taken from the Apocalypse, as illustrating the Spiritual Church. In both transepts the series culminates in an idealized Crucifixion, the basis and foundation for the church on earth, which is to be illustrated in the nave. There is a wealth of ideas in these compositions with their numerous figures and occasional dramatic force, which points to a master like Cavallini, whose earliest known works they would be. But here, as in the nave, we would recognize undoubtedly the hands of several artists if the frescos were less damaged.

In the nave the usual Roman scheme was followed. The Old Testament is illustrated by sixteen scenes on one side, covering the upper part of the wall, under the vaults; and the same number illustrate the New Testament on the opposite side. Evangelists, prophets and Fathers of the Church fill the vaults; one figure in each vaulting compartment. This part was apparently planned by the same master who directed the work in choir and transept, though it would be too bold to affirm this positively. What is perfectly clear is that as many as five or six, if not more, painters were actually engaged in carrying out the master's designs, at about the same time. Of these men at least three show absolutely distinct, almost diametrically opposed manners: (a) the dramatic author of the Sacrifice of Abraham, a master of linear power; (b) the quiet but intense painter of the Blessing of Isaac, with his mastery of drapery and story-telling; (c) the decorative master of the vault of the four evangelists, lacking in the sense of life and over-fond of clumsy accessories. These and the rest were Roman masters, all of whom betray the desire to attain to naturalness, each in his own way. Such scenes as those of the Passion on the opposite (left) wall show that one of these ways was through the reproduction of the ugliness of the types of the common people. The individuality shown by these various painters belonging to the school of Cavallini is quite remarkable; it is greater than will be the case during the two succeeding generations of the followers of Giotto.

An effect of greater unity is produced by the line of twenty-eight scenes from the life of S. Francis, which were placed beneath these Bible scenes on both walls. They are usually attributed to Giotto who, after having served his apprenticeship among the painters of the Bible scenes, was given full direction of the later series below. It may be doubted, however, whether the compositions nearest the transept are not maturer works of Cavallini himself, the series being completed by his greatest pupil, Giotto.[1]

It is through this Bible series that it is possible to connect still closer the Roman and Tuscan schools in Florence itself. At the Baptistery the mosaic decoration commenced in 1225, in the apse, by a Roman painter named Jacobus, was later extended to the dome in a most elaborate series of Bible stories culminating in the Last Judgment, the execution of which was continued into the fourteenth century. While Byzantine mosaicists apparently were put in charge of the colossal composition of the Last Judgment, we are able to see, by comparison with the frescos in the nave at Assisi, that the Roman mosaicists of the close of the thirteenth century were responsible for a considerable portion of the Bible stories. Perhaps it was in Florence, therefore, that the Roman school of mosaic-painting ended its days, in the home of Cimabue and Giotto.

---

[1] The decoration of the Lower Church was at first sporadic. This is shown by the famous Madonna fresco by Cimabue, which was painted previous to any general scheme, and afterwards worked into the design of the Giottesque age.

ROMAN ARTISTS

CAN anything be said of the personality, social condition and methods of the artists who worked in Rome during these centuries? I have already described their condition during the Roman decadence, when individuality was killed by the tyranny of imperial guilds and labor unions. The guilds were then supplemented or succeeded by the monasteries, and only a few individuals, such as Agatho and Januarius, emerge.

There is a striking contrast between Byzantine and mediæval Rome in the personality of its artists. Between the sixth and the eleventh centuries hardly a single lay artist can be mentioned, while numerous indications lead us to infer that it was in the monasteries that we must look for artists of all kinds. When the revival commenced at the close of the eleventh century, Rome was not an exception in Italy, but joined the other provinces in wresting art from the hands of the Benedictine and Greek monks and in establishing lay guilds and ateliers after the Lombard fashion.

The twelfth and thirteenth centuries saw the development of art under the auspices of these local schools throughout Italy. It was only after the middle of the thirteenth century that the monks, represented by the new orders of S. Francis and S. Dominic, succeeded in partly reëstablishing their hold on the Fine Arts and in working side by side with the lay artists.

Guilds. — In most Italian cities the artists joined a guild, such as that of the masons or stone-cutters, or of the painters, and the character of their unions is shown by many mediæval documents in which their constitution and organization, their membership and history are illustrated. This was the case in Siena, Florence, Bologna and many other cities. In Rome the case is not quite so clear; yet it would seem as if there were a guild of *marmorarii* which included all artists whether archi-tects, decorators, stone-cutters or mosaicists. Guilds had always existed in the eternal city. The monopolistic unions of the imperial age had never been wiped out, even by the Gothic wars. Under the denomination of *Scholæ* the population of Rome had been, as we have seen, carefully divided and organized according to occupations and nationali-ties in the early Middle Ages. As in other mediæval cities each industry was assigned to a street or quarter and there lived and worked in compact homogeneous groups, each with its church and its guild-hall or *Schola*.

But in Rome there was an even closer bond between certain smaller groups of artists. It is known how the unions of the late Empire had been tyrannically dealt with by the govern-ment: their occupation and membership made forcibly heredi-tary, so that the son could have no other occupation than that of his father; their residence in a single city also obligatory, so that if an artisan went to work in another city, he could be brought back by force; the association itself, in return for the privilege of monopoly, obliged to give free service to the State for all public works. Of course, with the decay and obliteration of imperial authority the enforcement of these conditions ceased. Service to the State remained in force, it is true, in Northern Italy and Venice, where centralized civil authority had never suffered an eclipse, but in Rome it could not be enforced by the Papacy. Gregory the Great sought to enforce the law of residence, but even that was a dead letter.

Families of Artists. — As for the third condition, that of hereditary occupation, it is curious to see how it survived even though the fact that the arts were monopolized from the sixth to the eleventh centuries by the celibate monks would seem to have given a death-blow to the hereditary habit in art. The reason is that in connection with the great monasteries were art schools and villages of artisans, where the people were the serfs or liegemen of the monasteries, from father to son, and from these obscure artisans, who preserved the hereditary habit, sprang, in many cases, the material from which the labor and art guilds were formed after the eleventh century.

At all events the Roman school of lay artists, from the time
of its reorganization in c. 1100 A.D., appears to consist of a few
family groups, constituting special art-schools whose traditions
and clientèle were handed down through several generations.
They worked not only in Rome itself, but throughout the province, in cities, towns and monasteries, but having probably one
central workshop in Rome. Among the many signed works
there is a large proportion where father and son worked together and take joint credit, and quite a number signed by
brothers. When the work of completely constructing and decorating a single one of the churches of this period in the characteristic mediæval Roman style, with its various accessories of
tower, cloister, monastery, church furniture and monuments, is
reckoned up, and this activity is multiplied by the hundreds of
such churches built or decorated in Rome and its province during these two centuries, it is evident that we must look upon
the Roman school as an exceedingly active and aggressive ag-
glomeration of a few large workshops each under a head master,
swarming with younger artists and apprentices, all under the
direction of the head of the family and his sons.

Workshops and Studios. — These workshops were often established in or near important ruinous buildings of the ancient
city where there was a large supply of the fine marbles, the
columns, pavements, revetments, sculptured details that were
required for materials and models and where lime-kilns could
be established conveniently. We may be allowed to conclude
that there were several departments to these large establishments. The Roman master artist was usually a man of even
broader artistic education and technical ability than the average always broadly educated mediæval artist. He was obliged
to be a designer of buildings and of details, a sculptor and a
practical decorator. He designed also the church furniture
and monuments, and executed the mosaic inlay with which
they were usually decorated. In his workshop there must
have been a section for mosaic work with furnaces for melting
the glass, making the plaster, sorting the cubes and preparing
the gold. There must have been offices for the preparation of
sketches, cartoons, models or other preliminary work; and of

course the stone-cutters' department and that for figure carving. It is quite possible that there was also a department for wall-painting, as all the churches of this period were more or less thoroughly frescoed, and we know that in more than one case a mosaicist and decorator was also a painter.

Often in quite small monuments nearly all these sections were called upon to take a hand. In a ciborium or a sepulchral monument, the sculptor, the mosaicist, the decorator and sometimes the painter collaborated. In connection with the sculptor's workshop there were often collections of models, including even antique statues. A statue of Æsculapius, for instance, was copied and signed by one of the Vassalletti and found in the ruins of his family workshop. At the Lateran Cloister, Vassallettus copied sphinxes, probably from the Isæum. The work at S. Lorenzo and at the cathedral of Civita Castellana is accurately classic. The finest capitals, cornices and friezes from the ancient buildings were set up for study, and the work of the school shows that its artists knew how to select good models, rejecting the products of the later Empire.

It is to this universal talent, this aggregation collected under one roof and one master-hand, that we owe the unity and harmony of the school's work, which, had it not been so almost universally and hideously marred by the barbarous churchmen of the Barocco period, would have given us in its way as wonderful a picture as that of some of the untouched French Gothic cathedrals.

It must not be supposed that the high grade of organization and workmanship was easily attained. Almost the entire twelfth century was consumed in a steady, slow advance. Neither did the existence of the family schools exclude the collaboration of artists not belonging to the same family. Drudus de Trivio, for example, was an apprentice and junior member in the school of Laurentius.

Work for the Province. — In these workshops were prepared not only the works destined for the churches of Rome itself, but part of those executed for the churches throughout the province. It was comparatively easy to forward them to their destination on wagons over the excellent Roman roads. It is interesting in this connection to note that the works of the school are far more numerous in the towns that are easily accessible from the Roman roads or directly on them than in the remoter towns, showing that it was not easy to execute works of importance on the spot without the transfer of a large force.

It was not only small articles of church furniture, ciboriums, sepulchral monuments and the like, that were executed in Rome for the province, but even large architectural works, such as the doorways or rose windows of church façades and even entire cloisters. The parts were all carefully marked so that the work could be set up without difficulty either by the artist himself accompanying his material or by local craftsmen. This was, for instance, the case with part at least of the cloister at Subiaco, the earlier part executed by Jacobus, son of Laurentius, in about 1200. I noted there that not only each base, shaft and capital, but all the stones of the piers and arcades were carefully numbered or marked.

Were they Architects? — It is a matter of dispute whether the Roman *marmorarii* were also architects in the strict sense; that is, whether they also planned and constructed the buildings they decorated.

Now, in Rome itself the construction of churches was not a matter of much consequence or artistic interest. None of the mathematical knowledge, none of the traditional technique, none of the trained handling of materials were required that raised the builders of the North to a high pinnacle of artistry. The walls of the churches were a thin and plain brick screen perforated with perfectly plain unmoulded apertures for windows. We may grant, as we examine the body of a Roman church, that there was no art in this business of brick-laying, and that it was outside the province of the *marmorarii*. So plain was the brick-work that the apses, for instance, were not decorated even with the lines of false arcades so common elsewhere as the simplest form of ornament. To diversify this meagreness came the mosaicists who covered the upper part of the façade and sometimes the outer face of the apse with mosaic pictures. Then came especially the *marmorarii* to fill the windows with thin slabs of marble and alabaster cut in open-work patterns; to set in marble doors with their columns, resting often on lions; and to cover the lower part of the façade with the long portico.

Probably the mechanical work of building belonged in Rome to a different art guild, and not to that to which our artists, the *marmorarii*, belonged. Whatever the name of the builder's guild may have been in Rome, its members appear to have been called *muratores*, the ancestor of the common modern Italian term for them (*muratori*). Thus we find one of them as a witness to a deed in 1200: *Magister Rainucius, murator,* — evidently a master-builder, not a common laborer. Whereas in a contemporary deed of 1193 we read *Alexius, marmorarius,* an ordinary member of the guild of *marmorarii*, not a master in it such as the men whose names we see on the monuments.

Another class of artist who may also have belonged to the same guild as the *muratores*, are the *fabricatores*, who were possibly the *magistri* of the guild of masons. There is one case of the signature of an architect-stone-mason, where the genealogy is given to the fourth generation, presumably from generations of artists. It is the inscription recording the construction of the great Capitoline stairway, unique in the Middle Ages, leading up to S. Maria in Aracœli, built in 1348, after the great plague, by order of Cola di Rienzo. Its architect was Lorenzo, of whom the inscription says : —

MAGISTER . LAURENTIUS . SIMEONI . ANDREOTII
CAROLI . FABRICATOR . DE . ROME . DE . REGIONE
COLUMPNE . FUNDAVIT . PROSECUTUS . EST
ET . CONSUMAVIT . UT . PRINCIPALIS . MAGISTER
HOC . OPUS . SCALARUM . INCEPTUM . ANNO
DOMINI . ANN . MCCCXLVIII . DIE . XXV . OCTOBRIS

It is when we turn from the church itself, an inheritance from earlier days, to the more characteristically mediæval structure of bell-towers and cloisters, described in previous chapters, that we see how intimately the work of the bricklayer was interwoven with that of the other arts, and to feel that probably the master of the works, *magister fabricæ*, was to be found among the *marmorarii ;* and that in such cases the artists we are to study had complete control. One might be tempted to attribute this position to the Lombard architects who were so prominent throughout Italy, both north and south, if it were not that not a single inscription records such an architect in Rome itself and none undoubtedly of this character even in the province.

Who were some of the artists who presided over the large workshops that supplied Rome and the province with all its art? A large number of artists, known to have worked in Rome between 1000 and 1300 A.D., could be named, but instead of a catalogue, useful merely to a specialist, only the men who stood in the front rank need be mentioned here. Earliest of all the sculptors was Christianus, who erected a cardinal's tomb in S. Prassede just before 1000.

Early Painters. — But the most prominent Roman artists of this and the next century were probably the fresco-painters, who developed a grand style.

Such were the two brothers John and Stephen, and their nephew Nicholas, who decorated S. Elia near Nepi; Heraclius, who wrote a handbook of painting that has been preserved; John, who accompanied Otho III to Germany. More than a century later we hear of Guido and Petrolinus as painters for Paschal II at the SS. Quattro Coronati and other churches, and a little later, of the painters who signed the martyrdom scenes at S. Agnese. One of the painters, Bentivenga, was even honored by the senatorship, in 1148, showing that it was not then impossible for artists to reach social and political distinction in Rome.

Foreign Artists. — All of them are not of Roman parentage. Several artists of the eleventh and twelfth centuries have names that are evidently Lombard, such as Gislebertus, who worked at S. Cecilia and three other churches; Obertus, who made the enamelled shrine for the confession of S. Peter, and the door at the Lateran basilica; Azo, who also worked in the Vatican basilica. Johannes, a Venetian sculptor, carved the doorway at S. Maria in Cosmedin. Certain branches of art industry were so much the specialty of a certain school that their works went everywhere. Bell-casting, for example, was such a specialty of the Pisan school; and the oldest bells in the Roman campanili were cast by Pisans, such as that of S. Maria Maggiore by Guidoctus Pisanus and his son Andreas. But these foreigners did not in the least affect the characteristics of the school, which was a product of the native soil, and owed but little to any but Byzantine and Campanian sources.

School of Paulus. — It was under Pope Paschal II that the school began, under his guidance, the work of reconstructing and redecorating the city after Guiscard's fire. The main glory of leadership must be given to an artist who signs himself *Paulus*, and who founded the first of these schools of combined architects, sculptors, decorators, and mosaicists of which we have any record. It was continued unto the fourth generation for three-quarters of a century. He had charge of making the pavement and choir-seats of the Vatican basilica, of which only insignificant fragments remain in the crypt. His earliest dated decorative work and that of which most remains is the pavement, and choir-screen, choir-seats and ambone in the cathedral of Ferentino, which he executed between 1106 and 1110, and will be described elsewhere.

Immediately after came the reconstruction, in 1112, of SS. Quattro Coronati in Rome, where, though his signature has perished, his hand is unmistakable in the scattered decoration of the interior and in the interesting cloister. Equally clear is it that he had charge, under the direction of Alfanus, ten years later, of the work at S. Maria in Cosmedin. Paulus died before the middle of the century, leaving four sons who had long been trained to continue his style. Johannes was the elder; the others were Petrus, Angelus and Sasso.

It was to this family school that was confided the decoration of S. Lorenzo-fuori-le-mura, with its ciborium, pulpits, choir-screen, etc., which was partly destroyed by Honorius III in c. 1217. The inscription on the ciborium gives the date 1147 and their names: —

JOHANNES PETRUS ANGELUS ET
SASSO FILII PAULI MARMORARII
HUIUS OPERIS MAGISTRI FUERUNT.

The next year the same brothers — except Petrus — were given similar work at S. Croce in Gerusalemme, where they signed the ciborium *Johannes de Paulo cum fratribus suis Angelo et Sasso huius operis magistri fuerunt.* A few years later they repeated these works at S. Marco and SS. Cosma e Damiano (1153–1154).

The son of one of these brothers, Nicolaus, son of Angelus, rose to as great eminence as his grandfather, between 1160 and 1180, advancing far beyond the level of his father and uncles and employing glass and paste mosaic cubes very largely in place of the larger marble cubes, thus gaining a delicacy and brilliancy for his work and increasing very considerably the proportion of decorative design over the plain surfaces. In this he was helped by Jacobus, son of Laurentius — of whom more later — who revolutionized the art of mosaic decoration in the school. It is, in fact, interesting to note that Nicolaus took as his associates the principal members of the two other leading artist-families in Rome. He had the son of Laurentius help him make the choir-screen at S. Bartolommeo all' Isola in 1180, that artist's share being the nineteen columns with their capitals that formed the open second story of the iconostasis stretching across the church. This is expressed in the signature: *Nicolaus de Angelo fecit hoc opus. Jacobus Laurentii fecit has XIX columnas cum capitellis suis.* Two of these columns have been saved and are now at S. Alessio — the most exquisite of their class ever done. Then, in the very different work of the carved paschal candlestick of S. Paolo, he was assisted by Petrus Vassallettus, whose family school was always more skilful in sculpture than the others.

The most considerable work by Nicolaus was probably the great portico of the Lateran basilica, due to him alone. Part of its columns and architrave were incorporated in the present Barocco porch, where they are lost. The original porch had an elaborate mosaic frieze and was signed: *Nicolaus Angeli fecit hoc opus.* The mosaic compositions decorating the frieze were traced before their destruction and these I have published.[1]

[1] *American Journal of Archæology*, 1887.

Signatures. — The fashion of signing their works was even more popular with these Roman artists than with any other Italian school. It is fortunate, for their names do not occur at all in contemporary literature and very seldom even in accounts and registers. If it were not for the inscriptions, hardly one of these artists could have been identified with his work. Yet, modest artisans though they may have been considered by their contemporaries, they had a pleasing consciousness not only of their own personal merit, but of their exceptional position as Romans. From the very beginning they were not troubled with modesty. Paulus, in signing his work at Ferentino, calls himself a great artist: *hoc opifex magnus fecit vir nomine Paulus.* A little later, when their art was more fully developed and they were more sure of their skill and style, they would call themselves "most learned Roman masters," *magistri doctissimi Romani,* and "Roman citizens," *cives Romani,* especially when signing their works outside of Rome, where they were not so well known and where they could more fitly vaunt themselves of their Roman birth.

School of Rainerius or Ranucius. — A second school arose in the wake of that of Paulus. It was founded by an artist whose name seems to be variously given as Rainerius and Ranucius, though it is not absolutely certain that these were not two distinct men. It would seem too strange a coincidence that two men should each have two sons with the same names and also artists in the same special branch. For in Rome, in the first half of the twelfth century, we find that the decorative work of the interior of S. Silvestro in Capite was given to Rainerius and his two sons, Nicolaus and Petrus. He signed it : —

EGO RAINERIUS CUM FILIIS MEIS NYCOLAUS ET PETRUS HOC
INCIPIMUS ET COMPLEVIMUS.

Then, toward the middle of the century, when we would expect the sons to have succeeded their father at the head of the workshop, we find Nicolaus and Petrus, called sons of Ranucius and Romans, artists of the decorative work on the façade at Corneto, which I describe under "Roman Province," where I also mention some of the subsequent work of this family school, as far as its fourth and apparently final generation.

School of Laurentius. — In about the middle of the twelfth century two other family schools were founded that were to be generous rivals in local leadership for almost a century, and to whom it is probable that the originality and greatness of the school were largely due. These are the family of Laurentius, commonly called the "Cosmati," and that of Vassallettus.

Laurentius, the son of Thebaldus, founded the family school to which Roman art owed the greatest progress. It struck very soon a new note. Joined to a greater technical perfection in the handling of line and surface was a deeper study and feeling of the antique, and a more exquisite sense of color and proportion. Until now the carving of capitals and cornices had been slack, outlines were blurred and classic forms rather parodied than reproduced. But Laurentius and his son Jacobus effected a transformation.

We do not know any of the early work by Laurentius, only what he did with his son's assistance. The refrain recurs again and again : *Laurentius cum Jacobo*, sometimes just these words, as in the decoration of the cathedral of Segni ; sometimes with the added *filio suo* and *hoc opus fecit* or *fecerunt* or *huius operis magister fuit.* A more poetic inscription in verse occurred on their pulpit in the old basilica of S. Peter : —

HOC OPUS EX AURO VITREIS LAURENTIUS EGIT
CUM JACOBO NATO SCULPSIT SIMUL AC PEREGIT.

Father and son worked indiscriminately throughout the normal sphere of Roman influence, having charge of important architectural and decorative work north of Rome at Civita Castellana and Falleri, to the east at the monastery of Subiaco, to the south at the cathedral of Segni. Most of their work in Rome is destroyed, and the two pulpits at S. Maria in Aracœli, though remodelled, could be reconstructed.

Laurentius seems to have died before 1205, leaving his son to complete their unfinished work on the cathedral of Civita Castellana and Subiaco. That Laurentius commenced his

2 A

artistic career earlier than is commonly imagined, perhaps in
about 1160, is shown by the fact that already in 1180 his son
Jacobus is a sufficiently experienced artist to be associated
with Nicolaus or Niccolò di Angelo in the work at S. Bartolommeo and to produce the wonderful nineteen colonnettes I have
mentioned.   In the year 1205, Jacobus signs his name alone,
without his father's, to the doorway at S. Saba in Rome, of

Mosaic Choir-stalls and Throne at S. Lorenzo (c. 1250).

whose two-storied portico and façade he seems to have been
the architect.   At the same time he executed the pavement
and decoration of S. Ambrogio in Pescheria.   Perhaps now,
certainly before 1209, he built the first section of the cloister
at Subiaco.   Then in 1210 Jacobus associated his own son
Cosmas in his work at Civita Castellana, to which he evidently
returned after completing these other undertakings, beginning
work there on the façade in 1208 or 1209 without his son's
assistance and then calling him in when he commenced the
great porch.   Henceforth the name of his son Cosmas is
coupled with his; once it is with a date, 1218, when he built

the doorway of the hospital of S. Tommaso in Formis with the mosaic medallion above it.

Meanwhile Cosmas himself was training his sons, and the family school was flourishing and expanding. Its popularity was warranted by its skill, and drew other artists to it. Shortly after 1220 his father Jacobus had retired or died and Cosmas alone is responsible for several works in the decade before 1230, as the ciborium and altar at SS. Giovanni e Paolo in Rome and the pavement of the cathedral at Anagni. It was to this cathedral that he appears to have devoted himself up to the year 1231, first alone and then with his two sons, old enough to join him. I shall describe elsewhere the extensive work they accomplished in the furnishing of this cathedral and its immense crypt with pavements, altars, choir-screens, ciboria, etc.

Hardly was this work finished when they were called to Subiaco to continue the work on the cloister which Jacobus had been obliged to discontinue in order to complete the cathedral of Civita Castellana and other unfinished work. This work done, before 1235, Lucas, the elder son, was sent back to Civita Castellana with Drudus, another member of the school, though not, apparently, a member of the family, to decorate the interior. They signed the superb choir-seats.

After this we lose sight of the school of Laurentius.

School of Vassallettus. — A couple of decades, perhaps, after Laurentius founded his school, another artist commenced a career and a family school that still remains obscure in its details and chronology, though exceedingly brilliant in its results. His name was variously spelled Bassallectus, Vassallettus or Vassallectus. There are rumors of a father before him; but what is certain is that in about 1170 Petrus Vassallectus was associated with Nicolaus de Angelo in the oft-mentioned carved paschal candlestick at S. Paul, and that in 1186 he worked at the cathedral of Segni. Perhaps we would not attach much importance to his name, were it not that he commenced the cloister of the Lateran completed by his more brilliant son, whose name was also Vassallettus without the prefixed "Petrus," between 1120 and 1230. Then follows a series of brilliant works, including the basilica and porch of S. Lorenzo, lasting till about 1270, whether all by this second Vassallettus or by a third generation is yet uncertain. There is an early work, by the father, at SS. Apostoli, the lion of a portal; then an episcopal throne at S. Croce in Gerusalemme, probably part of a large choir decoration and an undetermined work at the Vatican basilica — all in Rome. He also worked in the small towns of the province, as at Civita Lavinia (Cathedral). It is by his episcopal throne and paschal candlestick at the cathedral of Anagni that we can still admire the special talent he displayed as a sculptor. While brilliant as mosaicist and decorator, it is in the chapter on Sculpture that I will show how important a place Vassallettus takes in the revival of art.

All these family schools of the twelfth century had died out or intermingled before or shortly after the middle of the thirteenth century. The extension of the art had favored independent artists. Men like the two Andreas, father and son, who decorated S. Maria in Monticelli at Rome (1215); like Pietro at Alba; like Ivo at Vicovaro; like Petrus Oderisi at Viterbo, perhaps the same Petrus who was called by King Henry III to decorate Westminster Abbey — all these brilliant men had, so far as we know, no family connections as a reason for their artistic career.

Family of Cosmatus. — But before the close of the school's history, one more family emerges and after a brilliant and fruitful career dies out with Roman art itself; it is the school of Cosmatus.

This artist is known at present only by the chapel of the Sancta Sanctorum, a masterpiece described elsewhere and executed in 1277–1278. His four sons are known by works ranging between c. 1295 and 1332. These four sons were Jacobus, Petrus, Johannes and Adeodatus. Of the two latter only do we need describe the works, as they were particularly productive.

The specialty of Johannes, or as he is commonly called, Giovanni Cosmati, was sepulchral monuments, including mosaic paintings and frescos, showing that he, more than any other member of the school, had felt the influence of the new pictorial revival. His work is noticed elsewhere in detail. Nothing of his dates later than 1301. As a sculptor and decorator his work is hardly equal to the great masters who preceded him. He is a *Kleinmeister.*

Deodatus, probably the youngest of the brothers, had more originality and a better technique, as designer, decorator and sculptor. Under Boniface VIII he probably had charge of the artistic work done at the Lateran in anticipation of the Jubilee of 1300. Though he felt the influence of Arnolfo, he shows in his ciborium at S. Maria in Cosmedin that he was less inclined to abandon the use of mosaics for that of sculpture in church furniture, and also shows his exquisite taste as a designer, equal if not superior to the great Arnolfo's. His work for Boniface must be credited to his youth, as he lived and worked for thirty years longer, though not in Rome, for he was one of those who emigrated when the School disintegrated on the departure of the Popes.

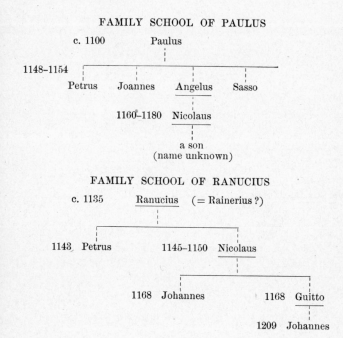

FAMILY SCHOOL OF PAULUS

c. 1100   Paulus

1148–1154

Petrus Joannes Angelus Sasso

1160–1180 Nicolaus

a son
(name unknown)

FAMILY SCHOOL OF RANUCIUS

c. 1135   Ranucius (= Rainerius ?)

1143 Petrus   1145–1150 Nicolaus

1168 Johannes   1168 Guitto

1209 Johannes

FAMILY SCHOOL OF LAURENTIUS

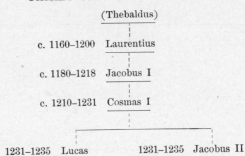

(Thebaldus)

c. 1160–1200   Laurentius

c. 1180–1218   Jacobus I

c. 1210–1231   Cosmas I

1231–1235   Lucas   1231–1235   Jacobus II

FAMILY SCHOOL OF BASSALLECTUS

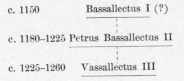

c. 1150   Bassallectus I (?)

c. 1180–1225   Petrus Bassallectus II

c. 1225–1260   Vassallectus III

FAMILY SCHOOL OF COSMAS II

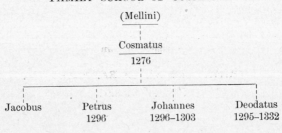

(Mellini)

Cosmatus
1276

Jacobus   Petrus   Johannes   Deodatus
                 1296   1296–1303   1295–1332

ART IN THE ROMAN PROVINCE

Geographical Limits. — Many of the small towns and cities of the Roman province preserve mediæval works of art that complete the contemporary series in Rome itself. It is merely by accident that they happen to be elsewhere than in Rome. The same artists of the twelfth and thirteenth centuries whose names are found in Roman churches also claim the authorship of many of these provincial monuments, and other artists whose works in Rome itself are now destroyed are known only from the records of their artistic work in the province. The limits of the activity of the Roman school were practically determined by political conditions. They extend southward a little farther than the Pontine marshes, to Fondi and Gaeta, being bounded on the south by the province of Naples. From the coast the line runs northeast and northwest through Sora, Celano and Rieti, leaving the Abruzzi to the northeast except a fringe of it which comes within Roman influence, as at Alba and Rocca di Botte. Continuing northward, the southwest part of Umbria is found to be partly invaded by the Roman school, so that the line runs above Spoleto and Foligno, crosses westward to Orvieto and ends on the seaboard at Grosseto, near the Tuscan border.

Within these boundaries the rôle of the Roman school of art was quite similar to that of the Papacy itself. The sturdy municipalities of the province only grudgingly and occasionally recognized the temporal power of the Popes or the suzerainty of the Roman Republic. They had their independent communal organization, as Rome itself had, and spelled over again the relations of Rome and the same Volscian cities in the primitive days of antiquity. At the same time the local bishop and the feudal families strengthened the tie with Rome. Three of the Popes belonged to the great feudal family of the Conti, Lords of Segni and of a large part of the Campagna. The Savelli of Rome were lords of the greater part of Sabina. The Colonnas, Orsinis, Vicos, Anguillaras and a dozen more of the great Roman families held immense feudal domains throughout the province. The art of the country-seats could not vary far from that of the metropolis.

Finally, the fact that so many of the Popes of the twelfth and thirteenth centuries travelled and lived with their court in the principal cities, both north and south, was an important factor.

Roman artists were, therefore, called by bishops, abbots, nobles and by the Popes themselves to supersede local artists. But they often found themselves face to face with novel conditions. In the architecture they usually found that local stone was used and had to be used in place of the brick they were accustomed to. The builders with whom they associated were often men with quite different artistic traditions, who employed vaulting, rose-windows, figured sculpture, in harmony with Lombard and Apulian ideas. To this they were obliged to adapt themselves.

Corneto. — The most complete and consecutive example of the connection of a school of Roman artists with a monument in the Roman province is that of the family of Ranucius with the church of S. Maria di Castello at Corneto. This church is perhaps the most considerable unspoiled work of vaulted construction of the Lombard type in the whole Roman province. It was founded in 1121 and its construction appears to have lasted about forty years.

The rather thin simplicity of its exterior hardly prepares one for the grand lines of its vaulted interior, with the immense span of the groin-vaulting and high heavy piers. Certainly no artist of the Roman school designed it; the structure stands at the opposite pole to a Roman basilica. But if we examine the façade, we will notice that the main portal and the large two-light window above it produce quite a different effect from the rest of the work. They are of white marble decorated with mosaic inlay and designed with that fine sense of proportion and surface that are henceforth to characterize the school. The architrave of the door is inscribed : —

RANUCII PETRUS LAPIDUM NON DOGMATE MERUS
ISTUD OPUS MIRE STRUXIT QUOQUE FECIT OPTIME.

It is dated 1143. Pietro, son of Ranucius, was, then, its author. The window above is inscribed: —

NICOLAUS RANUCII MAGISTER ROMANUS FECIT.

This second artist, Nicolo, was the other's brother. Both were Romans of the family school of Ranucius.

The greater part of the mosaic work has disappeared. Originally it filled the planes of the pilastered archivolts, in delicate patterns, the lines of which were uninterrupted in the window, but in the door were made to encircle disks in designs borrowed from the pavements, as was the case with all the primitive essays at vertical decoration of the sort. The delicate columns of the doorway are of *breccia corallina*. Their capitals, which support a torus archivolt, are a thoroughly mediæval adaptation of the classic type, not at all the exact reproduction that we shall see later in the school of Laurentius.

This by no means ended the school's activity in the church. The pavement was their work, though it is not signed; but they did attach their names both to the ciborium over the altar and to the ambone or pulpit. The ciborium is dated 1166 and inscribed: —

JOHANNES ET GUITTO MAGISTRI HOC OPUS FECERUNT.

That these two artists were brothers, sons of the author of the window in this church, Niccolo di Ranuccio, is shown by the signature on another ciborium, that in the church of S. Andrea *in Flumine* near Ponzano, where we read: —

NICOLAUS CUM SUIS FILIIS JOHANNES ET GUITTONE
FECERUNT HOC OPUS.

As the Corneto ciborium has been almost entirely modernized, its original form must be sought in the unspoiled one at Ponzano, which is a trifle earlier, being the work of the two brothers while their father was still living and directing them. It has the same general design as that of S. Giorgio in Velabro and as those of the other contemporary family of Paulus at S. Lorenzo and elsewhere. Only in such details as the capitals we seem to see less of antique influence and none that is archaistically mediæval.

Still later is the ambone at Corneto. It was not done until 1209; and yet it is by one of the same family, by John, son of the Guitto of the ciborium!

· · · PER MANUS JOHANNIS GUITTONIS CIVIS ROMANUS.

This ambone is a peculiar work, for it shows how a style of design could persist in a family school for over sixty years, while other family schools were making history. There is no perceptible change in the scheme for the arrangement of the mosaic patterns, and the lines and grotesque carvings of the colonnette-corbels are as barbarous as the worst work of the tenth and eleventh centuries.

For this reason I hesitate to attribute to the John, the uncle of this artist and joint author of the ciborium, a highly decorated ambone at the other end of the province, in the cathedral of Fondi, though it is certainly a work of the twelfth century. It is inscribed with one of the most discursive and descriptive of such dedications : —

TABULA MARMOREIS VITREIS DISTINCTA LAPILLIS
DOCTORIS STUDIO SIC EST ERECTA JOHANNIS
ROMANO GENITO COGNOMINE NICOLAO.

"This marble slab picked out with designs in marble and glass cubes is erected by the art of the learned John born of a Roman father named Niccolo." The mosaic inlay is here extremely rich and in the style affected in the neighboring Terracina, under the influence of the early Campanian school of decorators of Sessa, Salerno, Amalfi, Ravello and Cava. Whether we can identify this author of the Fondi pulpit with the artist of the same name at Corneto depends on how much allowance we are willing to make for a change in a man's style under the influence of a new environment. The inscription would seem to indicate that this use of mosaic work was a novelty.

Toscanella. — About halfway between Corneto and Viterbo, in the northernmost part of the Roman province, is Toscanella, with a most interesting group of churches and civil and military structures standing in untouched and picturesque desolation. The churches are quite *sui generis:* wooden-roofed basilicas, yet not of the Roman type. Neither are they like

Façade of S. Pietro, Toscanella.
(With main doorway by Roman artists.)

anything in Tuscany or Lombardy, or even in the nearest cities, Vetralla or Viterbo. The most interesting of the churches are S. Pietro and S. Maria Maggiore. The immense span of their arcades, the stone seats separating nave and aisles at S. Pietro, the type of the heavy and crude capitals, the thick-set columns, are all features of immense character. Equally striking are the façades: symmetrical, with their quadruple division of portal, gallery, rose-window and gable; yet barbaric in the colossal carved figures representing the forces of nature (dragons, bulls, etc.) and the forces of the spirit (symbols of evangelists, etc.). The hand of Apulian artists is betrayed in these monsters and in the Byzantine line of reversed foliage that forms some of the portal archivolts.

Without denying other traces of their presence there is one feature, the main portal of S. Pietro, which is indubitably by the hand of a Roman artist, contemporary with the brothers of the Corneto façade, Pietro and Niccolò, if he be not earlier and of the time of Paschal II. If anything, the style is a trifle more beautiful. The greater recessing, marked by the three shafts instead of the single one, is due to the projection of the central section of the façade. This doorway, though certainly contemporary with the rest of the façade, is not only different in its texture, — a white marble that contrasts with the loose-textured peperino of the rest, — but in the principles of design. At the same time, while no Roman artist was responsible for the rest of the design of the façade, the Roman handiwork is evident in the mosaic inlay of the bands of the rose-window and its frame and around the two-light windows, also in the colonnettes of windows and gallery. Inside the church there can be no doubt that the pavement is of the regular Roman type — well preserved in the choir. The date of 1093, given as that of the consecration of the high altar, is indicative of the time of construction. The ciborium on which it is cut is not, however, by the hand of a Roman artist; it is rather Apulian.

Viterbo is architecturally one of the most surprising of the small mediæval cities of Italy. Its basilical churches, its episcopal palace, its picturesque and highly finished private palaces, its beautiful fountains and the cathedral with its campanile, form a varied group of structures of the twelfth and thirteenth centuries when Viterbo lived a full and strenuous life in the closest connection with Rome and the Popes, many of whom passed here a large part of their pontificate. Of its works of art I shall speak only as they connect with Rome and her art. Studied as a whole Viterbo has a distinct school of architecture. Its cathedral campanile in its polychromy and with its low spire is not in the least Roman. And yet we must allow that in the construction of its churches the artists of Viterbo not only adopted the Roman basilical type, but also exported from Rome the columns used in them. They went even further, for in details like the rose-window of S. Giovanni in Zoccoli (similar to that of S. Pietro, Toscanella, which it resembles in its interior) we see the hand of a Roman mosaicist; and the pavement of the cathedral is also by a Roman.

It was during the years following the middle of the thirteenth century, that Viterbo saw the most numerous works by Roman artists, — works which are mostly described elsewhere: the tombs of Popes Clement IV and Hadrian V, of Prefect de Vico, the tabernacle by Vassalletto, the description of which comes more properly in the historic review of Roman sculpture.

Orvieto. — Even further north is Orvieto, which though on the Tuscan border was regarded as an outpost of the Roman province. From its proximity to the Tiber Orvieto could easily obtain antique materials from Rome, and there are here even more traces of Rome than at Viterbo, which it almost equals in the interest of its mediæval architecture. Its civil structures and its basilicas are not, it is true, on as high a level of workmanship and are careless in detail, but its two superb public palaces and its incomparable cathedral are superior to anything in Viterbo. Orvietan architecture also is characteristically local.

The earliest Roman work here is the mosaic pavement of the monastic church of SS. Silvestro e Martirio, outside the city — a real architectural enigma of the twelfth century. Almost as early is the city church of S. Andrea, rebuilt in the twelfth century with a mosaic pavement and several pieces of Roman church furniture of the close of the thirteenth century: a memorial tabernacle with twisted columns supporting a trefoil arch and framing an altar picture of the Virgin and Child with two saints; and a pulpit. The pulpit is a good piece of Roman mosaic decoration. It has not the Roman shape, but that affected by the preachers of the Franciscan and Dominican orders. It is a five-sided structure set up against the right-hand pier at the transept.

The façade of the cathedral of Orvieto, a piece of polychromy and sculpture, is an instance of how Roman materials and artists could be made to subserve a design that was absolutely anti-classic. Several Roman artists are known to have worked upon it and for it, especially in the mosaic inlay, and the materials for it came from Rome.

Only one other relic of Rome remains in Orvieto, the tomb of Cardinal de Braye, by Arnolfo, an early masterpiece which is described among his works.

Umbria. — Crossing the Tiber just below Orvieto, we find a unique example of a provincial form of the Roman style in the church of S. Maria Assunta at Lugnano in southwest Umbria. The porch extending across the façade is not far different from the heavier early Roman porticos such as that of S. Giorgio in Velabro, and the architrave is relieved of excessive weight in the same way by low arches, only the effect is far different, for instead of being of brick and concealed in the brickwork, they are free-standing. The Roman mosaic inlay, which decorates porch and façade, appears also in the confession at the high altar. It is a very complete little church, unspoiled except in its vaulting and apse. There is no trace of antique materials; everything was executed on the site.

Further north in Umbria, near Foligno, is the Cloister of Sassovivo, built by an artist named Pietro de Maria in 1229, *" in the Roman manner "* (see " Cloisters "). In Foligno itself there are traces of Roman workmanship in 1201 in the doorway of the cathedral; also at Spoleto and elsewhere.

But Narni, being more within the Roman orbit, is especially rich. The cathedral, S. Maria in Pensole, S. Domenico, are basilical churches with the purely Roman type of mosaic pavements. The cathedral is of early foundation, partly reconstructed in about the twelfth century. Of this date is the campanile, which is exactly of the Roman type, even to the material, which is not stone but brick. Here and at S. Maria in Pensole a weird, ungraceful effect is given to the interior by the use for spanning the space between the columns of the nave, not of either arches or architraves, but of the low form of segmental arch used in Rome to break the pressure on the architrave by concentrating it over the columns, — a form that was always concealed or at least never used without the architrave and without filling in the intervals. There is also a piece of decorative mosaic work in the Cathedral that is among the earliest products of the Roman school in vertical decoration — the shrine of S. Cassius.

Sabina. — The province of Sabina, below Umbria, on the east bank of the Tiber, was a favorite camping-ground for the Roman artists, for it had always been a fief of some Roman noble with occasional sections belonging to some large monastery. The ruined Foronovo cathedral near Torri preserves its ancient crypt, pavement and campanile; its ambone is decorated with mosaics and so was its confession. Its frescos are of the last period of the Roman school. At Catino, both parish and ruined castle church were Roman.

Most important of all were the monuments of Palombara, a fief of the great Savelli family of Rome which gave to the Papacy Honorius III and Honorius IV. The parish church and the churches of S. Biagio and S. Giovanni in Argentella were founded in or about the time of Paschal II. That of S. Biagio was restored by Honorius III and was the family church of the Savelli, containing several monuments of the family. An inscription of 1101 gives this date for its consecration and the name of its architect *Joannes Blasius.*

Other Roman works of the thirteenth century are at Montebono, where S. Pietro has a fine campanile and some frescos of 1204, and Toffia, where S. Lorenzo has an interesting façade. The early Gothic style, especially the form in which it was imported from Burgundy by the Cistercians, found lodgement in this province during the thirteenth century, partly expelling the basilical plan and construction. But in painting the Sabina remained dependent on Rome.

Near Soracte. — Crossing the Tiber once more westward, above Soracte, we come on a group of towns and monasteries that were from their closeness to Rome more generally subject to its artistic supremacy. They are especially the cities of Civita Castellana, Nepi and Sutri; the monasteries of S. Elia, of Soracte, of S. Andrea near Ponzano and S. Maria di Falleri; and, finally, the villages of Rignano, Leprignano and Fiano; they are full of works illustrating especially the earlier days of the later Middle Ages, from the middle of the tenth to the close of the twelfth century, though there is also some decorative work of the early thirteenth at Civita Castellana. Leprignano provides the only remaining iconostasis screen of the pre-Cosmati style; S. Elia and S. Andrea the most extensive frescos of the tenth century and the best dated basilicas of that period.

Porch of Cathedral, Civita Castellana.
(By Laurentius and his son Jacobus, 1210.)

The cathedrals of Nepi and Sutri, while their interiors are ruined, have preserved extensive crypts of the eleventh or twelfth centuries of a size unknown to Rome itself. The shafts and some of the capitals in these crypts are from the ruins of Rome, taken during the days subsequent to the fire. At Sutri especially the cathedral must have equalled that of Civita Castellana. Its large crypt has four radiating chapels and sixteen niches. The interior had originally columns with Corinthian capitals. The superb mosaic pavement is now restored with pieces of the choir-seats, ambones and choir-screen of beautiful mosaic work by Roman artists of the close of the twelfth century. To the same period belongs the fine main doorway and the campanile on the right of the façade. Other churches have retained some parts of their Roman work; the pavement at S. Giacomo; the altar and pavement at S. Angelo (S. Francesco).

The cathedral at Nepi, on a somewhat smaller scale, is of the same age and style, also built of peperino and partly of antique materials, as shown by the crypt, which has three aisles running across the entire width of the church. Heavy projecting abaci support well-built groin vaults, and, like the church above, there are three apses. There seem to be no two capitals alike; some are pseudo-corinthian, some have interlaced animals, one is cubic.

Near Nepi is the monastery of S. Elia, famous for its frescos described elsewhere, and for its church, first built in the ninth century, burned by the Saracens and then rebuilt after 939 when it was given to Monte Cassino. Both this church and those of the other monasteries belong strictly to the Roman school.

Civita Castellana, the ancient *Falerii*, was the first mediæval town of importance north of Rome. The little church of S. Andrea, with its elegant brick campanile, shows that even in its minor monuments, it was an integral part of the Roman school. Somewhat more important is S. Gregorio, with a heavier campanile of stone. But preëminent among all the monuments of the Roman province is its cathedral, where the parts we admire are by two artists of the Roman family school of Laurentius : the chief himself and his son James (Jacobus), who decorated and superintended the construction shortly before and after 1200, while the interior decoration was completed in about 1225 or 1230 by a grandson of Laurentius, Luke (Lucas), who, with his fellow-artist Drudus, signed the beautiful choir-seats now removed to the sacristy.

At the same time Laurentius and Jacobus built and decorated the near-by monastic church of S. Maria di Falleri, which rises alone, itself a ruin, inside the deserted walls of the ancient city of Falerii. Here the great vaults of the church, which show the hand of the Cistercian monastic designer, emphasize the fact that the actual construction — whether in stone, as here, or in brick, as in Rome — was

2 B

foreign to the work of the Roman *marmorarii*, to whom we can here attribute only such parts as the portal which is signed by them: —

LAURENTIUS CUM JACOBO FILIO SUO HOC OPUS FECERUNT.

It is a simple structure of white marble, moderately decorated and far from being on the scale of their work in Civita Castellana.

Abruzzi. — There were apparently local artists in Umbria and the Abruzzi who imitated Roman work. For example, at Rocca di Botte in the latter province, the pulpit and ciborium of the church have the general Roman design and mosaic decoration, but the crudeness of handiwork and the clumsiness of proportion betray the local imitator.

But elsewhere in the Abruzzi, Roman artists were themselves present. The church at Alba near Lake Fucino was decorated early in the thirteenth century by two Romans, Andreas and Johannes, with works that rival the best in Rome. The church itself is extremely interesting, being the result of the successive metamorphosis of a Pelasgic place of worship into a Roman temple of the early Empire whose immense Corinthian columns were used for the interior of a Christian church built on the same site. In c. 1225 the two Roman artists were called to decorate it with an ambone and an iconostasis screen. The iconostasis is signed by Andreas alone: —

ANDREAS MAGISTER ROMANUS FECIT HOC OPUS.

The ambone has a more elaborate inscription, showing that here Andreas was only the assistant of Johannes, who calls himself a " Roman Citizen, most skilful in art."

CIVIS ROMANUS DOCTISSIMUS ARTE JOHANNES
CUI COLLEGA BONUS ANDREAS DETULIT HONUS
HOC OPUS EXELSUM STURSSERUNT (!) MENTE PERITI
NOBILIS ET PRUDENS ODERISIUS ABFUIT ABBAS.

One does not wonder that Abbot Oderisius called in these Romans when one examines some of the terribly crude work he had to put up with at the hands of local artists.

Alban Hills. — East of Rome, in the Alban Hills, lies a group of towns, many of which were of ancient renown, and some of mediæval importance. Tusculum was punished by the Romans with total destruction, in 1191, for daring to be its rival. Albano was also wiped out. Marino, Albano, Grottaferrata, Genzano, Civita Lavinia, Ariccia, should be supplemented by

Mosaic Frieze of Porch, Cathedral of Terracina.

Velletri, Palestrina, Tivoli and Subiaco. Most of these towns became too popular as summer resorts, during the Renaissance and after, to have preserved as much of their mediæval art as the less frequented towns of the rest of the province. There is hardly enough to show that they actually did form an integral part of the school, except, of course, the Greek monastery of Grottaferrata, which was an oasis of Byzantine art. Even here, however, the Roman decorator penetrated in the thirteenth century, to erect monuments to members of the famous counts of Tusculum, who at one time ruled Rome.

These works are of the usual type with tabernacles, columns and mosaic work, but only fragments remain.

At Palestrina the cathedral has traces of its reconstruction under Paschal II (c. 1112); at Velletri is the crypt of the cathedral with its frescos (XII c.) and the campanile of S. Maria del Trivio; at Tivoli the ninth-century fresco of the apse of S. Silvestro, the campanile of the cathedral, the basilical interior and pavement of S. Pietro, etc.; at Albano the campanile of S. Pietro; at the monasteries of Subiaco, the remains of mediæval art are really of transcendent importance, and are elsewhere referred to. They form the subject of a sumptuous publication which is now being issued.

South of Rome, leading toward the Neapolitan border, were two main routes : one, the ancient Appian Way through the Pontine marshes as far as Terracina, on the coast, turning inland to Fondi and continuing to Gaeta; the other, following the inland valley of the Sacco (present railroad to Naples), with hill towns on both sides and entering the Neapolitan province near Ceprano, where the river Liris forms the historic frontier.

Towns of the Pontine Region. — Along the first of these routes the hills to the north are crowded by the cities of Cori, Sermoneta, Sezze and Piperno, before Terracina is reached, and the road passes through the fever-stricken and deserted site of Ninfa, at the foot of the ancient Norba. Although this district was a recognized dependency of Rome in the later Middle Ages, there are very few artistic traces of it. These towns seem to have been slow to rise. Not till the latter part of the twelfth century do we find monuments of importance such as the cathedral of Piperno, built by the architect Antonio di Rabotto. Its porch is a fine example of the type created by the monastic architects of the Benedictine order, as we see it at S. Clemente di Casauria. In fact, when these towns are built up, mainly in the thirteenth century, they do not patronize Roman artists of any class, but rather put themselves under the direction of the monastic school established by the French Cistercians from Burgundy settled at Fossanova, near

Piperno, with still another establishment at Valvisciolo near Sermoneta and, across the hills, at Casamari. The cathedrals of Sezze and Sermoneta, the parish church at Amaseno, are derived from these monastic types. So are the minor churches, such as S. Michele and S. Nicola at Sermoneta. They are quite the opposite to the columnar basilical type, and on the basis of groin or ribbed vaulting and piers. In the absence in this region, also, of any of the works of decorative church furniture in the Roman style, we are forced to conclude that this route was not travelled by our artists, and that they reached Terracina by the sea route.

It is, however, true that so far as Ninfa the land route was frequented. At Cori, on the way, there remains, in the parish church of S. Maria, an interesting and early paschal candlestick of the Roman school; and Ninfa itself is famous in the Papal documents of the early Middle Ages, as early as the ninth century. In the twelfth century it belonged to the Frangipani. It had the honor, in 1159, of being the place of the cardinals' conclave that elected Alexander III. Most of its churches are of this time, though S. Marco was built as late as 1216 by Cardinal Ugolino, who afterward became Gregory IX. These churches, whose walls are covered with decaying frescos, are all in ruins, as it has not been inhabited since the fourteenth century on account of malaria.

Region of the Sacco. — The other group of southern towns, that flanking the valley of the Sacco, is, when taken collectively, as important as any in the province of the history of Roman art, for its artists were as consistently active here as they were in the region immediately to the north. These cities are Anagni, Ferentino, Alatri and Veroli on the north side of the valley ; and Segni on the south side.

Destruction has overcome the cathedral of Segni, completed in 1185. Only from its inscriptions and archives do we know that it possessed six signed works of the Roman artists of this time, which show that its architectural details and furniture were executed by the most famous living members of the school, by Laurentius and his son Jacobus, by Petrus Vassallettus (1186) and others.

Ferentino. — But at Ferentino we can still trace, better even than in Rome itself, the beginnings of the school. The cathedral is entirely, in construction and decoration, a work of the time of Paschal II (1106–1110) when the Roman school of *magistri marmorarii* was founded. And an inscription shows not only the date, but that its artist is the very founder of the school, *Paulus*. Its construction is of the simplest. The material is large travertine blocks. The façade follows the outline of nave and aisles with nothing to relieve it besides the three doorways but a round-headed window in the gable. The side walls are equally plain, the windows being without mouldings. The triple apse is a trifle less simple, its windows having flanking colonnettes. Still, the revival of classic design shows clearly, even in the few existing details, in the dentils, the egg-and-dart and the pearl ornament of the archivolts of the doors. The corbels of the apsidal arcading with their sculptured masks and patterns may be compared with the contemporary work at S. Bartolommeo all' Isola in Rome.

In the interior the old granite columns have been submerged in barocco piers, but it is possible to reconstitute even its decoration by means of the multitude of fragments now stored in an annex, as well as the altar-fronts and other slabs still in use in the renovated church. On one of these, at the altar of S. Ambrose, is the artist's signature : —

HOC OPIFEX MAGNUS FECIT VIR NOMINE PAULUS.

From an examination of the pieces in the museum, which were used as material by the barocco " restorer " of 1693, we can see that Paulus, or whoever directed the building in 1106, made similar use as material of the ornamentation of an earlier church of the eighth-ninth century. He took the marble slabs that formed the choir-screen, the pulpits, the altar and confession of this probably ruined building and by reversing them utilized the smooth surfaces for his own decorative work, inlaying them with the mosaic patterns and slabs which Paulus himself was apparently the first to bring into fashion. Even one arch of the primitive ciborium has been preserved in a subterranean room under the cathedral and turned into an altar.

Now the choir-screens, pulpits, altar, confession, ciborium of Paulus himself have in turn been dispersed and utilized. Some of the present altars were made up of this material in 1693. In one chapel, a relief with Jonah and the whale formed originally the stairway rail of his ambone, which was supported by twisted columns inlaid with mosaic, three of which rested on lions. Either this work is not by Paulus, or this founder of the Roman school was himself an offshoot of the Campanian school, where, as well as in the Abruzzi, this form of the box pulpit on columns was in vogue.

Later Roman artists than Paulus worked here in the thirteenth century, as is clear from the delicate vitreous inlay of some of the present altar-fronts, different from the primitive marble cubes of Paulus. They seem, together with some twisted colonnettes, to recompose a supplementary choir-screen added to that of Paulus. The master who then came to Ferentino produced in the paschal candlestick one of the finest works of the school. Perhaps he is the Drudus who then (c.1230–1240) made the superb ciborium for the same cathedral, finer than anything of its type remaining in Rome itself.

Anagni. — The metropolis of Campania, Anagni, has nothing as old as the work of Paulus, but it was a Mecca for Roman artists during nearly the whole of the thirteenth century. Its cathedral, like that at Ferentino, took the place of an earlier structure decorated with the same pre-Cosmati sculpture. The new building was commenced at the same time as Ferentino's, under Paschal II. But if the immense crypt was soon finished, the upper church was not dedicated until 1179, and the decoration of both upper and lower churches was continued until about 1230.

This decoration — except for the wall-paintings — was confided to the then head of the most famous Roman school, Cosmas, son of Jacobus, of the family of Laurentius. His name appears first in the pavement of the upper church: —

MAGISTER COSMAS HOC OPUS FECIT.

He then, some years later, began work on the crypt, where he was assisted by his two sons and signed the main altar thus: —

MAGISTER COSMAS CIVIS ROMANUS CUM FILIIS SUIS
LUCA ET JACOBO HOC OPUS FECIT.

His long labors were completed by his setting in place in 1231 the altar of S. Magnus.

In reckoning the part that Cosmas took in the work of the cathedral I think we may eliminate any part of its architecture, though perhaps the design of the campanile is Roman. The ciborium remains in place over high altar and confession. Its style and close connection with the pavement plan make it quite certainly the work of Cosmas, c. 1220; the primitive handling of the capitals excludes a later date. This work is certainly the prototype of that by Drudus at Ferentino, an artist who was a pupil of Cosmas and associated with his son Lucas at Civita Castellana. The choir-screen and choir-seats, which extended into the nave from the high altar, and the ambones, were also probably by Cosmas. They were long since destroyed and only fragments remain in the sacristy.

Another artist, however, was called in to execute the paschal candlestick and the episcopal throne in the apse. He was Vassallettus, and his work came some years after that of Cosmas and his sons. These still remain in the sacristy, though the throne is mutilated. Which of the Vassalletti was he? From the type of sculpture of the lions flanking the throne and the piquant caryatid surmounting the candlestick, I think these must be mature works of the Vassallettus who built and carved the Lateran cloister more than thirty years before the year 1260, the decade to which they have been attributed. The candlestick is signed, on the plinth above the sphinxes: —

VASSALLETO ME FECIT.

The signature on the throne is under the circular disk that formed the centre of the back: —

VASALETO DE ROMA ME FECIT.

Another inscription says that the throne was ordered by Bishop Landus. The inlay in both these works is not of the minute and varied character which is shown in the works posterior to c. 1230, when glass paste had quite superseded natural marbles.

Here I will close the tour of the Roman province in the footsteps of the artists of the metropolis. Though I have omitted numerous minor places and works, it is evident that they brought great influence to bear on the decorative art of almost the entire region, with an occasional inroad beyond the regular Roman orbit. To the south they joined hands with the contemporary decorative school in Campania, to which they were so closely allied that it is not easy to distinguish sometimes the works of the two schools. On the north they overlapped the Tuscan school and undoubtedly encouraged its work in marble inlay such as we see at S. Miniato in Florence and the baptistery at Pisa.

It is even possible to conjecture that the Jacobus, *frater S. Francisci*, who in 1225 signed the mosaics and decorative work of the apse of the Florentine baptistery, was a Roman artist, perhaps the very famous Jacobus, son of Laurentius, who though still in his prime disappeared from the field of lay art in about 1220. He may have become a monk of the new Franciscan order and been placed in charge of the decoration of the baptistery, where the cornices, columns and sculptured details are so purely classic as to betray almost certainly the hand of a master from Rome, whose mosaics are of the minute description affected by the "Cosmati."

ARTISTIC INFLUENCE OF ROME

THIS influence has been already referred to, and naturally falls into two main divisions: that of the ancient city, and that of the Christian city. In both cases, there is a material influence, but only in the latter a spiritual influence as well. In fact it would seem as if the ruin wrought by the fire of Robert Guiscard in 1084 caused renewed activity in the pillage, and that many Italian cities then entering on a building era profited extremely.

Influence of the Ancient City. — There was a twofold effect of ancient Rome, according as to whether use was made of materials actually taken from classic monuments, or whether ancient models were imitated.

Some critics have fallen into the error of concluding that the supply of columns and marbles from the ruins of Rome had become exhausted as early as the Carlovingian period. On the contrary, it lasted, in abundance, until the close of the Middle Ages, as the monuments of the city itself abundantly show. I will give a few cases for each period.

King Theodoric had allowed some ancient material to be sent to him at Ravenna from the Domus Pinciana, much as he discountenanced the practice in general. But certainly there was little wholesale exportation of material until the Lombards began to build churches and monasteries. In 725 columns and marbles were brought from Rome for the construction of the church of S. Anastasia at Olonna by King Luitprand, a practice repeated during the eighth century.

Under Charlemagne and his successors material from Rome was carried even beyond the Alps to Gaul and Germany. In building S. Riquier, Abbot Angilbert, pupil of Alcuin, is said, by the monastic chronicler, to have used columns and other marbles from Rome. Charlemagne himself used material from

378

both Rome and Ravenna in his constructions at Aix-la-Chapelle. The early German Emperors, especially the Othos, did the same. In 962 considerable material for the new Magdeburg cathedral came from Rome.

The abbots of northern monasteries in their pilgrimage to Rome, which was often the great object of their career, some-times secured antique materials as well as relics for their new churches. A monastic chronicle gives a picture of a German abbot hauling these marbles with infinite trouble by mule-back across the mountains. Even as late as the twelfth, the French primate Suger, when he was preparing to build his epoch-mak-ing church at S. Denis, tells us that he planned to send to Rome for columns and marbles.

Lanciani tells us that it was mostly with marbles from Rome and Ostia that the cathedral of Pisa was built and that an in-scription in the transept *Genio. Coloniæ. Ostiensis* leaves no doubt of the fact, as well as a sarcophagus of Proculus, a nota-ble of Ostia. The cathedral and most of the other churches of Lucca were built out of Roman materials; so were the churches of Monte Cassino, S. Angelo in Formis, Salerno, Amalfi and many others, especially in the towns near Rome.

Last of all comes the cathedral of Orvieto, and the daily offi-cial records of its construction and decoration, especially be-tween 1321 and 1360, are full of details about the way marbles were procured from the ancient city. Local Roman stone-cutters, familiar with the resources of the ruins, were engaged to pilot the emissaries from Orvieto, and a regular gang of stone-cutters was established near Rome to receive and prepare the ancient material and then ship it to Orvieto ready for use.

Though much of the ancient material was reworked, much again was not. Columns, bases and capitals were transferred bodily, and often served partly to determine the character of the new building. The spread of the columnar basilical style throughout Italy and even beyond the Alps would hardly have been realized otherwise. The classic orders would hardly have been so widely perpetuated. So, in a way, vandalism profited art.

That observant eyes also imitated specific works is quite clear. The pine cone of the Vatican and the wolf of the Lateran were reproduced on the fountain at Aix-la-Chapelle. The bronze column at Hildesheim faintly echoes the great memorial columns of Trajan and Marcus Aurelius; so does the marble column at Gaeta. The sarcophagi at Pisa furnish models for Niccola Pisano.

Influence of the Christian City.— This is far more complex and hard to measure. Let us commence by the more material aspect: the artists and the works of art.

The earliest instances are in the century of Gregory the Great. The illuminated codex called the Cambridge Gospels contain a series of pictures by a Roman artist that were to serve S. Augustine and the other missionaries to the Anglo-Saxons as models for church frescos. When the hierarchy of the Anglo-Saxon church had been established directly from Rome by the mission of Theodore, made first archbishop of Canterbury, the promulgation of a Roman code of laws, the adoption of Roman music and liturgy, were followed by the importation of works of art and artists from Rome by the two most prominent Anglo-Saxon prelates. Benedict Biscop, says Bede, on the occasion of two of his visits to Rome took back collections of paintings. Wilfrid of York brought over masons and artificers from Rome to build and decorate churches at York, Ripon and Hexham (709). It would seem fair to conclude that the Anglo-Saxons, who had been quite innocent of any artistic endeavors before their conversion, owed mainly to Roman models, with some Gallic assistance, the style of their best early works.

Some instances of the sort occur in the Carlovingian and Othonian eras for France and Germany. Pipin gets from Rome its church music. The great monasteries supply themselves with the sacred vestments made in Rome: S. Wandrille (Fontanella), in c. 822, receives some *cappas Romanas* and some *cingula Romano opere facta.* S. Riquier (Centula), in c. 820, receives *albas Romanas cum amictis.* More important still, Odo, one of the architects of Charlemagne's cathedral of Aix-la-Chapelle, seems to have been a Roman.

Under Pope Leo IV Rome returned the compliment to Ravenna, who had in other days (fifth to sixth centuries) sent her artists, by sending an architect and workmen to restore S. Apollinare in Classe.

The diffusion of the practical handbook of painting by the Roman Heraclius undoubtedly spread the methods of the Roman school. The Italian painter John, whom the Emperor Otho II took to Germany, is possibly the same John who had decorated with his brother the basilica of S. Elia near Nepi (middle tenth century). In so far as the painter Methodius (ninth century) is concerned, who painted the terrifying Last Judgment for the Bulgarians, he is claimed by both Rome and Byzantinism, though Rome certainly ended by possessing him and some of his works.

There must have been numerous cases of a close imitation in other places of works in Rome. I will cite a very clear instance, the frescos of the church of S. Piero a Grado near Pisa, executed c. 1300. On the walls of its nave are three series of paintings: above a row of angels in architectural framework; then the main body of the decoration in oblong compositions, representing the lives and martyrdoms of SS. Peter and Paul; finally, just above the columns, a series of portraits of the Popes. It has recently been proved that these scenes from the lives of the apostles were copied literally from frescos in the atrium of S. Peter. The portraits of the Popes were taken from those in the same church or at the Lateran or S. Paul.

The cycles at S. Francis of Assisi seem planned by Cavallini.

In the opinion of Crowe and Cavalcaselle the frescos that fill the baptistery at Parma, the most important of their time (c. 1250) in Northern Italy, are by a master trained in the Roman school. These two are examples of the way Umbria, Tuscany, Emilia and Lombardy were invaded.

During this, its most flourishing period, the Roman school even made an occasional inroad with its own artists into the very central strongholds of other provincial schools. Of this the church of S. Frediano at Lucca is an instance. No Italian city had a more characteristic mediæval art than Lucca. It is a Tuscan art, of course, — the twin brother of that of Pisa. Of its churches none has been more studied than S. Frediano;

around it for over a half-century fought the battalions, of whom one faction asserted that it was a shining example of the Lombard art of the seventh century, while the other consigned it with all the rest of such so-called early Lombard churches to the less rare but far more civilized atmosphere of the twelfth century — and the latter have been proved correct. In fact, the present church is now shown to have been built between 1112 and 1147 or shortly after. The great peculiarity of its exterior is the large mosaic picture that fills the upper part of its façade, representing the Resurrection of Christ, who is seated on a throne and is being carried up by two angels, while the twelve apostles stand below and gaze. To what school does this work belong ? A reckless restoration in 1829 has made it somewhat difficult to do more than to assign it to the latter part of the twelfth century or later. The choice is practically between the Venetian and the Roman schools. The preference for Rome, where the custom of decorating the façades was then so common, becomes a practical certainty when one examines the remains of the mosaic pavement in the choir. Barbarously as it was transformed by the Barocco period, it is a Roman pavement. No one can mistake the subtle or graded designs and colors of the Venetian pavements for the strong contrasts and heavy outlines and uniform coloring of the Romans which here appear. No other church at Lucca or in this region has any pavement like it. It is an accident, — an accident which makes us conclude that the figured mosaics of the façade were also Roman. Pope Paschal II, when he came to Lucca in 1105, established close connections between S. Frediano and the Lateran. Pope Eugenius III consecrated the church in 1147. Perhaps in the latter's train came the Roman mosaicists who helped complete the decoration of the church. We cannot say whether to them also was due the choir-screen and pulpits which the Barocco prelates destroyed, or the connection may be due to Pope Lucius III (1181–1185), who was a native of Lucca.

There was another and more general connection with Rome. The churches of Lucca are in several cases built with antique columns and capitals; no Tuscan city shows such a profuseness of antique material. Where did it come from ? It has been supposed from the antique buildings of the city itself, especially from the amphitheatre — a purely imaginary and unsupported supposition. S. Giovanni, the old cathedral, S. Frediano itself, S. Alessandro, S. Maria forisportam, are all built with Roman columns largely topped with Roman capitals. Why should they not have been all brought from Rome? When cities on all sides, including Pisa itself, were allowed by the Popes to use Rome as a quarrying-ground, there is every reason to suppose that Lucca, the favorite residence of the Countess Matilda, the greatest benefactor of the Papacy, would long continue to feel the benefits of Papal favor.

No Roman artist, however, travelled as far as did the Pietro who went to England in company with Archbishop Ware to decorate Westminster Abbey. It was a most important commission. Ware went several times to Rome; in 1258–1259, in 1267 and in 1276. The decoration of Westminster choir, and the placing there of the body of Edward the Confessor in a magnificent shrine, had been planned as early as 1265. Ware probably brought back Pietro from Rome or Viterbo in 1267. The work was completed and the relics of the Confessor transferred on October 13, 1269. The inscription read:—

ANNO MILLENO — DOMINI CUM SEXAGENO
ET BIS CENTENO — CUM COMPLETO QUASI DENO
HOC OPUS EST FACTUM — QUOD PETRUS DUXIT IN ACTUM
ROMANUS CIVIS — HOMO CAUSAM NOSCERE SI VIS
REX FUIT HENRICUS — SANCTI PRESENTIS AMICUS.

A Roman citizen had the honor to execute the most sacred, the national shrine of England! He also did the tomb of King Henry III himself, and of others in the Abbey, the mosaic pavement of the choir, and probably also that in the same style at Canterbury, where the shrine of the martyred primate seems to be by the same hand. The inscription of the Westminster pavement read:—

TERTIUS HENRICUS REX, URBS, ODERICUS, ET
ABBAS HOS COMPOSUERE PORPHIRETICOS LAPIDES.[1]

---

[1] It is generally supposed that the Petrus of the first inscription and the Odericus of the second were two distinct Roman artists, but as the man who

A third inscription, placed in 1283 on the tomb of Ware himself, shows that all the marbles used for the pavement and the monuments were brought from Rome, for it expressly states that Ware rests under the stones which he himself brought from the city, " Urbs " : *hic portat lapides quos huc portavit ab urbe.* To this evidently alludes also the " Urbs" of the previous inscription, expressing Rome's share in the work.

There are traces both in Germany and France of the presence of Roman artists, though nothing nearly as important as the Westminster work. There is, for instance, the mosaic tomb of Archbishop Gero of Cologne († 976), and the mosaic pavement of a church in Cologne ; some details of " Cosmati " work from Vilseck (Oberpfalz), now in the Industrial Museum at Munich ; and a fragment in the Cluny Museum in Paris.

These examples, of indifferent periods, will be sufficient. The Roman artist was an easy traveller. In another chapter I have traced his normal peripatetic orbit in Central Italy. Elsewhere I also refer to his final achievements in France and Italy, when the departure of the Popes from Rome entailed the dispersal of the school to wherever they could find patrons. Under Painting it has appeared how predominant not only in the sphere of thought, but in style and technique, was the influence of the Roman school led by Cavallini and his contemporaries.

Aside from the actual work of Roman artists, the mark of the school was stamped even more widely if we study the marble incrustations of Tuscany in the twelfth and thirteenth centuries, and the spread through Central Italy of the imitation of antique ornament and orders. It is too broad a subject to be treated here. It is even more impossible to express fully the internal or spiritual influence of Roman artistic ideals, but no one can, I think, read this book without understanding that they reach down to the roots of all Italian mediæval art when it sought to express religious and symbolic thought.

worked at Viterbo called himself Petrus Oderici and as it was sometimes the habit to call a man by his patronymic, I am inclined to consider them one and the same.

INDEX

INDEX OF ILLUSTRATIONS

I

INDEX LIST OF CHURCHES

(To supplement Text)

S. AGATA IN SUBURRA. Origin unknown, but early. Its apse was decorated in 460–467 by mosaic of Christ and apostles, a gift of the barbarian general, Ricimer. It then became the cathedral or national church of the colony of Arian Goths in Rome. It was given back to Catholic worship and redecorated by Gregory the Great, who made it a diaconal church. In the eighth century a monastery was annexed to it by Gregory II. In the eleventh century it was restored by Leo IX.

Church and monastery were remodernized at close of sixteenth century, but the ancient walls and the twelve widely spaced granite columns remain.

S. AGNESE. Built by Constantine over the tomb of the martyr at the third mile on Via Nomentana; decorated by Constantina. It was restored by Pope Symmachus and rebuilt by Honorius I.

Placed at so low a level, it is reached by a long, wide stairway, descending at right angles. Unable to have an atrium, this is replaced by a closed narthex. The nave has 14 columns beside the pilasters at apse and narthex. It is 9.42 m. wide and 21.10 m. long, with an apse 7.80 m. in diameter. The aisles are extremely narrow, 2.60 m. Above them and the narthex is a high, open gallery, with an equal number of columns and arcades.

It is uncertain how much belongs to Constantine; how much to Honorius I. The present apse was undoubtedly the work of Honorius, who utilized for the rest much Constantinian material.

While the apsidal decoration of veined marble and porphyry is also of Honorius, the greater part of the furniture and decoration was renovated between 1225 and 1250, when the galleries and aisles were filled with important frescos, and the *schola cantorum* decorated with screens and pulpits.

In the twelfth century a monastery was added, of which some fragments remained until 1905.

S. ALESSIO. Original connected with S. Boniface. Alberic transformed his palace in this part of the Aventine into a monastery. In 977 Pope Benedict gave it to the Greek clergy and monks, and the monasteries here became very important. To this time a considerable part of the present structures belong, including the crypt, which is the most important in Rome, where so few exist.

To the revival of the close of the twelfth century belong the fine central doorway with mosaic inlay and the campanile.

S. ANASTASIA. One of the largest and earliest churches; third in rank, immediately after the Lateran and S. Maria Maggiore. There were 30 columns in the nave. In 403 a baptistery was attached to it. It became the principal church of the Byzantine officials. It was partly ruined by the earthquake of 1638; and the interior was modernized with the use of the antique columns, now set against the Barocco piers. The ancient brick walls remain in great part.

S. BALBINA. Especially interesting as a hall church of pagan origin of the Constantinian age, never transformed by the addition of columns. Its apse is remarkable for the niche in the thickness of the wall to receive the bishop's seat. The lower walls, with their alternation of tufa and brick, are early.

S. BARTOLOMMEO ALL' ISOLA. Also originally called S. Adalbert. Rebuilt by Paschal II (c. 1113); damaged by the earthquake of 1557, which destroyed the façade. The nave has 14 columns of unequal heights and sizes, with different bases, but with capitals made to fit the shafts. The level of the pavement has been raised. The cornice of the roof of choir and nave is extremely interesting, with stone consols elaborately carved with Byzantine designs. It seems not later than Paschal II.

S. CECILIA. Recent excavations and restorations have increased the interest of this church and its site. At a much lower level than the present was found the lower part of a large Roman house, variously surmised to be that of the Cæcilii or that of Cæcilia's husband, Valerian, whom she converted; more probably the latter. Pope Urban, says the legend, turned the house into a church. A regular basilica was built here in the fourth or fifth century. Paschal I found the church and the neighboring monastery in ruins, and rebuilt it. The ground-plan of the earlier church has been discovered, a little to the left of the present and on a smaller scale. Under Gregory VII a restoration was commenced which continued into the twelfth century. At that time the porch and the campanile were built. Later, at the close of the thirteenth century, an even more radical beautifying took place under the direction of Arnolfo and Pietro Cavallini, ending in about 1283. This involved covering the walls with a series of grandiose frescos, erecting a ciborium, altar, confession, paschal candlestick, choir seats, tabernacle for holy oils, etc. Meanwhile the monastery had also been rebuilt. Its cloister remains. The mosaic frieze of the porch does not belong to the ninth century but to the twelfth to thirteenth centuries. In the recent fearsome restoration of the interior it was found that the Barocco vandals had so disfigured the ancient columns when they built the piers around them that it would be impossible to free them.

S. CLEMENTE. The present interior of c. 1100 has 16 Ionic columns divided by an oblong pier into two almost equal sections. The archivolts of the arcades are modernized; so are the capitals. The side aisles are of unequal width (N. c. 14 ft.; S. c. 19 ft.), as are also those of S. Sabina, S. Anastasia, and others. The interior is 40.28 m. long and the nave is 10.88 m. wide. Portions of the monastic buildings of the twelfth century remain. The entire group, including atrium and propylon, is the most complete in Rome.

S. CRISOGONO. An early basilica existed here at a lower level in the fourth or fifth century, as it is mentioned in the time of Symmachus (499). It is now being excavated.

In 731 it was restored by Gregory III, who covered the walls with frescos, renewed the roof and the apse, and donated a ciborium of silver. He added a large and important monastery.

Having fallen into ruin, both church and monastery were rebuilt at the expense of the famous John of Crema, apostolic legate and cardinal priest of this church. The work was executed between c. 1120 and 1130. An inscription of 1123 speaks of the dedication of an oratory and the construction of all the monastic buildings including the cloisters. The church was consecrated in 1129.

The Benedictines had charge until 1200, when it was transferred by Innocent III to the secular clergy.

The church is preceded by a porch and has, on the right, a very heavy campanile, of the twelfth century, but plastered.

The interior, with superb antique columns, has been partially renovated. In Ugonio's time it preserved its "Cosmati" details: ciborium, altar, confession, choir seats, and throne. The capitals of the superb antique columns appear to have all been stuccoed by Cardinal Borghese in 1633! The pavement is one of the most superb examples of mosaic work in Rome, probably by Paulus and his school.

S. CROCE IN GERUSALEMME. Originally the large hall of the Sessorian palace belonging to the Empress Helena. The palace remained imperial property until the Gothic war. Helena transformed the hall into a church; hence it was called *Basilica Heleniana* in the fifth century. It was also called "Hierusalem." The Empress Placidia and her children were its benefactors in 425.

It was made a regular titular church by Gregory the Great. Its roof fell c. 720, and Gregory II, in restoring it, added two rows of columns. Its wide apse proves that originally it was a hall church without colonnades.

In 975 Benedict VII built a large monastery next to it, which was given in c. 1050 by Leo IX to the Benedictines of Monte Cassino.

The necessary work of renovation after the Gregorian revival was accomplished by Popes Lucius II and Eugenius III, 1144–1148, to whom were due the façade, the bell-tower, the large cloister, all the monastic buildings, and a large part of the church furniture.

They retained their mediæval form, as shown by a number of old prints, until Benedict XIV, who destroyed the old portico in 1744, and concealed the old façade, which is erroneously considered to have been destroyed, behind a Barocco structure.

The present interior is of c. 1744, but all the outer walls are classic or mediæval, and show that the basilica never had the usual low side-aisles. In fact its exact mediæval form has not yet been demonstrated and its original form is also somewhat of a puzzle. It deserves careful study.

S. GIORGIO IN VELABRO. This is one of the most characteristic and untouched of the smaller mediæval churches of Rome, with parts belonging to both the Byzantine and the later eras. It was a diaconal church c. 600; was probably restored by Leo II (682–683), who added the cult of S. Sebastian to that of S. George. Zacharias rebuilt it. Gregory IV decorated the apse with mosaics. The architraved *portico* and the sturdy *campanile* were added to the plan in the twelfth century. This is from the fact that the ...ions of the campanile fill ... ...st bay of the left aisle.

The interior is of the sixth or seventh century. There are sixteen shafts, all ancient, of various sizes and sources. All the capitals on the left are ancient and Corinthian: of those on the right two are ancient Corinthian and four ancient Ionic. The two required to complete the series are crude imitations of Ionic with uncarved volutes (eleventh century).

An interesting doorway opening out of the right aisle is the best preserved detail of the primitive church.

Only the apse has preserved in part its original features in its marble revetment and mosaic pavement of the seventh century.

Here and there are scattered fragments of the choir-screen and ciborium which belonged to the pre-Cosmati decoration of the seventh to eighth centuries. The present confession, altar, and ciborium belong, like the atrium and campanile, to the twelfth century and are among the best preserved groups of their class.

A considerable number of Byzantine funerary inscriptions show that this was a favorite church of the Greek colony in the seventh to eighth centuries.

SS. GIOVANNI E PAOLO. Built c, 400 by Pammachius inside the walls of the private palace of the martyrs themselves, its lower floor being left beneath the church, and one of its rooms, where the martyrdom took place, being turned into an oratory. The basilica was restored, a century later, by Symmachus, then by Leo III. The interior has been modernized, but most of the twenty antique columns, with their capitals, have been left in place, though piers have been inserted between them and a few columns have been removed to make room for the heaviest piers.

The fine porch and bell-tower belong to the twelfth century, as also does the pavement.

S. GIOVANNI A PORTA LATINA. Its origins are obscure. Restorations are connected with the names of Leo II and Hadrian I, when it belonged to the Lateran. Lucius II gave it to the Benedictine nuns, and it was restored under Celestine III (1190), who dedicated it.

It is in poor condition. The *porch* was an early arcaded structure, badly restored, but probably of the seventh to eighth centuries; while the *campanile* is a fine twelfth-century structure, to which date the good square doorway, similar to that of SS. Giovanni e Paolo, also belongs. The interior has interesting elements of all three periods of its early history; the fifth(?), the eighth, and the twelfth. The ten fine antique columns of the nave, with their well-shaped arcades, evidently belong to the primitive church. Then, to the middle period, of say Hadrian I, are some remarkably good pieces of the usual low-relief decoration, some of it *in situ*, some of it used as material by later restorers. Such are two pilasters at the entrance to the apse and a carved frieze now forming a step of the main altar. To the twelfth century belong the mosaic pavement and the fine mosaic altar.

S. JOHN LATERAN. The present basilica of S. John Lateran appears to have retained but little that is early Christian or mediæval since its modernization by the architect Borromini, and it is difficult to say how much of what remains belongs to the original near the façade. There are six columns on each side, with capitals of an Egyptianizing type common in the fourth century and of excellent workmanship. These columns have been barbarously set into Barocco piers. The façade was reconstructed, many frescos added, the campanile built under Innocent III, who renovated the work done nearly a century and a half before by Gregory VII. The work of mediæval artists affected the façade more than the interior, except, of course, for the church furniture.

SS. QUATTRO CORONATI. This basilica has been already described. It was an early foundation, rebuilt and restored by Honorius I and Leo IV. Its monastery is ancient and unusually imposing, with foundations as early as Leo IV. Together with the church it was rebuilt by Paschal II. The columns of the original larger and wider nave appear in the refectory of the monastery, in the outside walls, and in the atrium. The 8 granite columns of the present nave were placed there by Paschal II, who built the gallery also.

The plan is remarkable for the double atrium in front of the church with the campanile in front of them, and a double portico against the façade of the church.

The mosaic pavement is good; beautiful pieces of the old ambones and choir-screen are worked into the pavement of the apse. The columns of the gallery are Ionic; those of the nave Corinthian and composite. A central pier divides the galleries into two groups of three arcades each.

The monastery was combined with a papal palace by Paschal II. The chapel of S. Silvester, opening out of the atrium, is an interesting annex of the group,

with original pavement and frescos of the thirteenth century.

S. SABINA. One of the least changed of Roman churches. After its construction in 425–432 it was restored by Leo III and Eugenius II. It was then that a monastery was added, whose cloister even then took the place of the primitive atrium, and turned the open porch into a closed passage, which was entered from the short end, which alone remained open and was approached through an arched portico. This portico is attributed to the eleventh century, but it is either later, or, more probably, much earlier and built in the ninth century, under Eugenius II, whose artists renovated the choir and furniture and used the columns of the altar canopy of the fifth century in the reconstruction of the porch.

The interior has 24 Corinthian columns. Though its structure is unchanged it has lost nearly all the marble incrustations and figured mosaics of the fifth century that together covered its walls, all the choir precinct and furniture of the ninth century, destroyed in 1683, together with the mosaic pavement. The style of this decoration is indicated by the few rescued fragments that have been pieced together and restored on the left wall.

It was one of the stational and baptismal basilicas, after Gregory the Great, and among the most important churches of Rome. This importance was emphasized under the Popes of the Savelli family who dominated the Aventine. Honorius III and Honorius IV had their palatial residences here ; the former gave it to S. Dominic in 1216 and he made it the Roman centre of his new order, building the still existing beautiful cloister.

S. SINFOROSA. This suburban basilica, at the ninth mile on the Via Tiburtina, abandoned, probably, at the time of the Lombard raids, under Stephen III, is a rare example for two reasons: it consists of two structures, an oratory and a basilica, arranged back to back; and its basilica has piers in place of columns.

The oratory is square, with a large apse. Against this apse is placed that of the basilica, which is about 40 m. long and almost 20 m. wide, and is divided into 3 aisles by 6 piers. It is probably of later construction than the oratory.

The group is a modest form of the arrangement at Nola, described by S. Paulinus.

SS. VINCENZO ED ANASTASIO ALLE TRE FONTANE. There are three churches within one general precinct of the monastery. The largest, though not the earliest, is that of *SS. Vincenzo ed Anastasio*, which gives its name to the entire group. According to an unverified tradition both basilica and monastery were built by Honorius I, c. 625. They were restored by Hadrian I, and rebuilt from the foundation by Leo III in 798, and at this time Charlemagne conferred on the monastery large estates.

In 1128 Pope Innocent II began to renovate the monastery and in 1140 induced S. Bernard to occupy it with Cistercian monks. Its first abbot, Pietro Pisano, became in 1145 Pope Eugenius III. Most of the present buildings were then constructed. Honorius III decorated with frescos and consecrated the church in 1221.

No part of the buildings can be assigned to as early a date as the seventh century (Honorius I). At most that part of the walls of the monastery, cloister, and church (as well as entrance) where there is a mixture of stones and bricks can be attributed to the time of Charlemagne.

The reconstruction under Innocent II left only one side of the old cloister and a section of the wall of the church, which was entirely reconstructed. The unusual church, with its piers in place of columns, its attempted vaulting, its porch and window-panes, are described under "Architecture." Also its chapter-house and cloister. The refectory is modern.

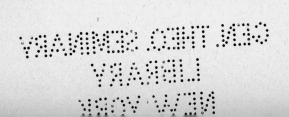

HANDBOOKS OF
Archæology and Antiquities

Edited by
PERCY GARDNER and F. W. KELSEY

FOWLER

The Roman Festivals of the Period of the Republic. By W. WARDE FOWLER. $1.25

GARDNER, E. A.

Greek Sculpture. By ERNEST A. GARDNER. Two parts in one volume. $2.50

Appendix to the above, separately $0.35

GARDNER, P.

Grammar of Greek Art. By PERCY GARDNER. $1.75

GREENIDGE

A Handbook of Greek Constitutional History. By A. H. J. GREENIDGE. With Map. $1.25

Roman Public Life. By A. H. J. GREENIDGE. $2.50

HILL

Greek and Roman Coins. By GEORGE F. HILL. $2.25

LANCIANI

The Destruction of Ancient Rome. By RODOLFO LANCIANI. $1.50

LOWRIE

Christian Art and Archæology. By W. LOWRIE. $1.25

Monuments of the Early Church. By W. LOWRIE. $1.25

Published by

THE MACMILLAN COMPANY

Sixty-four and Sixty-six Fifth Avenue, New York

STANDARD WORKS OF REFERENCE

ON

Archæology, Antiquities, Etc.